Applied Social Psychology

Applied
Social Psychology

JAMES M. WEYANT
University of San Diego

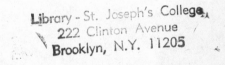
New York   Oxford
OXFORD UNIVERSITY PRESS
1986

Oxford University Press

Oxford   New York   Toronto
Delhi   Bombay   Calcutta   Madras   Karachi
Petaling Jaya   Singapore   Hong Kong   Tokyo
Nairobi   Dar es Salaam   Cape Town
Melbourne   Auckland

and associated companies in
Beirut   Berlin   Ibadan   Nicosia

Library of Congress Cataloging-in-Publication Data
Weyant, James M.
Applied social psychology.
Bibliography: p.   Includes index.
    1. Social psychology.   I. Title.
HM251.W576   1986   302   86-701
ISBN 0-19-504072-4
ISBN 0-19-504073-2 (pbk.)

9 8 7 6 5 4 3 2 1

Printed in the United States of America

To my parents, John and Elizabeth Weyant,
and in memory of my grandmother, Hedwig Siwik

Preface

To me, applied social psychology offers the best of two worlds. On the one hand, it has a firm basis in science. Throughout the history of social psychology, care has been taken to test theories with rigorous empirical methods. Although this emphasis on methodology may at times seem fastidious, it helps separate fact from fiction. Aside from its scientific approach, applied social psychology also has the laudable goal of trying to improve the human condition. This goal is addressed by techniques designed to solve problems in numerous aspects of everyday life, including mental health, physical health, the environment, education, organizations, consumer behavior, and law. In preparing this book I was truly impressed by what has been done and by the possibilities for the future.

The purpose of this book is to present the practical side of the science of social psychology. For the most part, the term *applied* is used here in the strict sense of real-world problem solving, rather than merely studying such problems. Much of the work directed toward the study of real-world problems is reviewed in many of the current textbooks on social psychology. The focus of the present volume is on aspects of social psychology that receive relatively little coverage in current textbooks—interventions by social psychologists in real-world problem solving and use of social psychological knowledge by public policymakers.

I have tried to write a book that social psychologists would feel comfortable using in their classes. Toward this end, the theoretical basis and scientific evaluation of the applications are discussed. The intent is to promote the Lewinian approach of the practical application of science in a manner where both the human condition and science benefit.

This book could serve as the primary text for a course on applied social psychology, or it could be used to supplement any of the fine textbooks that are currently available for basic courses on social psychology. While the approach I have taken offers some degree of scientific rigor, I have avoided the use of jargon and have included a glossary of key terms to reinforce the explanations provided in the text. Thus, the book should be understandable for students with a minimal background, such as an introductory course in psychology.

I thank Cathy Anderson, George Bryjak, John Christianson, Mike Soroka, and Gerdi Weidner for reading and commenting on earlier drafts of this work. I also thank the editorial board of Oxford University Press, especially Shelley Reinhardt, for making this book possible.

February 1986
San Diego, California

J. M. W.

Contents

Applied Social Psychology

1

Introduction

Think of the term *social psychology*. What kind of images come to mind? Given that psychology is commonly thought of as a helping profession, it is quite natural for people to assume that a discipline called social psychology would be mainly concerned with benefiting society. For example, you might imagine social psychologists working to reduce racial prejudice and discrimination. Or perhaps you can picture a social psychologist advising the producers of an educational television program about how to teach children social skills. On the other hand, you may know that psychology is often defined as the science of behavior, and, therefore, you might think that the main activity of social psychology is to *study* people rather than to help them. Accordingly, your image of a social psychologist might involve a nonemotional person in a white lab coat who systematically confronts people with carefully prearranged situations.

It may have occurred to you that there is a third alternative. Social psychology can be both a science and a helping profession. Indeed, stating this view quite eloquently, Walter Stephan (1980) describes social psychology as a discipline "with a scientific mind and a humanistic heart" (p. 196). The main focus of this text is the humanistic application of scientific knowledge that has been accumulated by social psychology.

Some Definitions

Social Psychology

Because of its diverse subject matter social psychology is difficult to define. Social psychologists study aggression, helping, conformity, obedience, compliance, prejudice, interpersonal attraction, love, sexual behavior, impression formation, impression management, attitudes, leadership, communication, risk-taking, perceptions of others, self-perceptions, emotions, motivations, performance, and much more. Indeed, there is virtually no human thought, feeling, or behavior that is not within the realm of social psychological inquiry. One may begin to wonder if there is nothing that social psychologists do not study. Yet there are limits. A key defining aspect of social psychology is its emphasis on how individuals are influenced by other people, as opposed to explanations that are based primarily on personality characteristics, one's physiological makeup, or nonsocial environmental factors. For example, a social psychological analysis of the determinants of helping might focus on the influence of role models, whereas a physiological explanation might focus on genetic factors. Perhaps the best definition of social psychology, and the one most often cited in textbooks, is Gordon Allport's (1968) characterization of the discipline as "an attempt to understand how the thought, feeling, and behavior of individuals are influenced by the actual, imagined, or implied presence of others" (p. 3). Note that social psychologists endeavor to understand thoughts and feelings as well as overt behaviors, and that social psychological explanations can involve the influence of others who might not actually be present. For example, a social psychologist might attempt to determine how role models influence thoughts and feelings about aggression, even when the role models are idealized or imaginary heroes, such as those depicted on television.

Basic and Applied Social Psychology

Having defined social psychology, a distinction can be made between the discipline's basic and applied areas. Actually, Allport's definition (and virtually any other definition of the discipline) describes the basic aspect. The goal of basic social psychology is to *understand* how individuals are influenced by others. To attain such basic understanding scientific research is conducted and, ideally, the results of related studies are later integrated into theories and general principles. The theories and principles, and the research that supports them, are the main subject matter of most textbooks on social psychology. It should be noted that although basic research is most commonly associated with laboratories, it can also be conducted in field settings. If the goal is to understand, then the research is basic.

It is one thing to understand something and quite another to put that understanding to practical use. To meet the latter goal, applied social psychology attempts to use the theories and principles of the discipline to solve problems in the real world. Most often the applications use social psychological knowledge to develop interventions that can help solve problems facing society. The interventions are designed to directly influence people's behavior. For example, in response to the energy crisis there have been several attempts to use social psychological principles to induce people to conserve resources. A less direct form of application is utilization, which occurs when policymakers, such as government officials, use social psychological information to make decisions. For example, the 1954 Supreme Court decision to desegregate schools was based partially on social psychological evidence. In keeping with the scientific tradition of the discipline, many social psychological applications, especially the interventions, are carefully field tested to determine whether they are effective.

The distinction between basic and applied social psychology is not always as clear as is suggested above. One area of ambiguity is the numerous research studies that are designed to enhance our understanding of real world problems, but do not directly involve solutions. For example, there is research that indicates that viewing television violence makes children more aggressive. To the extent that understanding a problem may be a first step toward developing solutions, some social psychologists have been inclined to regard such research as applied social psychology (Fisher, 1982). Other social psychologists (e.g., Bickman, 1980; Kidd & Saks, 1980; Reyes & Varela, 1980), including the author of this textbook, however, prefer to reserve the label "applied" for actual

Table 1-1. Goals of Social Psychology

Basic → understand how people influence one another
Applicable → understand specific real-world problems
Applied → *solve* real-world problems

problem solving. The term "applicable," which suggests a potential for practical use, may be used to describe research that is aimed primarily at increasing our understanding of social problems and, at best, only indirectly suggests possible solutions (cf. Goldstein, 1980).

An Integrated Approach

Although thinking of social psychological activity as either basic or applied might help to clarify goals, too much emphasis on the distinction may be counterproductive. Deutsch (1980) warns that narrowly focusing on one aspect while ignoring the other is like wearing blinders. By categorizing a project as strictly basic research one might not see important applied implications, and by concentrating exclusively on solving real-world problems one might miss potential theoretical contributions. A laboratory study that may seem far removed from the real world might uncover a principle of behavior that could help solve a practical problem, and research aimed at solving a practical problem might shed some light on a theoretical issue. Although setting a clear goal helps to focus attention, it is also wise to consider the broader picture.

Expressing an even greater concern that a growing division between basic and applied social psychologists might destroy the discipline, Mayo and La France (1980) provide a model to help integrate the field. A schism in the discipline could lead to principles that will be of little practical use in the real world and applications that, because of no basic understanding of how they work, may be of very limited usefulness. To avoid these unfortunate consequences the model is designed to promote compatibility among three elements of social psychology: knowledge building, which is commonly thought of as the domain of basic social psychology; improvement of the quality of life; and utilization/intervention. The last two activities are typically associated with applied social psychology.

An Example

A classic example of applied social psychology (and its integration with basic social psychology) is provided by Kurt Lewin's use of principles of group dynamics (1947a) to alter eating habits during World War II (1947b). A shortage of meat during the war made it important for families to conserve by using cuts of meat from visceral organs, such as beef hearts, sweetbreads, and kidneys. Since other cuts of meat were generally preferred, persuading people to use the visceral meats was not easy. Lewin, who was one of a team of social scientists who were recruited by the government to work on the problem, applied his field theory of behavior. The theory suggests that many habits are difficult to change because they are generally formed and supported in a social context. If an individual were to try to change that person would meet with resistance from others. For example, in our society belching at the dinner table is considered very bad manners. Even if an individual thought the taboo silly, he or she would probably comply because of social pressure. An implication of the theory is that to induce a lasting change in behavior it is important to change the social context.

Applying the theory, Lewin deduced that the key to changing food habits was to prompt group involvement in the decision to use visceral meats. Whereas individual decisions to switch to visceral meats would likely meet with resistance from others, involving whole groups of people in the decision to switch would provide social support for the change. To test the hypothesis homemakers were assigned to two conditions. In one condition the homemakers heard a lecture that, in addition to pointing out how using visceral meats at home would help the war effort, provided information about the nutritional value of such meats and how they can be prepared. Lecturing represents a conventional approach of trying to persuade people by providing them with relevant information. With the exception of occasional questions, the audience plays a passive role. In the other condition a leader conveyed essentially the same information in the context of a group discussion with the homemakers. To prompt group involvement in the decision to change, the leader ended the discussion by asking the participants to indicate, by a show of hands, whether they intended to try serving the visceral meats at home. Lewin predicted that active group involvement in both the discussion and decision to change would more effectively produce actual change than would the lecture. Supporting the hypothesis, follow-up data indicated that only 3 percent of the women who had heard the lecture subsequently served one of the visceral meats at home, whereas 32 percent of those who participated in a group discussion served at least one. Besides providing a means of dealing with the meat shortage, the intervention also demonstrated the robustness of field theory in a real-world setting.

Historical Perspective

Compared to most scientific disciplines, the history of social psychology is quite brief. What is commonly acknowledged as the first social psychology experiment took place just before the beginning of the twentieth century (Triplett, 1897), and it was not until some time later that the discipline began to develop an identity as a specialized area of psychology and sociology. Indeed Kurt Lewin, who did most of his work in the 1930s and 1940s, is often referred to as the founder of social psychology.

Lewin was a prolific advocate of both the basic and applied aspects of social psychology. His work, as exemplified by the visceral meat project, was both theoretical and practical (cf. Marrow, 1969). His most often quoted words are "there is nothing so practical as a good theory" (Lewin, 1951, p. 169). While maintaining a commitment to the scientific method, he stressed the need for research to accomplish some social good (Lewin, 1948) and warned of what he called a "highbrow aversion" (Lewin, 1951, p. 1951) against applications by those who saw such activity as somehow unscientific.

Given that the discipline began with a strong bent toward prac-

Table 1-2. Historical Trends in Social Psychology

1897	Triplett conducts the first social psychology experiment
1930s–1940s	Pioneering work of Kurt Lewin—combines basic science and application
1950s–early 1960s	Era dominated by basic science and laboratory research
Late 1960s–early 1970s	Crisis—concern about relevance—emphasis on field research
Late 1970s–1980s	Reemergence of applications—integration of basic science and applications

tical applications, it may come as a surprise that after Lewin's death in 1947 social psychologists virtually abandoned real-world problem solving. Instead, they turned almost exclusively to laboratory research and set about developing and testing theories and principles. There is general agreement that the main reason for this emphasis on basic research was a great concern about establishing the scientific credibility of the young discipline (cf. Bickman, 1980; Kidd & Saks, 1980). Whereas applications necessitate field work and value judgments, the laboratory offered tight control over variables and, since social implications were mostly ignored, an objective detachment could be maintained.

In the late 1960s and early 1970s, after two decades of laboratory experiments and basic research, social psychologists went through a crisis, or period a self-doubt. Critics within the discipline raised questions about several issues. For example, some wondered whether social psychology, with its penchant for experiments involving cleverly staged deceptions, was a serious science or merely "fun and games" (Ring, 1967, p. 117). A more general concern, and of more importance here, was whether phenomena observed in highly contrived laboratory settings had any relevance to the real world. In the 1960s questions of relevance prompted social psychologists to venture out of the laboratories and to conduct more research in natural settings. Initially the movement toward field research was not a return to applications but rather a means of testing basic theories in realistic settings (Bickman, 1980). Nevertheless, the greater acceptance of research conducted in natural settings, and the accompanying improvement of field research methods, seemed to help pave the way for a reemergence in the 1970s of applied social psychology.

Some Comments about Methodology

During the 1950s and 1960s social psychologists tailored their research methods to basic science. In the prototypical study, subjects, usually college students, report to a laboratory and are randomly assigned to experimental conditions. Without revealing the true purpose of the study, an experimenter manipulates an independent variable (e.g., frustration or no frustration) and measures a dependent variable (e.g., aggression) while controlling extraneous variables (e.g., room temperature). The purpose of these procedures is to isolate the influence, if any, of the independent variable on the dependent variable. In a well controlled experiment a systematic effect (e.g., subjects in the frustration condition exhibit more aggression than those in the no frustration condition) may be attributed to the causal influence of the independent variable. Alternative explanations for the effect are less tenable. Random assignment of subjects to conditions is a safeguard against explanations having to do with the characteristics of the subjects (e.g., subjects in the frustration condition were more belligerent to begin with). The control over extraneous variables that can be exercised in the laboratory makes it unlikely that some other circumstance (e.g., room temperature) produced the effect. Finally, by not telling the subjects the true purpose of the study, it becomes unlikely that the observed effect would be obtained merely because of the subjects' reactions to the hypothesis (e.g., motivation to help the experimenter confirm it). For these reasons the laboratory deception experiment is a valuable tool for uncovering basic principles of behavior.

In assessing the effectiveness of social psychological applications, some degree of experimental control is usually lost. One problem is that whereas research participants reporting to a laboratory can easily be randomly assigned to experimental conditions, it is often much more difficult to manipulate people in real-world settings. Another problem is that since interventions almost invariably take place in natural settings where events occur more spontaneously than in the laboratory, it is difficult for researchers to control situations that might influence the dependent variable. A third problem is that whereas the independent variable in basic research is typically quite simple and therefore leads to clear conclusions about cause and effect, the independent variable in an applied research is often quite complex and leaves ambiguity about which part, or parts, of it are sufficient to produce an effect.

Given the inevitable loss of experimental control when going from basic to applied research, one can readily see why social psychologists have been hesitant to get involved with applications. Nevertheless, in addition to the potential social value of applications, there are reasons to have confidence in the results of applied research. Unless they systematically change with the independent variable, uncontrolled extraneous variables will tend to reduce the probability of demonstrating that an independent variable has a causal effect on a dependent variable. Therefore, demonstrating the effectiveness of an applied intervention in the relatively uncontrolled realm of the real world might attest to the strength of the independent variable, especially when the intervention is based on conceptually similar laboratory findings. In addition, newly developed quasi-experimental techniques, which allow for causal conclusions, can be used in field settings when true experimental control is not feasible.

Some Comments about Ethics

Another obstacle for applied work is the potential for greater ethical problems. Basic social psychological research has already been criticized because of the common use of deceptive techniques. Critics argue that subjects should be fully informed about the purpose and procedures of an experiment before they participate. Without "informed consent" a subject may become involved in a situation that he or she may otherwise have avoided. Of course, providing full disclosure at the outset may bias the results because people will be less inclined to react spontaneously to the experimental manipulations. The typical resolution to this dilemma is to use benign deceptions, manipulate behavior temporarily, and debrief each subject immediately after his or her participation. The debriefing involves both disclosing the true purpose of the experiment and attempting to restore the subjects to their original psychological state. Most basic social psychological principles have been uncovered by using this strategy of temporarily influencing people's behavior.

While sharing some of the same ethical problems as basic social psychology, the extent of the consequences of applied social psychology may be cause for even greater ethical concerns. Whereas attempting to induce temporary changes in people's behavior may be an effective strategy for developing theories and basic principle, the goal of most applications is to induce more permanent changes. It would, for example, be of little use to get someone to stop smoking for a day if he or she were to resume the habit the following day. One might view long-term influences as unjustified manipulations of other people's behavior. Even a policy of restricting applications to those that would benefit the subjects and society begs the question of who is to decide what is good for someone else. Nevertheless, abandoning applications might cause the even greater ethical evil of failing to help people when there are means to provide assistance. It seems that, as has been done with research, the ethics of each application should be assessed before it is carried out, preferably by a committee of responsible people.

Overview and Theme of This Book

Consistent with social psychology's reemerging emphasis on applications and its tradition as a science, the major focus of this book is on projects that have involved both attempts to use social psychological principles to benefit society and scientific evaluations of the effectiveness of those attempts. The following chapters review applications in a wide variety of areas, including mental health, physical health, conservation of natural resources, education, organizations, consumerism, and the law. Some of the applications have been done by people with traditional backgrounds in social psychology, some is interdisciplinary, and some has been carried out by people in other fields who have sought information in the literature of social psychology in an attempt to solve problems in their own fields. Regardless of who is doing the work, the key defining aspect here is whether an attempt is made to benefit society by putting a principle of social psychology to practical use.

2

Mental Health

Imagine a 25-year-old man who is upset because he believes he has homosexual tendencies. This belief is based on his failure to have satisfactory sexual intercourse and the fact that he sometimes finds himself looking at the crotch area of other men. Given that the man views homosexuality as perverted, he is ashamed of what he interprets as an unnatural inclination. As you might expect, his shame prevents him from telling his problem to others. He becomes progressively more convinced that he is abnormal.

The above description summarizes the presenting problems of an actual clinical case (Neale reported in Valins & Nisbett, 1971). Further information about the man suggested that his problem was not homosexuality. Instead, it became clear that the source of his anxiety was a belief that his penis was too small. Emotionally upset and loathe to discuss his problem with anyone else, he imagined the worse and failed to see that his symptoms could be explained as normal reactions to his feared inadequacy. His sexual dysfunction with women could easily be explained by his feeling that he was physically inadequate and his glances at the crotch area of other men could be explained as attempts to compare the size of his own penis to that of others.

How, you might ask, is this case relevant to the application of social psychology to mental health? Part of the answer is that the blocking of a normal social psychological process may have contributed to the man's problem. Normally, we engage in self-evaluations by talking about, or otherwise comparing, our experiences and performances with others. These social comparisons (Festinger, 1954) provide us with useful feedback about how we are doing. There are, however, conditions under which this normal process may be blocked. In describing one such condition, feelings of shame, Valins and Nisbett (1971) suggest that "failure or inability to use social consensus to check shameful evaluations can lead to self-ascriptions of mental abnormality and personal inadequacy that can be profoundly debilitating" (p. 138). Later in this chapter we will see that the solution to this kind of problem can also be social psychological.

Although the main focus of social psychology is the study of how normal individuals are influenced by others, as the above example illustrates, the blocking of a normal social psychological process may lead to the development of psychological disorders. Therefore, social psychology may be useful in understanding the causes of clinical problems. More importantly, in many cases social psychological theories and principles can be applied to the solution of psychological problems that are not necessarily social psychological in origin. Given that the main focus of this volume is the *solution*, and not the description, of problems, this chapter emphasizes the development and testing of clinical interventions that are primarily based on social psychological theories and principles. Three approaches have been most well developed and researched. These are: (a) vicarious extinction, which is based on social learning theory; (b) attribution therapy, which is based on research on how people explain the causes of behavior; and (c) effort justification, which is derived from cognitive dissonance theory.

Vicarious Extinction

Ever since the pioneering work of Ivan Pavlov in the late 1800s, one of the most well-supported notions in psychology is that behavior is influenced by one's environment. Although the extent of such influence has been debated, little doubt remains that our experiences with people, places, and things have a profound effect on the acquisition and maintenance of our thoughts and feelings and on the instigation of our actions. As a corollary it follows that one's environment can help shape both normal and abnormal modes of behavior. Going one step further, a landmark event for clinical psychology was the realization that abnormal modes of behavior could be modified to become more normal by manipulating certain key aspects of an individual's environment. Carefully devised programs of such manipulations, most often referred to as behavior modification or behavior therapy, have been successful in treating a wide variety of psychological disorders ranging from relatively mild neuroses to severe psychoses.

The first behavior therapies—for example, systematic desensitization (Wolpe, 1958) and response-contingent reinforcement (Ayllon & Azrin, 1964)—were based primarily on two traditional theories of learning—classical and operant conditioning—and thus were not social pschological in origin. Very soon, however, Albert Bandura and his associates (e.g., Bandura, 1969a) made two major contributions to the principles of behavior modification, one of which was cognitive in nature while the other was decidedly social psychological. The cognitive contribution was the realization that an actual contingency between one's behavior and environment may not be as important in shaping behavior as is the way the person processes information about such contingencies. The social psychological contribution was the notion that much, and perhaps most, of our behaviors are acquired by observing and modeling the behaviors of others.

As we will see throughout much of this book, Bandura's social learning theory, which incorporates traditional learning models, cognitive processes, and modeling, has been a particularly useful, perhaps *the* most useful, theory in social psychology. With regard to clinical psychology, the most well-researched applications of social learning theory have involved the use of models to help reduce avoidance of feared objects and to induce social behavior in those who are socially withdrawn.

Reducing Avoidance of Feared Objects

Many, perhaps most, of us are afraid of some things that may not pose realistic threats. In most instances such fears are relatively minor and are of little or no consequence. For example, rats make me particularly anxious, but for most of my life this fear was no problem. My fear became a problem, however, when as a graduate assistant I was told to color code the tails of all the rats used for several sections of an undergraduate laboratory class. I overcame my fear enough to complete the task, albeit with a hand so shaky that the color codes, while functional, were quite messy. Other irrational fears can be very intense and debilitating. These intense fears, known as phobias, prevent people from engaging in common behaviors, such as riding in elevators or traveling by airplane.

Whether such irrational fears are severe and debilitating or mild and annoying, people sometimes seek assistance in overcoming them. Clinical psychologists use a variety of techniques to help people with such problems. One technique, vicarious extinction, derives from social learning theory and is therefore distinctly social psychological in origin. The basic strategy of this technique involves exposing the fearful person to a model who, over a series of progresssively more threatening episodes, effectively deals with the feared object without any negative consequences (cf. Bandura, 1969a). According to the theory, the fearful person will vicariously experience the model's behavior and outcomes. Since the model experiences no negative consequences, the observer's fear should gradually diminish over the series of modeled episodes.

As an initial test of the vicarious-extinction technique, Bandura, Grusec, and Menlove (1967) sought to reduce children's fear and avoidance of dogs. Nursery school children, who were especially afraid of dogs, were randomly assigned to four treatment conditions, with each treatment taking place over four consecutive days. In one condition the children participated in parties during which a fearless model, also a nursery school child, approached and played with a cocker spaniel. The behavior of the model toward the dog became progressively more bold over four days of modeling. It was hypothesized that the modeling would help reduce the children's fear of dogs and that the positive context (i.e., the parties) would enhance the effect. To test the effects of modeling in a more neutral context children in the second condition were exposed to the same modeling behavior as in the first condition, but without the parties. As a control for the possible effects of exposure to the feared object in a positive context, in the third condition parties were held with the dog present but with no model. Finally, to control for the effects of a positive context alone, children in the fourth condition participated in parties with neither the dog nor the model present.

The day after the last treatment session and again a month later all the children were given a behavioral avoidance test. This test, which was also used for the initial selection of the subjects, is particularly noteworthy because rather than relying on subjective self-reports it provides an observable measure of fear. The test involved a sequence of 14 tasks in which the children were asked to engage in progressively closer interactions with a cocker spaniel and, to test the generalizability of any effects, with a mongrel. The interactions ranged from looking at the dog while it was in a play-pen to climbing into the playpen and scratching the dog's stomach while no one else was around. Of course, the children were observed through a one-way mirror. For each task the children scored two points if the requested behavior was performed without hesitation, one point if it were done with reluctance, and zero points if it were not performed. Therefore, the total scores over the 14 tasks could range from zero to 28. As shown in Figure 2-1, modeling, whether in a positive or neutral context, produced less fearful behavior toward the dogs both a day after the treatment and at the one month follow-up than did the nonmodeling conditions. Statistical analyses indicated that the positive context did not enhance the effect of the modeling treatment. Overall, the results strongly support the efficacy of the vicarious-extinction technique.

Subsequent to the initial demonstration of vicarious extinction, research has focused on improving the technique by making it more practical and by testing variations of the procedure that have been designed to enhance the beneficial effects. In the original study the models gave repeated performances over several days, which would not be practical for everyday clinical use. If models were to be selected, trained, and available for multiple perfor-mances as relevant clinical cases arose, the technique would be prohibitively time consuming and expensive. As a more practical alternative, Bandura and Menlove (1968) introduced and tested "symbolic" vicarious extinction, which involves using filmed rather than live models. Similar to the findings with live models, exposure to fearless, filmed models significantly reduced fearful

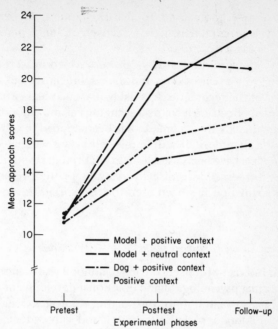

Figure 2-1. Children's level of approach to dogs under various treatment conditions in a vicarious extinction experiment. (Adapted from Bandura, Grusec, & Menlove, 1967. Copyright © 1967 by the American Psychological Association. Reprinted by permission of the publisher and authors.)

children's avoidance of dogs. It is also noteworthy that the reduction in avoidance behavior was enhanced by showing films of several different fearless models as opposed to repeated exposures to the same model, although the latter condition was significantly more effective than no model.

Additional studies indicate that vicarious extinction is most effective when the models are similar to the person being treated. Important aspects of similarity include demographic characteristics, such as age (Kornhaber & Schroeder, 1975), and patterns of behavior. As an example of the latter factor, Meichenbaum (1971) tested the effects of "coping" models. Unlike the fearless models in earlier studies, coping models initially exhibit fears similar to those of the person being treated, but soon overcome those fears and act bravely. Compared to fearless models, Meichenbaum found that coping models more effectively reduced the subjects' fear and avoidance of snakes.

If the only applications of vicarious extinction were to help reduce children's fear of dogs and snakes, one might question the usefulness of the technique. It is likely that such fears would have only minimal effects on a child's psychological and emotional well-being. Fortunately the technique has been applied to other problems. In the chapter on health in this volume we see that symbolic coping models have been used to help children deal with the stress of having surgery. More directly relevant to the present topic, vicarious extinction has been used to treat social withdrawal and shyness.

Inducing Social Behaviors in the Socially Withdrawn

Failure to interact with peers during childhood years may seriously hinder normal psychological and emotional development (O'Connor, 1972). Research into this matter indicates relationships between childhood social withdrawal and subsequent negative consequences, such as poor academic achievement, continued avoidance of social situations, mistreatment by peers, delinquency, and psychiatric problems (see Conger & Keane, 1981). Such evidence suggests that a treatment to help children overcome social withdrawal may be especially worthwhile. Since it is likely that fear of interacting with other people underlies most social withdrawal, vicarious extinction, which was developed to help people overcome fears, seems nicely suited to the task of treating social withdrawal. Several applications have been made along these lines.

O'Connor (1969) was the first to demonstrate the usefulness of vicarious extinction as a treatment for social withdrawal. Socially isolated nursery school children were selected on the basis of two criteria. First, teachers were asked to select children who interacted least with their peers. Second, observers visited classrooms and noted each child's frequency of interactions with peers. The most socially isolated children were randomly assigned to view a modeling or control film. The modeling film consisted of several brief scenes and lasted for a total of about 20 minutes. Each scene began with a young child, who served as the model, noticing other children engaging in a social activity. The model joined in the activity and was reinforced by smiles, friendly talk, or offers to share playthings. In order to grab the viewer's attention the models played their roles dramatically, showing enthusiasm and emotion. In addition, to focus the viewers' attention on the important events in the film, a woman's voice narrated each scene. The control film, which was designed to be interesting but irrelevant to social interaction, depicted the entertaining acrobatics of dolphins at Marineland.

After the children viewed the film, observers, who were unaware of which film individual children had seen, reassessed each child's frequency of interactions with peers. As shown in Figure 2-2, the results strongly supported the efficacy of vicarious extinction in treating social withdrawal. Whereas the control children showed no change in frequency of interactions from the pretest to the posttest, the children in the modeling condition signif-

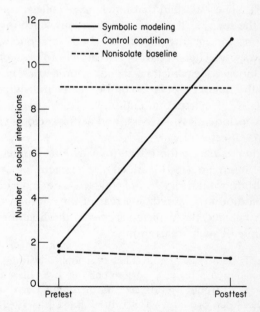

Figure 2-2. Mean number of social interactions displayed in the modeling and control conditions, before and after experimental sessions. The dotted line represents the level of interactions displayed by 26 nonisolate children who were observed at the pretest phase of the study. (Adapted from O'Connor, 1969. Reprinted by permission of the publisher.)

icantly increased their frequency of interactions with peers. In fact, social isolates who had viewed the modeling film subsequently interacted with peers at a rate similar to that of nonisolates. In a later study the results were replicated and it was found that the effects were still strong when assessed six weeks after treatment (O'Connor, 1972).

Subsequent research has both refined the procedures and extended the usefulness of vicarious extinction as a means of treating social withdrawal. For example, instead of merely increasing the frequency of social interactions, Keller and Carlson (1974) successfully adapted the vicarious-extinction technique to facilitate the use of specific social skills. Exposure to videotaped models who displayed behaviors such as smiling and affectionate touching, increased similar behaviors in socially withdrawn preschool children. Jones, Hobbs, and Hockenbury (1982) had similar success in promoting a social skill in an older sample of subjects. First, they empirically established that lonely male college students typically lack the social skill of partner attention, which involves asking questions and making statements about someone with whom one is conversing. Then as part of a treatment to promote partner attention, lonely college males listened to audiotapes that modeled the skill. Subsequent observation of the treated individuals showed increased use of partner attention, and self-reports indicated reductions in loneliness, shyness, and self-consciousness and an increase in self-esteem.

To further enhance the effects of vicarious extinction Jakibchuk and Smeriglio (1976) added the element of self-speech. Socially withdrawn nursery school children observed videotapes in which, in addition to overcoming fear of interacting with others, the model narrated the depicted scenes in the first person. Here is an example of such a narration:

> My name is Danny, and I go to nursery school. I'm sitting here all by myself looking at a book. . . . Those children over there are playing together. . . . I would like to play with them. But I'm afraid. I don't know what to do or say. . . . This is hard. But I'll try . . . I'm close to them. I did it. Good for me. I like playing with Johnny and Bobby. I'm glad I decided to play with them. I'm having lots of fun. (p. 839).

It was hypothesized that the socially withdrawn children who were given this treatment would incorporate the self-speech as their own and use it to direct their own behavior. The effects of the self-speech treatment were compared to a condition that included a third-person narration, a nature film control condition, and a no-treatment control. Using behavioral measures both immediately following treatment and three weeks later, it was found that the self-speech treatment was most effective in increasing the children's frequency of interaction with their peers and also increased their giving and receiving of positive social reinforcement. As might be expected, the condition involving modeling and third-person narration produced positive effects compared to the control conditions, nevertheless, the effects in the self-narration condition were stronger.

In summary, it appears that vicarious extinction is an effective means of inducing socially withdrawn people to engage in social interactions more frequently and to develop certain social skills. As in the application of vicarious extinction to reducing fear of animals, certain refinements of the technique, such as self-speech, further enhance the positive effects.

Treating Sexual Dysfunction

Further evidence of the clinical usefulness of vicarious extinction was provided in an application of the technique designed to help inorgasmic women overcome sexual anxiety and enjoy sexual activity (Nemetz, Craig, & Reith, 1978). Nemetz and her associates began with the premise that anxiety about sexual functioning is typically learned from unpleasant and often traumatic experiences, such as rape, molestation, criticism about sexual performance, and failure to achieve orgasm. Once acquired, such anxiety may block the desire for, and enjoyment of, sexual contact. Therefore, a key factor in treating sexual dysfunction is to reduce anxiety associated with sexual contact. Once again, vicarious extinction, which is designed to reduce learned fears, is well suited to the clinical task.

Nemetz and her associates tested the utility of vicarious extinction as a mode of treatment for sexual dysfuntion in an experiment with actual clinical clients. The subjects in the study were inorgasmic women who had been referred to a sexual dysfunction clinic by their physicians. Pretreatment measures indicated that these women were severely anxious about sexual activity. Another

important selection criterion was the availability and cooperation
of a husband or steady male partner. Each woman was randomly
assigned to one of three conditions: individual treatment, group
treatment, or control.

Except for the administration of the treatment in groups or
individually, the procedures for the two treatment conditions were
the same. In both conditions the women were first given relaxation
training, as is typically done in the behavioral technique of systematic desensitization (see Wolpe, 1958). They were to use these
relaxation techniques while viewing a series of videotaped
vignettes that depicted sexual activities. The tapes were shown
eight at a time over five sessions that were three days apart. The
women were asked to imagine themselves engaging in the depicted
sexual activities, and were given the option of terminating any sex
scene if they were becoming too anxious. At the end of each session the women were instructed to practice the depicted sexual
activities at home with their partners, who were instructed not to
initiate any sexual activity during the treatment period. Women in
the control condition were put on a waiting list and eventually
received treatment six weeks later.

The results indicated that both treatment conditions were
highly successful. By the end of treatment, and three weeks later,
women in the treatment conditions were less anxious about sexual
activity and were more frequently initiating sexual behaviors, such
as foreplay and intercourse, than were women in the control condition. A one year follow-up indicated that the reduced anxiety
and increased sexual behavior reported by the women in the treatment conditions were maintained. There were no significant differences between the two treatment conditions. Although self-
report measures were used, the results were substantiated by
obtaining measures from the women's partners, who throughout
the study provided data that were in very high agreement with the
reports provided by the women.

Summary and Conclusions

Vicarious extinction, a technique that is based on social learning
theory, involves exposing a fearful client to a model who, through
a series of progressively more threatening scenes, is shown to deal

with the source of the client's fear without experiencing any negative consequences. This technique has been successfully applied
to a variety of clincial problems, including fear of dogs, social withdrawal, and sexual dysfunction. Practicality of the technique is
enhanced by the demonstrated fact that symbolic (filmed) models
effectively produce the desired results. Refinements of the technique, such as using models who are similar to the client and providing a narration of the scenes presented by the model in the first
person, have facilitated the positive effects.

Attribution Therapy

Have you ever caught yourself making psychological judgments
about people? Do you assign certain motives and personality traits
to particular individuals? Do you decide that some people are kind
and some are cruel, some are friendly and some unfriendly, some
are generous and some self-centered, and so on? Of course you
do. To some extent we all engage in a "naive psychology" (Heider,
1944, 1958). That is, without conducting scientific research into
the matter or using established clinical procedures, we often try
to discern the motives and personality traits of people we know,
and even of people we merely encounter. Given the potential
impact on our behavior, the way we make such judgments is of
great interest to social psychologists. It has been found that to a
large extent we make such judgments from our observations of
others' behavior. We even make judgments about ourselves from
observations of our own behavior (Bem, 1972). Social psychologists use the term attribution to refer to the process by which we
all, as naive psychologists, attempt to explain the causes of people's behavior.

   Attributions we make about our own behavior are particularly
relevant to mental health. Recall that in the opening example of
this chapter a man attributed his inability to have satisfying sexual
intercourse and his glances at the crotch area of other men to
homosexuality. This attribution, which was later found to be
faulty, was very emotionally upsetting to the man. Could it be that
certain attributions can contibute to, and even cause, psychological disorders? Many social psychologists believe that the answer to

this question is yes. They also suggest that other attributions can reduce or cure such disorders. The essence of attribution therapy is to change self-defeating attributions into self-enhancing attributions.

Misattribution and the Exacerbation Model

Ross, Rodin, and Zimbardo (1969), who first introduced the term *attribution therapy,* based their new technique primarily on a theory of emotion put forth by Stanley Schachter (1964). According to Schachter's theory, the experience of any particular emotion is caused by a combination of general physiological arousal and an attribution of that arousal to an emotional cause. In this view the arousal sets the stage for an emotional experience and the attribution directs one to a particular emotion. If either the arousal or the attribution is missing no emotion will be experienced. Supporting the theory, Schachter and Singer (1962) found that people surreptitiously aroused by a drug displayed either anger, if exposed to an angry confederate, or euphoria, if exposed to a euphoric confederate. Presumably, the confederate's behavior suggested an attribution for the drug-induced arousal. In comparison conditions people who were informed that the drug was responsible for their arousal were relatively nonemotional when exposed to the angry or euphoric confederate. This research suggests, therefore, that physiological arousal can lead to emotional or nonemotional experiences, depending on the perceived cause of the arousal.

Following from Schachter's theory, Ross, Rodin, and Zimbardo (1969) hypothesized that aversive emotional experiences could be reduced by providing people with a nonemotional attribution for their arousal. To test this hypothesis college students, who were led to believe that they were participating in a study on the effects of distracting noise, were asked to solve puzzles while exposed to noise. Half of the students were told that the noise was likely to produce arousal symptoms, such as heart palpitations, hand tremors, stomach upset, and rapid breathing. The other half of the subjects were told that the noise would produce a different set of symptoms, such as numbness, dizziness, a dull headache, and weariness. All subjects worked on two puzzles and were told that solving one of the puzzles would earn them a monetary reward, while solving the other puzzle would be required in order to avoid receiving electric shock. The threat of shock was used to produce arousal symptoms. It was hypothesized that the subjects who were told that the noise would produce arousal symptoms would tend to misattribute their arousal to the noise rather than to the threat of shock, while the subjects who were not expecting arousal symptoms from the noise would more accurately attribute their arousal to fear of the shocks. This hypothesis gained support when the students who were not told to expect that the noise would produce arousal symptoms spent more time working on the puzzle to avoid shock than did the students who were told that the noise would produce arousal symptoms. Thus it seems that misattribution of fear arousal to a nonemotional source reduced the experience of fear.

Although the situation created in their experiment was highly contrived, Ross, Rodin, and Zimbardo maintained that their research had implications for actual therapy. They suggested two therapeutic procedures. One procedure would be to point out an existing, and presumably true, alternative nonemotional attribution for emotionally upsetting arousal symptoms. We examine this suggestion more closely in the next section. The second procedure, which follows more closely from their experiment, would involve presenting an artificial source to which the person's arousal symptoms could be attributed. For example, for some of the students in their experiment the noise served as an alternative explanation for arousal symptoms, which were probably really caused by the threat of shock. In general, if arousal is truly caused by an emotionally upsetting source, misattribution to a nonemotional source should help to reduce the aversive emotion.

The misattribution technique was further developed by Storms and Nisbett (1970), who applied it to the problem of insomnia. Based on research indicating that difficulty in falling asleep is associated with high levels of autonomic arousal at bedtime, it was hypothesized that attributions about this bedtime arousal might contribute to sleep disorders. People having such difficulties might make emotionally upsetting attributions about their arousal, such as, "There must really be something wrong with me because I cannot fall asleep like other people." Such attributions might further exacerbate arousal symptoms, making it even more difficult to fall asleep. Therefore, the basic strategy employed by Storms and Nisbett was to trick insomniacs into believing that there was an external cause for their arousal. It was hypothesized that if insomniacs would attribute their arousal to an external cause, then they would be less upset, begin to relax, and fall asleep.

Storms and Nisbett found support for their hypothesis, but in a highly contrived situation. College students who reported having difficulty falling asleep were recruited for what they were told was an experiment on how level of bodily activity influences dreams. Actually this was a cover story for a study of misattribution therapy applied to insomnia. Unknown to the subjects they were randomly assigned to either of two treatment conditions or to a control group. In both treatment groups the subjects were given pills to take before bedtime. The ostensible purpose of the pills was to enhance the likelihood of dreaming, but they were actually placebos. In one treatment condition the subjects were told that the pill would produce arousal, and in the other treatment condition the subjects were told that the pills would reduce arousal. The control subjects were not given pills. All the subjects were then asked to keep records about their dreams and sleeping patterns for several days. As predicted, the subjects who were told that the pills would produce arousal, which would provide an external attribution for their bedtime insomnia symptoms, fell asleep an average of about 12 minutes faster than they had prior to the treatment (see Figure 2-3). In contrast, the subjects who were told that the pills would make them relax experienced a "reverse placebo" effect. That is, it took longer for them to fall asleep than it had before the treatment. Subjects in the control condition showed virtually no change in onset of sleep.

There are several reasons to be skeptical about the usefulness of Storms and Nisbett's treatment. One concern is that it is based on a deception that presents both ethical and practical problems. Ethically one might question the practice of deceiving clients, even if the psychologist thinks it is for the client's own good. A practical problem is that, unless offered in the context of a highly contrived experiment, there seems to be no reason why an insomniac would be convinced to take a pill that he or she thinks would increase bedtime arousal. In addition to the ethical and practical problems

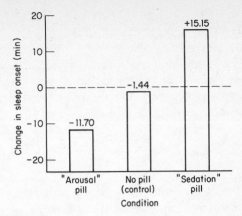

Figure 2-3. Mean change (posttest minus pretest) in sleep onset for subjects in various pill attribution conditions. (Adapted from Storms & Nisbett, 1970. Copyright © 1970 by the American Psychological Association. Reprinted by permission of the publisher and authors.)

other researchers have failed to replicate Storms and Nisbett's findings (Bootzin, Herman, & Nicassio, 1976; Kellogg & Baron, 1975).

Admitting that the misattribution technique is unreliable, Storms and his colleagues (Storms, Denney, McCaul, & Lowery, 1979; Storms & McCaul, 1976) nevertheless defend the theoretical model on which it is based and suggest alternative techniques to apply the model. Their theoretical model suggests that insomnia, and perhaps several other disorders, may be maintained and worsened by an exacerbation cycle. For insomnia the cycle begins with the experience of arousal symptoms at bedtime, such as accelerated heart rate, racing thoughts, and restlessness. If such arousal were attributed to emotionally upsetting internal causes that are not controllable, such as mental instability or some other kind of personal incompetence, then the insomniac might worry. Anxiety about symptoms might lead to more arousal and thus exacerbate the symptoms. The exacerbated symptoms might lead to further self-defeating attributions and the cycle would continue.

The unreliablity of the misattribution technique might be accounted for by the fact that the insomniacs in the studies would have experienced bedtime arousal before being given the "arousal" pills. Thus many of the subjects might not have believed that their arousal was caused by the pills. Without such a misattribution, the technique should not work. Consistent with this argument, in their original study Storms and Nisbett found that only those subjects who believed that the pill caused their bedtime arousal showed an improvement in sleep onset.

Veridical Reattribution

An alternative technique, which also follows from the exacerbation model, appears to solve many of the problems with the misattribution technique. In general, the alternative is to suggest a nonemotional attribution for symptoms that is truthful. Applied to insomnia, rather than using deception, the alternative is simply to inform insomniacs truthfully that their problem may be caused by high baseline autonomic arousal. To the extent that this nonemotional, veridical reattribution would alleviate anxiety that otherwise might be caused by attributing failure to sleep to a serious psychological problem, the insomniac should be better able to relax and fall asleep. Supporting this hypothesis, Lowery, Denney, and Storms (1979) found that this straightforward approach did help insomniacs both to make fewer self-defeating attributions and to have less difficulty falling asleep.

A number of interesting case studies have also supported the efficacy of veridical reattributions. Recall that in the opening example of this chapter a young male client was worried about his failure to have satisfying sexual intercourse and his interest in the crotch area of other men. The client attributed these symptoms to homosexuality, which upset him greatly and may have exacerbated his symptoms. Neale (cited in Valins & Nisbett, 1971) treated the client by helping him to reattribute the symptoms to the actual fear the client had that his penis was too small. Having been provided with a veridical reattribution, and with reassurance that he was not anatomically inadequate, the client made a dramatic recovery.

In a more severe case, Davison (1966) was able to help a man who had been diagnosed as paranoid schizophrenic. The patient experienced twitches in several areas of his body. He referred to these sensations as "pressure points" and attributed them to a "spirit" who he believed was helping him make decisions. As is typical in paranoid schizophrenia, the patient's speech was characterized by bizarre associations and delusions of persecution. A major part of the patient's therapy was to reattribute the "spiritual pressure points" to normal symptoms of tension. In several instances it was pointed out that the sensations occurred in reaction to stressful situations. Soon the patient began to refer to the twitches as sensations and stopped interpreting them as spirit induced.

In another delusional case a man who thought he had been experiencing sexual intercourse with a mysterious "warm form" sought help at a hospital emergency room (Johnson, Ross, & Mastria, 1977). He reported that the warm form would present itself without warning and would press against his genitals until he ejaculated. He was admitted to the hospital with a tentative diagnosis of paranoid schizophrenia, and thorazine, a strong psychiatric drug, was prescribed. Further observations and interviews, however, led psychologists to suspect that the warm form was merely a faulty attribution for a real experience and that the man could be treated by providing a veridical reattribution.

It was determined that the man's delusion regarding the warm form began at a time when he had been abstaining from sexual activity because of body lice that he had contracted from a sexual partner. Prior to contracting the body lice, he had engaged in sexual intercourse regularly for several years without ever abstaining for more than two weeks. He denied ever using masturbation as a sexual outlet because he felt that it was inappropriate. In the hospital, however, it was observed that when he reported the presence of the warm form his legs would move in a manner sufficient to stimulate his penis. It was apparent, therefore, that he was engaging in inadvertent masturbation.

Treatment consisted of accepting the man's experience of penile stimulation but questioning his interpretation of that experience. In order to dissuade him about his delusional warm form, a penile strain gauge was used to demonstrate that no foreign agent was present when he experienced penile stimulation. As a reattribution for the experience, it was suggested that by abstaining from sexual activity, sexual tension had built up and that the movement of his legs resulted in inadvertent masturbation. He was reassured that masturbation was an appropriate behavior. With acceptance of the reattribution his delusion about a warm form disappeared. Six months later he was still experiencing spontaneous erections, but he no longer attributed them to abnormal causes. Johnson, Ross, and Mastria concluded that "the proper focus of attribution therapy lies in changing cognitions and not overt behavior by presenting veridical as opposed to deceptive information" (p.425).

Veridical reattributions may be particularly useful in crisis intervention, because attributions that contribute to a psychological crisis are likely to be newly formed and tentative (Skillbeck, 1974). Such tentative attributions may be relatively easy to alter, whereas attributions that have maintained chronic disturbances over a long period of time should be more resistant to change. In a crisis case, Skillbeck was successful in persuading a female student to reattribute her symptoms of agitation and depression from an inner psychopathology to normal stress associated with an upcoming exam.

Attributional Style Therapy

For many psychological problems, especially those that are chronic, attribution therapy may be too narrow an approach to bring about positive changes. The problem is that the techniques fail to address the possibility that an individual's attributions are part of a system of interrelated beliefs (Peterson, 1982). Attempts to change one attribution may fail because of the resistance offered by related attributions. In such cases it may be necessary to focus treatment more broadly on an individual's general style of making attributions rather than on a specific attribution. Taking this broader approach, Layden (1982) has developed an attributional-style therapy.

Layden defines attributional style as "a habitual manner of answering questions about causality" (p. 64). She suggests that attributional styles that individuals use to explain their own behavior may be either self-enhancing or self-defeating. For example, people with high self-esteem tend to attribute their successes to internal causes, such as skill or effort, and to attribute their failures to external causes, such as the difficulty of the task or poor luck. People with low self-esteem, on the other hand, have the opposite attributional tendencies. It follows that individuals with high self-esteem will make judgments about themselves in terms of their successes, whereas individuals with low self-esteem will judge themselves on the basis of their failures. Such biases may lead to a positive cycle for people with high self-esteem and a negative cycle for people with low self-esteem. By focusing selectively on successes, individuals with high self-esteem should expect success, persist despite failures, and therefore be successful. Individuals with low self-esteem should expect failure, not persist, and therefore fail. Layden cites research that supports the notion that people with high self-esteem are more persistent and successful in a variety of tasks than are people with low self-esteem.

Layden summarizes the rationale for her therapeutic approach to low self-esteem as follows:

> Since high self-esteem individuals interpret their successes and failures in ways that are different from low self-esteem individuals, why not teach the lows to make attributions like the highs? For individuals who have low self-esteem, who are depressed, or who are helpless and passive, it may not be necessary to increase the level of success in their lives. Change their attributional style and successes which in the past have been denied may now be accepted. Successes which have been trivialized by attributing them to good luck or an easy task may now be attributed to a combination of ability and effort. Failures that were used as evidence of incompetence may now be attributed to external barriers or to temporary difficulties that renewed effort may overcome. (p. 72)

Attributional-style therapy, as Layden views it, should proceed according to two general guidelines. One guideline is that the therapy should be veridical rather than deceptive. Resorting to misattributions is awkward, relatively unconvincing, and unnecessary. Her strategy is to ask individuals who are low in self-esteem to examine their successes more closely, focusing on realistic internal causes that they typically overlook. They are also asked to think of realistic external causes for failures. As a second guideline, she recommends that the clients write their new attributions down in a diary, which is intended to facilitate the therapy in several ways. One beneficial effect of the diary is that it helps focus the patient's

attention on self-enhancing, rather than self-defeating, attributions. Second, the act of writing the new attributions would serve
as a means of practicing them. A third facilitating aspect of the
diary is that it would provide material that can be discussed and
analyzed during therapy sessions.

Preliminary research on attributional-style therapy indicates
that the technique may have promise. In an experiment with college students who both had low self-esteem and were depressed,
Layden (1982) compared attributional-style therapy to a no-treatment control condition. The key aspects of the therapy included
the following: (a) discussing the importance of attributions about
success and failure; (b) having the students attempt laboratory
tasks involving intellectual and social skills; (c) asking students to
make attributions about their performance on the tasks; (d) pointing out the students' self-defeating attributions; and (e) requiring
the students to keep a diary about attributions of success and failure for four or five weeks. Compared to the control condition,
attributional therapy produced a more positive attributional style
and increased self-esteem. The therapy failed to reduce depression
or to increase persistence on tasks, however. Perhaps these latter
two phenomena would only occur after more prolonged therapy,
in which case a long-term study may be in order. Also, Layden
suggests that in actual clinical settings the effectiveness of the therapy might be enhanced by analyzing attributions about important
successes and failures in the client's life rather than about laboratory tasks, which are likely to be relatively insignificant to the
individual.

Summary and Conclusions

Three general types of attribution therapy, all derived from basic
research on how people explain their own experiences, have been
applied to a variety of clinical problems. The misattribution technique, which involves supplying a bogus nonemotional cause for
upsetting symptoms, is the least desirable of the three therapies,
because its effects are unreliable and it involves deception. Supplying veridical, nonemotional attributions avoids the problem of
deception; however, a word of caution is in order since most of
the evidence for the effectiveness of this technique comes from

case studies, which do not involve adequate control groups. As a third variant, attributional-style therapy focuses more broadly on sets of interrelated attributions, because the altering of any one attribution may meet with resistance from other attributions. Although promising, attributional style therapy is a relatively new and untested technique.

Effort Justification

Suppose that you will accomplish two things tomorrow, one of which will require a great deal of effort while the other will come easily. Which of the two would you appreciate the most? Although not knowing what the two accomplishments are might make you hesitant to answer the question, it seems that we generally appreciate most that which we find hardest to achieve. Things that come easily can be taken for granted, whereas that which is accomplished through great effort tends to be highly valued. Why is this so? An obvious explanation is that an individual would only work hard for something that he or she values highly. Otherwise, the person would quit before expending much effort. Thus things that a person works hard to attain would be perceived as worthwhile *before* he or she sets out to accomplish them.

A less intuitively obvious explanation for valuing a difficult accomplishment is offered by Festinger's theory of cognitive dissonance (1961). Instead of focusing on the a priori value of a goal, Festinger proposed that *after* an individual works hard to accomplish something, he or she has a psychological need to *justify* the effort involved. In general, the theory of cognitive dissonance holds that people find inconsistencies in their own thoughts (cognitions) to be aversive. It would be inconsistent (dissonant) to know that you worked hard to accomplish a goal that was not worthwhile. You could regain consistency (consonance) by convincing yourself that the goal was worthwhile after all. Therefore, your subsequent assessment of a goal may have little to do with its a priori value, but rather might be a justification of the effort you put into attaining it. Supporting this notion, Aronson and Mills (1959) found that, despite exposing all students to the same discussion group, students who by random assignment endured a severe initiation to the group subsequently found it more attractive than did students randomly assigned to a mild initiation.

Reasoning from a cognitive-dissonance perspective, Cooper and Axsom (1982) note that, to some extent, being a patient in psychotherapy involves effort and thus they propose that the psychological need to justify that effort may enhance the effectiveness of the therapy. They conceptualize effort quite broadly as engaging in any activity that a person might find unpleasant. Besides the expenditure of time and money, being in psychotherapy involves unpleasant activities such as admitting that one has a problem, discussing the problem with a stranger, and working to overcome the problem. While many therapists quite naturally would attempt to minimize their patients' perception of the unpleasantness of therapy, Cooper and Axsom suggest the opposite. By calling attention to the unpleasantness of therapy patients should, according to cognitive dissonance theory, attempt to justify the effort involved.

Cooper and Axsom (1982) suggest three interrelated ways that effort justification on the part of the patient might enhance the effectiveness of therapy. One possibility is that the patient might develop a more favorable attitude about the goal of the therapy. For example, a shy person who is asked to role-play being more outgoing might subsequently justify the effort involved by becoming more attracted to the goal of being extroverted. A second effect might be to enhance motivation. The unpleasantness involved in the process of therapy could be justified by becoming further committed to trying to change. A third factor might be an enhanced expectation that the therapy will be effective. It would be dissonant to think that one is expending effort in therapy that is ineffective. To the extent that effort justification can induce a positive attitude, motivation, and an expectancy of success, the effectiveness of therapy should be enhanced.

It is important to note that effort justification follows from cognitive-dissonance theory only under conditions of perceived free choice. It would be cognitively dissonant to believe that you freely chose to engage in a relatively worthless task and, according to the theory, you would feel some need to justify your actions. On the other hand, if you thought you had little or no alternative but to perform the task, then your participation would already be explained by the lack of choice. For example, I might feel a need to justify my choice to exercise regularly by extolling the virtues of physical fitness; however, if for some reason I had to exercise and could not choose otherwise, then there would be no reason to explain doing so. For clinical practice the implication is that calling attention to the effort involved in therapy will enhance the effectiveness of the treatment only to the extent that the patient feels that he or she has some choice about participating.

The influence of effort justification on psychotherapy has been tested in a number of studies. In one study Gordon (1976) asked college students to participate in a relaxation training session. Some of the students volunteered without any further incentive, while others (nonvolunteers) agreed to participate only when offered extra credit in one of their classes. Half of the participants were given an apparent choice about which kind of therapy they would receive and the other half were given no apparent choice. Actually all the subjects received the same treatment. Supporting cognitive dissonance theory, volunteers who thought they had freely chosen their treatment rated the therapy as significantly more valuable and effective than did subjects in the other conditions. Apparently volunteering and perceiving free choice led to a greater need to justify the effort involved in the therapy. In similar research Cooper (1980) found that conditions designed to induce effort justification can enhance therapeutic effects even when a bogus therapy is used. The "therapy" consisted of physical exercise that in one study was supposedly designed to reduce fear of snakes and in a second study was supposed to increase interpersonal assertiveness. Compared to conditions of no choice, subjects who freely choose to participate in the therapy were actually more able to approach a snake and to act assertively in an interpersonal conflict. As shown in Figure 2-4, these effects were comparable to those obtained with traditional therapies. Furthermore, Mendonca and Brehm (1983) found that for at least one type of nonvoluntary patient—children—perceived choice of type of therapy was sufficient to significantly enhance the effectiveness of a treatment program.

While the studies described above demonstrate the positive effect of free choice in therapy, they did not systematically vary the amount of effort involved in the treatments. According to dissonance theory, given a perception of free will the amount of jus-

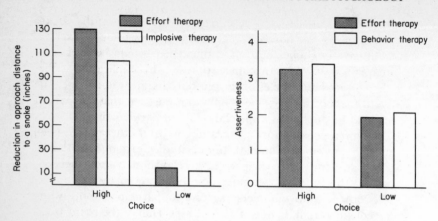

Figure 2-4. Clinical effects of effort therapy and more traditional therapies on approach distance to snakes and on assertiveness under conditions of high and low cost. Assertiveness scores range from 0 to 4, with higher scores indicating more assertiveness. (Adapted from Cooper, 1980. Copyright © 1980 by Academic Press. Reprinted by permission of the publisher.)

tification should be directly proportional to the amount of effort involved. Supporting this hypothesis Axsom and Cooper (1981) found that a bogus weight loss program requiring a high degree of effort led to significantly more long-term weight loss than did a treatment requiring less effort.

Overall, it seems that conditions designed to induce effort justification can enhance the effectiveness of therapy. Both calling the patients' attention to their own volition in participating in demanding therapies and using therapies that require a great deal of effort have been shown to yield positive results. It should be pointed out that, although they used bogus therapies in their studies, Axsom and Cooper do not recommend the clinical use of such therapies but do suggest that therapists take advantage of the fact that perceived effort enhances the effectiveness of treatments. The idea is to not shy away from the use of therapies that require effort and not to disguise the effort involved. An issue that might be prudent to address is whether the effort might scare some patients away from participating in the therapy.

Summary and Conclusions

Social psychological factors might contribute to the development of many clinical disorders. For example, lack of social comparison feedback can lead to a vicious exacerbation cycle, which involves a downward spiral of self-defeating attributions and aggravated symptoms. More importantly, the application of social psychological techniques has been shown to be effective in treating a variety of clinical problems, regardless of the origin of disorders. Three of the techniques that have been well researched are vicarious extinction, attribtuion therapy, and effort justification.

Vicarious extinction is a clinical technique that is derived from social learning theory. It is based on the premise that people tend to model their behavior after that of others. The technique involves showing a fearful patient a model who effectively deals with the fearful object or situation. Research indicates that this technique is effective in helping people overcome fear of animals, social withdrawal, and sexual dysfunction. The fact that filmed models can be effectively used makes the technique practical. Refinements of the technique, such as using a model who is similar to the patient and providing a narration for the film, further enhance its effectiveness.

Attribution therapy is derived from social psychological research on how people attempt to explain the causes of behavior. Self-attributions can be either self-enhancing or self-defeating. The latter can contribute to the development and maintenance of psychological disorders. One version of attribution therapy, the misattribtuion technique, is to provide a nonpejorative, but false, attribution as a substitute for a self-defeating attribution. This technique currently enjoys little favor because it produces unreliable results and it raises ethical concerns. A more straightforward approach, providing a nonpejorative attribution that is also true, seems more promising. Such veridical reattributions seem to have been effective in a number of case studies but, for the most part, are untested in well-controlled studies.

A third technique, attributional-style therapy, has been developed to induce more effective changes by altering the patient's habitual manner of making self-attributions rather than focusing on a few attributions in isolation. This technique is very new and, although preliminary research on it seems promising, it needs to be more thoroughly tested.

The technique of effort justification derives from cognitive-dissonance theory. It is based on the premise that people have a psychological need to justify choosing to expend effort on a difficult or unpleasant task. It is argued that by calling patients' attention to the effort involved in being in psychotherapy the patients will justify their decision to participate by perceiving the therapy to be worthwhile and effective. Research shows that both the perception of free choice and high effort can enhance the effectiveness of therapy. A question that remains unanswered is at what point might the effort-justification technique backfire by scaring patients away from therapy.

3

Physical Health

When I was growing up I liked to watch "Perry Mason," a television show about a fictional defense attorney. Each week, District Attorney Hamilton Burger would have what seemed to be an open-and-shut case against Mason's client. But invariably Mason would determine that some other person committed the crime and would masterfully manipulate that person into publicly confessing before the court. If only social psychologists knew that much about people! At the time I did not have much sympathy for Burger, despite the fact that he was defeated week after week. After all, it was only a television program. My sympathies abruptly changed, however, when one day I was shocked to learn that William Talman, who played Burger on the television series, was losing one more battle, but this time in real life. As a public service, Talman appeared on television to explain that he was a cigarette smoker who was dying of cancer. This one time I hoped he would win, but tragically it was too late. He died a short time later. Unfortunately, this is but one example of how people's behavior can be the cause of ther own demise.

In recent years people have become increasingly aware of the health hazards associated with certain behavior patterns. For example, beginning with the Surgeon General's report in 1964, it has been widely known that there is scientific evidence linking cigarette smoking to cancer, emphysema, and heart disease. By the late 1970s the Surgeon General recognized that cigarette smoking is the leading preventable cause of death in the United States (Richmond, 1979a). Other self-destructive behavior patterns that are being widely publicized are poor dietary habits, lack of exercise, alcohol and drug abuse, and chronically stressful work habits.

Unfortunately, despite awareness of the consequent health hazards, many people regularly engage in self-destructive behavior. The Center for Disease Control (1979) estimates that about half of the deaths in the United States can be attributed to behavioral causes. A report of the Surgeon General indicates that unhealthy behavior is the primary contributor to seven of the ten leading causes of death in this country (Richmond, 1979b). Perhaps part of the problem is that much of this behavior is deeply ingrained in our life-styles (Evans, 1980). Fast food is convenient, alcohol and drug use often are social behavior, cigarette smoking is a generally accepted habit, and many people are convinced that hard-driving work is the way to achieve the American dream. Resistance to change is so great that people often will not restrict or alter their personal habits, even when advised to do so by a physician (Kasl, 1975).

Given the risks associated with many common life-styles, it is clear that behavioral change can have a tremendous beneficial effect on the health of a great number of people. Indeed, a report of the Surgeon General suggests that seven of the ten leading causes of death could be dramatically reduced by changing unhealthy to healthy behaviors (Richmond, 1979b). To help induce such changes, a new multidisciplinary health concept, called behavioral medicine, is emerging (Evans, 1980). This new approach is associated with a general movement in health care away from an almost exclusive reliance on doctors to treat disease to a greater emphasis on self-help and prevention of disease (Taylor, 1978).

The preventive approach to health care increases individual responsibility to adopt healthy behavior patterns and life-styles. Nevertheless, with the emergence of behavioral medicine the role of traditional health care providers has not diminished in importance and the role of other professionals has expanded. While medical researchers have the skills needed to determine the health risks associated with various behaviors, physicians and other health care practitioners can use their training and clinical experience to give chronically ill, high-risk, and even healthy patients advice about how to prevent and control disease. As already noted, however, people often do not change their behavior patterns even when they know the risk factors. This is where behavioral scientists, including social psychologists, can make an important contribution. Since social psychologists have expertise in the areas of persuasive communication and social influence, they are particularly well qualified to provide techniques to help people make the behavioral and life-style changes that are suggested by medical researchers and health care practitioners.

Changing Health-Related Behaviors: Some Social Psychological Applications

Most of the applications of social psychology to health have involved interventions designed to alter behavior patterns or lifestyles that are detrimental to health, such as poor dental hygiene, cigarette smoking, alcohol and drug abuse, overeating, passive institutional living, and experiencing stressful events.

Dental Hygiene

Janis and Feshbach (1953) were the first to apply social psychology to a health problem. Their work was part of the larger Yale Communication and Attitude Change Program, which was a comprehensive program of research on persuasive communication carried out by several prominent social psychologists (see Hovland, Janis, & Kelley, 1953). The general approach of the Yale group was to break the process of persuasive communication into its component parts—the source or communicator, the message, and the audience—and to independently vary aspects of each component to determine the influence on attitude change. Focusing on the message component, Janis and Feshbach (1953) varied the amount of fearful information in a communication that was designed to persuade high school students to improve their dental hygiene habits. Although the effect that the Yale group usually studied was attitude change, in their study Janis and Fesbach were interested in both attitude and behavioral change.

The assumption underlying the use of fear appeals was that such messages would arouse adverse emotional tension that would motivate the audience to comply with the communicator's recommendation for avoiding the fearful consequences. To test this notion, Janis and Fesbach randomly assigned high school students to four conditions. There were three fear conditions, which all involved essentially the same factual information about the causes of tooth decay and the same recommendations for preventive oral hygiene practices. In the high-fear condition, the communicator emphasized, in graphic detail, the painful consequences of poor dental hygiene, such as diseased gums and infections that could spread to other parts of the body. Students in this condition were repeatedly reminded that they could fall victim to the same consequences. In addition, the high-fear communication was accompanied by pictures of severe tooth decay and mouth infections. Students in the moderate-fear condition were told about the same dangers, but in a less personally threatening, more factual manner. Also, they were shown pictures depicting milder examples of decay and infection. In the minimal-fear condition, there was very little fear-arousing information, and instead of unsightly pictures depicting decay and infection, the students were shown X-rays and diagrams. In the control condition, students received a communication that was irrelevant to oral hygiene (it was about the structure of the eye).

As expected, after the communications students in the high-fear condition were the most worried, followed by the moderate-fear and minimal-fear groups, respectively. Also, the high-fear group rated the communiction most favorably with respect to interest and educational value; however, they also complained most often about some aspects of the message, such as the unpleasantness of the slides or that there was not enough information about prevention. The most important question, of course, was whether fear would motivate actual improvements in dental hygiene practices. To answer this question, a comparison was made between self-reports of toothbrushing and flossing made before and one week after the communications. As shown in Figure 3-1, the minimal-fear group reported the most change toward conformity with the dental hygiene recommendations, while higher levels of fear produced progresssively less compliance. The

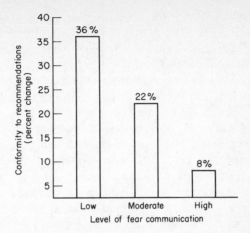

Figure 3-1. Net change toward conformity with dental hygiene recommendations for children receiving various fear communications. (Adapted from Janis & Feshbach, 1953. Copyright © 1953 by the American Psychological Association. Reprinted by permission of the publisher and authors.)

control group, which did not receive the oral hygiene recommendations, showed no change in brushing and flossing habits.

Janis and Feshbach concluded that the fear arousing material did not increase the effectiveness of the oral hygiene communication, and in fact may have interfered with its success. With little to fear, students reported that they were highly compliant with the toothbrushing recommendations, whereas those students who received the high-fear message were considerably less compliant. Therefore, it appears that health care instructions may induce behavioral changes, but that the use of fearful information has no positive effect on behavior. Adding further support for such a conclusion, Leventhal, Singer, and Jones (1965) found that increasing the specificity of instructions enhanced the effectiveness of an appeal urging people to get tetanus inoculations, whereas increasing the fear appeal did not increase compliance. Nevertheless, when we examine the applications of social psychology to cigarette smoking we will see that an interesting variation of the fear appeal, emotional role-playing, is effective in motivating health-enhancing behaviors.

More recently, Evans and his colleagues (Evans, Rozelle, Lasater, Dembroski, & Allen, 1968, 1970) carefully extended and refined earlier research on the effects of persuasive messages on dental hygiene practices. In addition to fear messages, one extension involved testing the motivating effects of a positive appeal. Rather than emphasizing the negative consequences of poor dental hygiene, the positive appeal suggested that good health and popularity could be obtained by good dental hygiene practices. As in previous research, all the messages included a standard set of dental hygiene recommendations, except that to further investigate the effects of recommendations, one group of students received especially elaborate tooth care instructions. Hence, in their most comprehensive experiment (Evans et al., 1970), junior high school students were randomly assigned to the following five conditions: high fear plus recommendations, low fear plus recommendations, positive appeal plus recommendations, recommendations only, and elaborate recommendations only.

In order to fully appreciate the findings, an additional refinement of the method employed by Evans and his colleagues should be understood. When asked to report their own behavior people do not always give accurate responses. It is not always easy to remember all the details of past behavior, and the need for social approval can bias self-reports (Crowne & Marlowe, 1964). Thus, self-reports may often be more a matter of how people feel they should have behaved than what they actually did. Now consider students who have received a message advocating good dental hygiene practices. Even if some of them did not comply with the recommendations, they probably would feel that they should have done so. Given this bias and the likelihood that they would not know precisely how many times they did brush and floss, they might overestimate their compliance with the recommendations when later asked about such behavior. To avoid this ambiguity of interpretation, Evans and his colleagues used a more objective measure of dental hygiene. Students were asked to chew on a "disclosing wafer," which leaves a red stain on any plaque that remains on teeth after inadequate brushing and flossing. After chewing the wafers, the students' teeth were photographed and judges, who were unaware of which experimental condition each student was in, rated the cleanliness of each student's teeth.

The results of the experiment show the importance of using the objective measure. Overall, the self-report measures indicated that the fear messages were the most effective in motivating and obtaining the recommended dental hygiene behaviors, but examination of the objective measure led to a much different conclusion. According to the self-reports, high fear induced the most anxiety, the strongest intentions to conform with the recommendations, and, five days later, the greatest frequency of toothbrushing. In contrast, both a test of how much of the dental hygiene information was retained and the disclosing wafers indicated that other conditions were actually more effective. Students in the positive-appeal and elaborate-recommendations conditions retained the most information and actually had the cleanest teeth five days after the messages.

As shown in Figure 3-2, it is particularly noteworthy that, students in the high-fear and recommendations-only conditions reported that they were brushing the most five days after the messages, whereas after the same period the disclosing wafers revealed that students in the positive-appeal and elaborate-recommenda-

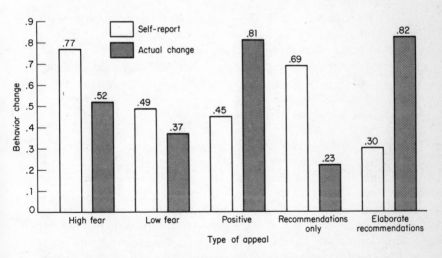

Figure 3-2. Self-reported and actual change in dental hygiene five days after each of five types of persuasive message. Changes indicated are post-test minus pretest scores on 5-point rating scales by which higher scores mean better dental hygiene. (Adapted from Evans et al., 1970. Copyright © 1970 by the American Psychological Association. Reprinted by permission of the publisher and authors.)

tions conditions actually had cleaner teeth. This discrepancy raises serious doubts about the interpretation of studies on health behavior that rely entirely on self-report measures. The goal of such studies is to improve health through actual changes in behavior, not to induce mere verbal compliance.

Besides inducing behavioral changes, an intervention designed to induce good dental hygiene practices should have long-term effects. An increase in the frequency of brushing for a few days will have little, if any, effect on dental health, but a lasting change in brushing habits could be very beneficial. To test for long-term effects, Evans and his colleagues (Evans, Rozelle, Noblitt, & Williams, 1975) used disclosing wafers to compare the effects of a positive appeal, a fear appeal, and a control condition shortly after the message, as well as one, two, five, and ten weeks afterwards. Surprisingly, there were no differences among the conditions, but students in all conditions had cleaner teeth in the posttests than they had in a pretest. Evidently, the repetition of the objective tests induced the students to begin, and to maintain, improved dental hygiene.

Other components of the persuasive communication process that influence attitudes and behavior are the communicator and the audience. It is surely the case that some communicators are more persuasive than others and that different audiences are more or less easily persuaded. Also some communicators are more persuasive with certain audiences than with others. Dembroski, Lasater, and Ramirez (1978) cite an impressive number of studies indicating that similarity between the communicator and the audience on any of several dimensions—occupation, attitude, past experience, aptitude, or race—enhances the likelihood of compliant attitudes and behavioral changes. Dembroski, Lasater, and Ramirez went on to investigate the influence of source-audience similarity and fear messages on subsequent self-reports of anxiety and attitude change and objective tests of information retention and cleanliness of teeth. As in previous studies, fear messages produced self-reported anxiety and attitude change, but no actual improvement in cleanliness of teeth as measured by disclosing wafers. In contrast, similarity of race had a behavioral effect. All the recipients of the persuasive communications were black junior high school students. Those who received the communication from a black dentist had significantly cleaner teeth the next day than did those students who heard the same message from a white dentist. However, additional posttests revealed that the effect lasted only one day.

In conclusion, research on social psychological interventions designed to induce good dental health suggest some guidelines for future applications to dental health or perhaps to health in general. The use of fear appeals probably should be abandoned or substantially modified because the effectiveness of such appeals has gotten only mixed support from self-report measures and no support from objective measures. More promising techniques include the use of positive appeals, elaborate recommendations, and matching the race of the commumnicator to that of the audience, all of which have resulted in objective evidence of cleaner teeth. More research is needed, however, to determine whether the matching technique can produce long-term effects.

Cigarette Smoking: Helping Adults Quit

Despite the well-known health hazards associated with tobacco use, in the United States about a third of the population 17 years old or over smoke cigarettes and 70% of these people smoke at least 15 cigarettes a day (U.S. Bureau of the Census, 1980b). Although there was some decrease in smoking following the Surgeon General's report in 1964, the overall effect was small and temporary (Mann & Janis, 1968). In addition, many of the techniques used to control smoking are generally associated with high rates of recidivism (Bernstein & McAlister, 1976). There is, therefore, a need for interventions that will have long-lasting effects in deterring cigarette smoking. Several lines of social psychological research have responded to this need.

Employing an old strategy in a new way, Janis and Mann (1965) devised a technique to help moderate and heavy smokers to quit. As in previous research on dental hygiene, the strategy was to use fear as a motivator of attitudinal and behavioral change. Rather than presenting messages to passive audiences, however, the new approach, called *emotional role-playing,* involved having subjects act out a distressing role. The underlying assumption was that by playing a role, the subjects would have a dramatic experience that would have more of a personal impact on them than would merely hearing a message. To test this notion some subjects were asked to role-play with the experimenter, whereas other subjects merely listened to audio tapes of the role-playing sessions.

In the role-playing conditions each subject, all of whom were female, was asked to imagine that she was a patient and that the experimenter was a doctor who was treating her for a chronic cough. In a series of five scenes the subject learned that she had lung cancer and must undergo an operation that has only a moderate chance of success. To enhance empathy with her role, in two of the scenes the subject was asked to give soliloquies in which she was to express her feelings and thoughts out loud. In the final scene she and the doctor discussed the connection between smoking and lung cancer. The overall intent was to provide an emotional experience that was realistic, personally involving, and fear provoking.

As shown in Figure 3-3, the results strongly supported the effectiveness of the emotional role-playing technique. As expected, the role-players were subsequently more fearful about their health and more worried about lung cancer than were the subjects in the audience condition. The role-players also were more likely to agree that cigarette smoking causes cancer, that smoking is generally harmful to health, and to express an intention to stop smoking. Most importantly, two weeks after the sessions self-reports indicated that the role-players were smoking an average of 10.5 fewer cigarettes per day as compared to their pretest level, whereas subjects in the audience condition were smoking only 4.8 fewer a day. In a series of follow-ups (Mann & Janis, 1968), the reduction in smoking by subjects in the role-playing condition persisted. By the last follow-up, 18 months after the treatment, the role-players reported smoking an average of 13.5 fewer cigarettes per day and subjects in the audience condition reported smoking only 5.2 fewer per day. It should be noted that to reduce the chance that the subjects might report that they were smoking less in order to help the experimenters confirm their hypothesis (cf. Orne, 1969), the follow-ups were conducted as obstensibly independent surveys of smoking and the interviewers made no mention of the original study. Nevertheless, as we saw in

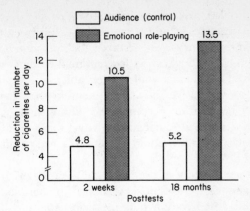

Figure 3-3. Mean reduction in cigarette smoking after participation in an emotional role-playing or an audience (control) condition. (Adapted from Mann & Janis, 1968. Copyright © 1968 by the American Psychological Association. Reprinted by permission of the publisher and authors.)

the dental hygiene studies, self-reports should be interpreted with caution.

In a replication and extension of the role-playing technique, Mann (1967) found that nonemotional role-playing, which involved taking the role of a debater arguing against cigarette smoking, was not as effective in deterring smoking as was the more fearful role of playing a lung cancer victim. It seems, therefore, that whereas fear is not an effective motivator of change in the health-related behaviors of passive audiences, it does add to the effectiveness of the role-playing technique.

In a more unusual approach, Suedfeld and his colleagues (e.g., Suedfeld & Ikard, 1974) applied the technique of sensory deprivation to help people reduce or eliminate their cigarette smoking. Use of this technique was based on earlier research that demonstrated that subjects who were deprived of sensory stimulation were more susceptible to attitude change in response to persuasive communications than were control subjects (Scott, Bexton, Heron, & Doane, 1959). Suedfeld (1973) suggested two reasons why sensory deprivation would increase susceptibility to persuasion. One is that the lack of stimulation might induce a need for stimuli that could cause one to attend to messages he or she might normally ignore. The second reason is based on research indicating that sensory deprivation reduces the capacity for complex thinking. This latter suggestion led Suedfeld to suggest that sensorily deprived individuals would be less able to generate counter-arguments to persuasive messages. Suedfeld then hypothesized that sensory deprivation accompanied by antismoking messages would be effective in producing negative attitudes toward smoking and that such attitudes would result in a reduction of actual smoking.

To test their hypothesis, Suedfeld and Ikard (1974) randomly assigned male cigarette smokers to four experimental conditions—stimulus deprivation plus messages, stimulus deprivation only, messages but no deprivation, and control (no deprivation and no messages). Sensory deprivation involved 24 hours of lying on a bed in a dark, sound-reduced room without cigarettes or other stimuli. Liquid food could be consumed by sucking on a plastic tube, and the only time the person could get up was to use a chemical toilet, which was near the bed. In contrast, people in the nondeprivation conditions were not deprived of stimuli and were not confined, except that subjects in the nondeprivation-message condition were asked to stay home so that they could receive messages by telephone. People in the message conditions received 10 messages altogether, some of which instructed the subjects to relax while thinking of past emotional experiences that led to cravings for cigarettes and some of which simply congratulated the subjects for having gone so long without a cigarette. To assess both the short- and long-term effects of the various experimental conditions, all subjects were asked about their subsequent smoking in a series of follow-up telephone calls and mail inquiries.

The results were impressive but somewhat surprising. It was expected that the combination of sensory deprivation and the messages would produce the greatest reduction in cigarette smoking. The follow-up data showed, however, that sensory deprivation led to large reductions in self-reported cigarette smoking regardless of whether or not the subjects were given messages. One year after the 24-hour period of isolation, the subjects who were deprived of stimuli reported smoking 48 percent fewer cigarettes than they had before the deprivation, whereas subjects who had not been deprived of stimulation reported smoking only 16 percent fewer. After two years, subjects who had been in the sensory-deprivation-message condition reported smoking 58 percent fewer than before the session, and those in the sensory-deprivation–no-message condition reported about the same reduction (52 pecent). In contrast, subjects who had been in the nondeprivation-message and nondeprivation–no-message condition reported only 24 percent and 14 percent reductions, respectively. In addition, in the two-year follow-up, 39 percent of the sensory-deprived subjects reported that they had completely abstained from smoking, whereas only 16 percent of the nondeprived subjects reported complete abstinence. In a more recent study, which did not include no-message controls, sensory deprivation combined with antismoking messages significantly enhanced the effectiveness of behavioral antismoking techniques, especially with regard to preventing relapses (Best & Suedfeld, 1982). However, it should be noted that all of the studies on the use of sensory deprivation to deter smoking relied on self-reports, which, as we have seen, may be of questionable validity.

Apart from the problem of relying on self-reported data, the reduction of smoking in the sensory-deprivation studies remains somewhat of a theoretical mystery. Recall that the hypothesis was that sensory deprivation would cause people to be particularly susceptible to persuasive messages, but the empirical results showed that sensory deprivation reduced self-reported smoking even when the antismoking messages were not presented. Suedfeld (1975) offered some *post hoc* explanations for these findings. One is that the context of the experiment and the measures that were administered before the study began may have sensitized even the no-message subjects to the antismoking purpose of the study. The combination of such awareness and the sensory deprivation may have been enough to persuade people to change. An alternative explanation is that the sensory deprivation was therapeutic because it allowed the subjects to experience a 24-hour period of nonstressful absence of cues that normally elicit smoking. Yet another explanation is that the deprivation induced cognitive dissonance, such that after investing 24 hours in a very strange situation people may have been motivated to justify their participation by continuing to abstain from smoking (cf. Festinger, 1957). Since all of these explanations came after the fact, further research would be needed to determine the precise reasons for the observed effects.

Cigarette Smoking: Preventing Children from Starting

The two techniques for controlling cigarette smoking that have been examined so far, emotional role-playing and sensory deprivation, were used to help adult smokers to quit or reduce their habit. Although the reduction and cessation of smoking are certainly worthwhile goals that applied social psychologists should continue to pursue, there are several reasons why interventions aimed at preventing people, especially children, from ever beginning the habit might be even more effective in deterring smoking. One reason is that there is evidence that frequent cigarette smoking may result in a physical addiction to nicotine (e.g, Schachter, Silverstein, Kozlowski, Herman, & Liebling, 1977), which may be particularly difficult to cure with psychological techniques. Even without physical addiction, smokers may develop a psychological dependence on cigarettes. Supporting this notion the vast majority of smokers report that they do so for pleasure or to relax (Ikard, Green, & Horn, 1968). Such dependencies might help explain why many interventions that at first seem to be successful in reducing cigarette smoking are later found to have only short-term effects (Evans, Henderson, Hill, & Raines, 1979). Finally, although there has been a moderate decline in adult smoking, there has been a recent increase in smoking among children. The need to intensify preventive efforts aimed at children thus seems to be particularly acute (cf. Evans, Rozelle, Mittelmark, Hansen, Bane, & Havis, 1978).

Responding to the need for preventing children from beginning to smoke, Evans and his colleagues (see Evans, 1976) developed an extensive, educational intervention based primarily on two social psychological perspectives. The decision to employ one of the perspectives was influenced, in part, by preliminary interviews that indicated that elementary and junior high school students feel great social pressure to smoke, even though they believe educational messages that smoking is dangerous to their long-term health. The three major sources of such pressures are peers, parental models, and the media. Recognizing that the onset of smoking in children may be more a matter of social influence than a deficit in health education, Evans decided to apply social learning theory (see Bandura, 1977), which holds that children develop many of their behavior patterns by observing and imitating others. To offset models of smoking, therefore, a crucial component in the antismoking intervention is exposure to peer models who do not smoke.

The second perspective that Evans relied on belongs to the tradition of analyzing the process of persuasive communication that began with the Yale Communication and Attitude Change Program (Hovland, Janis, & Kelley, 1953). Evans employed one aspect of this approach, McGuire's (1964) notion of attitude inoculation. McGuire has shown that people can build a resistance to attitude change in a manner analagous to medical inoculations. Just as medical inoculations involve receiving weak doses of a disease so that the body can build up defenses against stronger doses, so exposing people to weak arguments that oppose their attitudes can help build defenses against stronger arguments. Thus, a second crucial feature of the antismoking intervention is inoculation through exposure to pressures to smoke.

Integrating the social learning and inoculation perspectives, Evans decided to show adolescents videotapes depicting similar adolescents who are tempted to smoke by peers, parental models, or the media, but who also model resistance to these pressures. The exposure to social pressures is intended to serve as an inoculation and the depiction of resistance to such pressures is intended to provide positive models. The combination of these two factors should help the adolescents resist the pressures to smoke that they will naturally encounter in their everyday lives.

Another feature of Evans's approach is worth noting. In addition to modeling resistance to social pressures to smoke, the videotapes emphasize the immediate effects of smoking (i.e., the increase in toxic agents, like carbon monoxide, in the body). The emphasis on immediate effects rather than long-term consequences is based on evidence indicating that adolescents generally are oriented to the present rather than to the future (see Evans, 1980).

Realizing that the seventh grade is a particularly vulnerable time for adolescents to begin smoking, Evans and his colleagues implemented their approach in several junior high schools (Evans, Rozelle, Mittelmark, Hansen, Bane, & Havis, 1978). Some classes received the full treatment, which includes the following components: three videotapes depicting social pressures to smoke; a film about how smoking immediately increases carbon monoxide in the body; multiple follow-up measures to determine the level of smoking in each class; and feedback about the level of smoking in one's class. This is an extensive program that was presented over parts of several days. In comparison conditions, students received some of the treatment components but not others, and the control condition involved only the final measures of smoking.

Before discussing the results, the method that Evans and his colleagues used to measure smoking should be explained. As we saw in the research on dental hygiene, self-reports of a health-related behavior can be quite different from a more objective measure. In a smoking study we might expect the same kind of discrepancy. In order to test for this possibility Evans, Hansen, and Mittelmark (1978) conducted two experiments in which some children were first shown a film demonstrating how saliva specimens can be analyzed for nicotine content in order to detect cigarette smoking, and then were asked to provide specimens of their saliva. In control groups nothing was said about the saliva test and no samples were taken. All subjects were then asked to provide self-reports of smoking. It was hypothesized that knowing that their self-reports could be verified by the saliva test would reduce the tendency to deny smoking behavior and thus would induce more accurate self-reports. Supporting the hypothesis the proportion of self-reported smokers in the saliva test condition was much greater than it was in the control condition. Hence, in order to increase the validity of self-reports of smoking in their prevention studies, Evans and his colleagues regularly took saliva specimens along with self-reports. Actually there are reasons to doubt the accuracy of the saliva test (e.g., it cannot distinguish smokers from those who are exposed to the secondhand smoke of others); therefore, unknown to the subjects, the saliva specimens were never actually analyzed. The technique of increasing the accuracy of self-reports by leading subjects to believe that their responses can be verified by more objective measures is generally known as the *bogus pipeline* and was first introduced by Jones and Sigall (1971).

The results of the social learning-attitude inoculation program indicate that it is effective in deterring the onset of cigarette smoking. Evans and his colleagues (1978) found that, ten weeks after the intervention, over 18 percent of the students in the control condition had begun to smoke, compared to less than 10 percent in the treatment condition. In a three-year study (Evans et al., 1981), the intervention had a significant long-term effect in deterring cigarette smoking.

The kind of intervention strategy initiated by Evans is referred to as a *social influences* program, because the strategy centers on techniques to offset social pressures to smoke (Best et al., 1984). This strategy has been further developed and tested by several other teams of researchers (Arkin, Roemhild, Johnson, Luepker, & Murray, 1981; Best et al., 1984; McAlister, Perry, & Maccoby, 1979; Murray, Johnson, Luepker, & Mittelmark, 1984). While retaining the social learning and attitude inoculation perspectives, these researchers made modifications intended to increase the impact of social influences programs. McAlister and his colleagues, for example, made three changes in the basic program that most of the other research teams also incorporate. One change was to use popular high school students as live models rather than using videotape models. Adolescents may not pay much attention to videotapes, but they usually are interested in what popular peers say and do. A second modification involved having each student announce his or her intention not to smoke before a whole class of peers. Social psychological research has shown that, while people often behave in a manner that is inconsistent with their privately held attitudes, they are likely to behave in a manner that is consistent with their public commitments (see Kiesler, 1971). The third modification was to have the students role-play strategies to resist social pressures to smoke. It follows from social learning theory that role-playing provides the students an opportunity to actively acquire and practice the social skills needed to resist pressures to smoke (see Bandura, 1977).

The impact of the modified social influences programs has been carefully evaluated with experimental and quasi-experimental research designs and with bogus-pipeline measures of smoking. Compared to traditional health education programs or to control groups receiving no treatment, the social influences programs have consistently been more effective in preventing the onset of smoking in junior high school students (Best et al., 1984; McAlister, Perry, Killen, Slinkard, & Maccoby, 1980; Murray, Johnson, Luepker, & Mittelmark, 1984; Telch, Killen, McAlister, Perry, & Maccoby, 1982). There is also some indication that these programs can help to reduce the instance of smoking in those students who have already experimented with smoking (Best et al., 1984; Perry, Killen, Telch, Slinkard, & Danaher, 1980). However, Best and his colleagues found that a social influences program has a stronger long-term impact on nonsmokers than on those who had smoked before the program began. Further validating the emphasis on social influences, Best and his colleagues also found that their program had its strongest impact on those students who were exposed to the most pressures to smoke by family and friends.

In conclusion, there are three promising social psychological interventions that are designed to control cigarette smoking. Both emotional role-playing and sensory deprivation have been shown to reduce cigarette smoking in adults. Either of these techniques offers the advantage of requiring only a relatively brief intervention. In addition, there is evidence that both techniques have long-term effects. However, all the evidence for the effectiveness of emotional role-playing and sensory deprivation as techniques to reduce smoking have been self-reported. There is therefore some question about whether actual smoking was reduced. For control of preadolescent and adolescent smoking, interventions based on a social influence approach has both deterred the onset of the habit in nonsmokers and reduced the behavior in smokers. Although the implementation of the social influences programs is time-consuming and requires many resources (e.g., student models), it seems to fit nicely into the curriculum of junior and senior high school health classes. Confidence in the effectiveness of the social influences interventions should be high, because of the demonstrated long-term effects involving stringent testing with bogus-pipeline measures of smoking.

Adolescent Alcohol and Drug Abuse

An alarming number of adolescents use not only cigarettes but also alcohol and other drugs. According to the U.S. Bureau of the Census (1980b, p.129) well over a third of the youth (ages 12 to 17) in the United States are "current users" of alcohol, and the percentages of youths who use marijuana, inhalants, hallucinogens, cocaine, analgesics, stimulants, sedatives, and tranquilizers are greater than the percentages for adults (26 years old or older). As with cigarette smoking, both the prevalence of alcohol and drug use among youths and the difficulties with breaking psychological and physical dependencies suggest a need for preventive measures.

McGuire (1974) suggested that attitude inoculation would be effective in strengthening negative attitudes toward drugs, but he also cautioned that such attitudes may not be enough to offset social pressures to use these substances. Following up on McGuire's suggestion, McAlister and his colleagues extended their application of the social influences approach, which was successful in deterring cigarette smoking, to curtailing alcohol and drug use among adolescents (McAlister, Perry, & Maccoby, 1979; McAlister et al., 1980). In treatment conditions, specially trained high school students visited seventh-grade classes and presented scenarios in which a young person is pressured to drink alcohol or to smoke marijuana. Having begun the inoculation process by exposing the subjects to undesirable social pressures, the next step was to help the students to build up defenses to resist such pressures. This was accomplished by conducting a contest in which popular records were given as prizes to students who suggested the best ways to resist the pressures. To induce social learning, the best resistance strategies were acted out in front of the class. Finally, the students were given buttons that said "I'm naturally high" and were told that is what college students say to resist pressures. In the control condition students received traditional classroom instructions in health education.

As shown in Figure 3-4, the results indicated that the social influences intervention was quite successful in deterring the use of alcohol and marijuana. At the end of the eighth grade, which

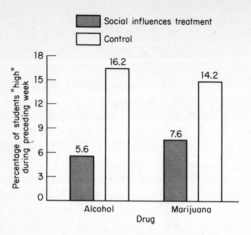

Figure 3-4. Two-year follow-up of alcohol and marijuana use for junior high school students who received or did not receive a social influences treatment. (Adapted from McAlister et al., 1980. Reprinted by permission of the publisher and authors.)

was nearly two years after the beginning of the intervention, less than 6 percent of the students in the treatment condition reported being "high" or drunk on alcohol during the immediately preceding week compared to over 16 percent in the control condition. In the same follow-up, less than 8 percent of the treatment students reported smoking marijuana during the preceding week compared to nearly 15 percent of the control students. As in the cigarette studies, to help ensure the accuracy of the self-reports, the students were led to believe that their reponses would be verified by analyses of breath samples.

Maintaining an Ideal Weight

A large portion of the people in the United States realize that they have a weight problem. According to the U.S. Bureau of the Census (1980a), a survey of people 17 years old or older indicated that about a third of the males and nearly half of the females in this country considered themselves to be overweight. While many of these people probably are not dangerously overweight, others are truly obese and should be aware of the health risks associated with this condition. Obesity increases the likelihood of high blood pressure, high levels of blood fats and cholesterol, and diabetes, all of which are risk factors for heart disease and strokes (U.S. Department of Health, Education, and Welfare, 1980). Despite awareness of the health problems associated with obesity, many people find it hard to make the necessary behavioral changes (i.e., a good diet and regular exercise) to achieve and maintain an ideal weight.

Social psychologist Janis (1975), once again analyzing the persuasive communication process, recommends that health care counselors, as communicators, can do two things to help people deal with the stress involved in making the decision to alter their life-styles in order to improve health. He hypothesized that people will more readily comply with a counselor's recommendations if the counselor: (1) begins by asking for confidential personal information about the problem (e.g., how the person feels about his or her body); and (2) responds to disclosures of personal shortcomings with acceptance. He contends that trust in the counselor, which is essential for attitude and behavioral change, depends on both encouragement to self-disclose and genuine acceptance of potentially embarrassing disclosures. In a series of studies, Janis and his colleagues (reported in Janis, 1975) applied this approach to the problem of getting overweight people to comply to a low-calorie diet. As expected, people who were encouraged to self-disclose about how they felt about their weight problem and were accepted when they did so were more compliant in reporting daily progress and lost significantly more weight than did people receiving only one or neither of the two aspects of counseling.

As discussed in Chapter 2 of the present volume, cognitive dissonance theory is also relevant to attitudinal and behavioral change (Festinger, 1957). As we have seen, the theory predicts that freely choosing to expend effort to accomplish a goal produces a psychological need to justify the effort put forth. Some of the options for justification are developing a more favorable attitude about the goal, increasing motivation to achieve the goal, and increasing the expectation that the goal will be achieved. All of these options should help facilitate actual attainment of the goal. It follows, therefore, that a treatment program that involves a high degree of effort would be more effective in achieving the therapeutic goal than would a program involving minimal effort. Thus, in designing a weight loss program, it might be best to resist the usual temptation to lure people to a treatment by emphasizing that it is relativley easy. Instead, an appropriate strategy would be to admit that weight loss will be effortful and unpleasant. Supporting this notion, Axsom and Cooper (1981) found that freely choosing to participate in an effortful weight loss program produced more weight loss and better long-term maintenance of weight than did conditions that did not involve free choice or did not involve high effort. Extending this approach to the treatment of overweight children, Mendonca and Brehm (1983) found that free choice of an effortful therapy produced greater weight loss than did a condition that did not involve choice.

Old Age and Institutional Living

Loss of control over one's environment, or even the perception of lack of control, can lead both to serious psychological problems, most notably withdrawal and depression, and to related physical afflictions, such as ulcers, weight loss, and perhaps even sudden death (see Seligman, 1975). One terribly unfortunate aspect of old age is the loss of control over many parts of one's life. Many old people face mandatory retirement, live on inadequate fixed incomes, develop debilitating physical impairments, and are no longer "needed" by their children. Being relegated to a nursing home can further contribute to a loss of control, because the elderly often have no choice in the matter and when they get to a home find themselves in an environment where they are expected to be passive and to have everything done for them. Although the care provided may be well intentioned, these institutionalized elderly are likely to withdraw from life, become physically ill, and may even die prematurely. Indeed, Ferrari (1962, reported in Seligman, 1975) found that of 17 women who reported that they had no choice but to move into an old-age home, 16 died unexpectedly within ten weeks of moving in. In comparison, only one person in 38 who reported that they came to the home by her own choice died in the same period.

To help remedy this situation, social psychologists have provided evidence that the mental and physical health of the elderly in nursing homes can be improved by providing residents of such institutions with opportunities to take more control over their lives. In one intervention, Langer and Rodin (1976) told a group of elderly nursing home residents that they should realize the amount of control they have. The perception of control was enhanced by reminding these residents that they could plan social events, visit friends, watch TV, listen to the radio, write, read, and decide how to arrange their furniture. Actual control was enhanced in two ways. First, each resident was allowed to select a plant as a free gift and was given the responsibility to take care of it. Second, they were allowed to decide whether and when to see a movie. In contrast, other residents were given no pep talk about control, were told that the staff decides how to arrange the furniture, had a plant selected for them, were told that the nurses would take care of the plants, and were given no choice about the when the movie was shown. In this manner the overall amount of care provided for the two groups was about the same, but the degree of perceived and actual control was greater for one group than for the other.

Questionnaires administered three weeks after the initial communications indicated that control was beneficial to the overall well-being of the residents. Those who were given control reported feeling happier, more alert, and more active than did residents in the no control condition. Ratings by the nurses indicated that the residents who were given control made greater overall improvement, spent more time visiting, and spent less time passively watching TV than did those who were not given control. Behavioral measures, such as attendance at the movie and participation in a contest, also showed that the residents with control were more active than those without control. The same beneficial effects were sustained 18 months later, and giving residents control over their lives led to significantly better health and fewer deaths (Rodin & Langer, 1977). As Langer and Rodin point out, "some of the negative consequences of aging may be retarded, reversed, or possibly prevented by returning to the aged the right to make decisions and a feeling of competence" (1976, p. 197).

In a conceptually similar approach, Schulz (1976) also devised an intervention that involved giving the institutionalized elderly more control over their lives. Since residents in nursing homes are often very lonely, it was hypothesized that visits from friendly college students would be beneficial, particularly if the residents could control, or at least predict, the visits. In a field experiment that took place in a home for the elderly, some residents were given control by allowing them to choose the time and duration of visits from college students. In a second condition, the students determined the time and duration of the visits and notified the residents about their plans; thus, the residents could predict, but not control, the visits. In a third condition the students would visit without notice, which meant that the residents could neither predict nor control the visits. In a fourth condition there were no visits.

The results indicated that both control and predictability of the visits had beneficial physical and psychological effects. Residents who could control or predict the visits were rated significantly healthier by the activities director and had significantly less increase in medications than did residents who had unannounced or no visits. In addition, responses to questionnaires indicated that residents who could control or predict the visits were happier, had more zest for life, and were more active than were those residents who were in the other conditions. It should be noted, however, that the positive effects of the controllable and predictable student visits dissipated after the visits were terminated (Schulz & Hanusa, 1978). It may be that long-term beneficial effects, like those observed by Rodin and Langer, depend on interventions that induce lasting perceptions of control and predictability.

More recent research also points to the beneficial effects of predictability and control on the institutional elderly. One study demonstrated that providing incoming residents with information about living conditions in a nursing home facilitated a healthy adjustment to the institution (Krantz & Schulz, 1980). In a nonexperimental study of the institutionalized aged, a postive correlation was found between perceived control and well-being (Janoff-Bulman & Marshall, 1982).

Coping with Stressful Events

It is inevitable that at some time in their lives, people will experience highly stressful events, such as the death of a loved one, the loss of a job, or personal injury. In most cases, such events occur infrequently and people are able to cope with them. However, when stressful events occur in bunches there may be serious health consequences. Indeed, Holmes and Masuda (1974) found that people who experienced a number of stressful events had a higher incidence of physical illness, such as heart disease and skin disorders, than people who did not experience such events.

Being hospitalized for a major operation certainly seems to qualify as a highly stressful event. Surgical patients find themselves in an unfamiliar environment, may lose time from work, have little or no control over what happens during the operation, know they will be cut open, and cannot be certain of the outcome. All of these factors can add up to a great deal of stress that may adversely affect one's health in general and the outcome of the operation in particular.

In order to help hospital patients cope with such stress, social psychologists Langer, Janis, and Wolfer (1975) tested two stress-reducing strategies on adult hospital patients who were about to undergo major surgery. One strategy was cognitive coping. This technique involves self-control of attention away from the negative aspects of the surgery and toward the positive aspects, such as the opportunity to rest, to take stock of oneself, and to lose weight. The other strategy involved providing the patients with preparatory information about what to expect both before and after their operations. This information included details about the procedures and about the pains and discomforts that were likely to occur. Using a stratified random sampling—which equated the patients on type of operation, seriousness of operation, sex, age, and religion—each patient was assigned to receive cognitive-coping tips, preparatory information, both cognitive-coping tips and preparatory information, or neither strategy.

The results indicated that the cognitive-coping strategy was effective in reducing stress, while the preparatory information had no beneficial effect. Before the operation, nurses rated the patients who were in the cognitive-coping condition as less anxious and better able to cope than patients who were in the no-treatment or preparatory-information conditions. After the operation, the patients who were given the cognitive-coping tips requested fewer pain relievers and sedatives than did the other patients. Langer, Janis, and Wolfer concluded that it might be beneficial to train nurses to give patients cognitive-coping tips as a routine part of intake interviews.

While surgery is somewhat stressful for adults, it can be particularly traumatic for children. In most cases children have little or no experience with hospitals, have seldom spent nights away from family or friends, and lack the emotional maturity to cope well with highly stressful events. Thus, a technique to help children cope with the stress of having an operation might be especially useful.

To help meet this need, Melamed and Siegel (1975) applied the technique of vicarious extinction. This approach is based on the social learning principle that under certain conditions children are especially likely to imitate the behavior of others (Bandura, 1977). As described in Chapter 2 of the present volume, vicarious extinction involves showing a fearful child a model, usually another child, who successfully approaches the object or event that provokes the fear. The fact that the model suffers no negative consequences should help to vicariously reduce the fearful child's anxiety and facilitate imitation of the model's behavior. Melamed and Siegal tested the usefulness of this technique on 4- to 12-year-old hernia, tonsillectomy, and urinary tract patients. The chidren were shown a film of a 7-year-old boy who undergoes a hernia operation. The film depicts the entire hospital experience from admission to discharge and is narrated by the 7-year-old protagonist. Although the narration reveals that the boy was initially anxious about his operation, the film goes on to show that he overcomes his fear, bravely faces all the preoperative procedures (e.g, administration of the anesthesia), and has a successful operation. It was hypothesized that the children observing the film would similarly overcome their fears and be more relaxed about their own operation. In a control condition, children about to undergo similar operations were shown a film that was unrelated to operations.

The results indicated that viewing the film about the boy having a successful operation helped reduce anxiety. The children who viewed this film had lower sweat gland activity, fewer self-reported medical concerns, and engaged in less anxious behavior than did the children who saw the unrelated film. These beneficial effects were observed both the night before the operation and three weeks later. Another point in favor of this intervention is that it is easy to implement, because it merely involves showing a 15-minute film in addition to the usual preparatory procedures for operations.

Some Applicable Research

We have seen that social psychologists, or those using a social psychological approach, have devised and tested a number of interventions to influence a wide variety of health-related behaviors. These interventions represent applied social psychology in that they were actually used to solve health problems, such as poor dental hygiene, cigarette smoking, adolescent alcohol and drug abuse, obesity, passive living in institutions, and experiencing stressful events. In contrast, certain generalizations from these projects, and additional social psychological research, may be considered applicable; although they have not yet been used to solve health problems, they may provide the basis for future applications.

Adolescent Risk Taking

Recall that McAlister and his colleagues successfully adapted the social influences approach, which was first successful in preventing cigarette smoking, to deterring adolescent alcohol and drug use (e.g., McAlister, Perry, & Maccoby, 1979). Generalizing further, they speculate that the same kind of intervention may be useful in deterring an even wider range of adolescent risk-taking behavior. Besides succumbing to social pressures to smoke, adolescents may engage in other risky behaviors in order to gain acceptance from their peers. For example, reckless driving of automobiles and motorcycles is often regarded as "cool" behavior. It should come as no surprise that, acccording to insurance actuarial statistics, teenage drivers are involved in a disproportionately high number of traffic accidents. McAlister and his colleagues suggest, therefore, that many serious accidents could be avoided by exposing adolescents to popular peer models (e.g., "Fonzie" types) who demonstrate resistance to peer pressures to engage in reckless behaviors. In this way the applied research on deterring smoking, drinking, and drug use may be applicable to the broader problem of adolescent risk-taking in general. Of course, it would be prudent to first test this generalization with further applied research.

The Coronary-Prone Behavior Pattern

Confirming earlier speculation, recent research indicates that a certain hard-driving life-style, now called the Type A Coronary-Prone Behavior Pattern, is a risk factor for health. Type A individuals are two times as likely to develop coronary heart disease than are people who do not exhibit this pattern (Rosenman & Friedman, 1974). Several social psychologists have studied various aspects of Type A behavior (e.g., Glass, 1977; Carver, Coleman, & Glass, 1976; Dembroski, MacDougall, & Shields, 1977; Matthews, 1979; Weidner, 1980). As described by Carver and his colleagues the life-style of Type A individuals is characterized by extremes in "competitive achievement striving, time urgency, and aggressiveness" (1976, p. 460).

Despite the interest in Type A behavior by social psychologists, the techniques that have been designed to reduce it—sedative drugs, transcendental meditation, biofeedback, behavior modification, and group therapy—are not based on social psychological principles (see Glass, 1977, for a review). This is surprising, especially since the Type A pattern may be acquired and maintained as a result of social pressures. For example, Matthews (1981) suggests that parental pressures may be responsible for the early development of Type A behavior. Once developed, this hard-driving, achievement-oriented life-style might be maintained by social reinforcements, such as recognition, status, and enhanced self-image. Perhaps the techniques used to help children resist the social pressures to smoke and use other drugs (e.g., McAlister, Perry, & Maccoby, 1979) could be extended to help children resist pressures to develop a Type A behavior pattern, or maybe techniques like emotional role-playing (e.g., Janis & Mann, 1965) or sensory deprivation (Suedfeld, 1973) could be employed to persuade adult Type As to change. Of course, such interventions may run counter to the ambitions of the people involved.

Attributions

All of us, as naïve psychologists, attempt to explain the behavior and internal dispositions of others. Social psychologists call these explanations attributions and suggest that, without always realizing it, we spend a great deal of time formulating them. If, for example, you saw a man help a woman carry some packages you might wonder whether he felt superior to her; he felt some social obligation to help; he had some ulterior motive; or he was merely trying to help. In general, social psychological research indicates that attributions are made quite reasonably, but under certain circumstances they are likely to be faulty or biased (cf. Jones et al, 1971). As we saw in Chapter 2, misattributions can lead to dysfunctional behavior (e.g., Storms & McCaul, 1976). Whether reasonable or biased, attributions can influence our lives in important ways. Most relevant to the present chapter, Rodin (1978) suggests that attributions "have a profound impact on many aspects of health-related behavior" (p. 538). How can attributions influence health-related behaviors? One example, provided by Rodin, involves an attributional bias caused by the relative availability of images. As Kahneman and Tversky (1973) have shown, people have a tendency to judge the likelihood of an event based on the extent to which they can imagine its occurrence. Other things being equal, events that we can vividly imagine seem more likely to occur than do those that we cannot easily picture. Rodin points out that we seldom directly encounter someone suffering from severe respiratory disease or lung cancer; consequently, it is unlikely that we would ever vividly imagine what it is like to have such maladies. It follows that people would underestimate the probability of contracting these diseases and would tend to ignore recommendations for preventive measures. Recently, Sherman, Cialdini, Schwartzman, and Reynolds (1985) found that the perceived likelihood of contracting a disease increases when one reads a concrete description of its symptoms and is then asked to imagine experiencing them. It may be beneficial, therefore, for health professionals to use similar procedures in order to provide their patients with vivid images of the negative consequences of unhealthy behavior. Although this suggestion is speculative, it is interesting that while fear messages are generally unsuccessful in inducing healthy behavior, emotional role-playing, which was designed to make the negative consequences of unhealthy behavior more personal and vivid, effectively reduces cigarette smoking (Janis & Mann, 1965).

Physicians' Attributions

Attributions that physicians make about their patients' behavior may also lead to important consequences. It is likely that a doctor's diagnosis and treatment is subject to the same kind of attributional errors as people generally make in their everyday lives (Snyder & Mentzer, 1978). Rodin (1978) provides an example. When trying to explain the causes of behavior, our attributions are often subject to the actor–observer bias, which is a tendency to attribute our own behavior to the situation in which the behavior occurs, but to attribute the behavior of others to their personality characteristics (Jones & Nisbett, 1971). Rodin suggests that, because of the actor–observer bias, doctors and patients may misunderstand one another. Physicians would tend to attribute a patient's failure to comply with health recommendations to some characteristic of the patient, such as stubbornness or lack of willpower. Patients, on the other hand, might attribute their lack of compliance to situational factors, such as insufficient support or information. Consequently, physicians might be less inclined to make what they would perceive as futile recommendations and the patients, receiving less information, would become less compliant to their physicians' recommendations. Perhaps social psychologists, through role-playing or some other means, could help physicians become more aware of their own attributional biases and the viewpoint of their patients.

Summary and Conclusions

Recent trends in health care have led to an increased emphasis on prevention. The success of this new development relies, in great measure, on the ability of people to make changes in their lifestyles. These changes involve avoiding risk factors, such as cigarette smoking, alcohol and drug abuse, overeating, passivity, and stress. Unfortunately, people often fail to make the appropriate behavioral changes, even when advised to do so by their physicians. To help in this matter, social psychologists have become involved in developing and testing techniques designed to induce healthy life-styles.

The first application of social psychology to health involved attempts to persuade high school students to improve their dental hygiene. Although it was first assumed that fear would be a good motivator of change, other approaches, especially positive appeals and elaborate recommendations, were more effective in inducing improvements. The early work was also criticized because it relied on self-report measures, which are not always accurate indicators of actual behavior. In later research disclosing wafers were used to gain more objective measures of brushing and flossing.

Several social psychological techniques have been devised to deter cigarette smoking. In one approach cigarette smokers were asked to play the emotionally charged role of a cancer patient. Follow-up data indicated that this approach effectively reduced smoking. In a more unusual approach, cigarette smokers were deprived of sensory stimulation for a 24-hour period. Both short- and long-term follow-up data indicated that this technique effectively reduced smoking. As with the early research on dental hygiene, a weakness of these applications was a reliance on self-report measures.

The most impressive line of social psychological applications to a health problem is the work being done on helping adolescents resist the social pressures to smoke. These social-influences approaches involve an integrated application of several principles of social psychology, including social learning, attitude inoculation, and public commitment. Both the short- and long-term results of these programs show that this approach is successful in preventing and reducing smoking. Adding to confidence in the results, in evaluating this approach the validity of self-reported smoking was enhanced by leading the subjects to believe that accuracy of their responses would be verified with chemical analyses of saliva samples. In addition, the social influences approach has been effective in deterring adolescent alcohol and drug use.

Some social psychological techniques have been successful in helping people achieve and maintain an ideal weight. By encouraging overweight clients to talk about personal shortcomings and by responding to such self-disclosures with acceptance, counselors were better able to help their clients to stay on a low-calorie diet. Other research indicates that, as predicted by cognitive-dissonance theory, emphasizing the effort involved in losing weight leads to more long-term weight loss than do easier treatments.

Other social psychological applications have been successful in helping people to cope with a variety of situations that can potentially produce negative consequences for health. For example, restoring perceived and actual control to elderly nursing home patients improved both their mental and physical health. To cope with the stress of surgery, adult patients were instucted in the use of cognitive-coping strategies. For children, showing a film of a peer having a successful operation helped reduce anxiety both before and after an operation.

In addition to actual interventions, some other social psychological research might be applicable in the future. The social influences approach, which was effective in reducing adolescent smoking and drug use, might be useful in deterring other adolescent risk-taking behaviors, such as reckless driving. The social psychological study of the coronary-prone behavior pattern might lead to the development of interventions to inhibit this high-risk life-style. Insights offered by attribution research might lead to the development of applications that could motivate people to change their life-styles, help cure hypochondria, and give doctors insight into their patients' noncompliance with medical regimens.

4

Conservation and Other Environmental Concerns

There was a brief cartoon, shown not long ago in many movie theaters, that delivers an environmental message. As it begins a maintenance man is in the lobby of a movie theater and he finds that there is no trash in the garbage cans, but later when he opens the door to the theater he is buried in an avalanche of paper cups and candy wrappers. Undoubtedly most of us can empathize with the man's plight. Movie theaters generally are quite littered and, although we do not get buried in the trash, we often find ourselves sitting in a sticky mess. This situation is unpleasant for everyone, yet it is obvious that many of us contribute to the problem.

People also contribute to environmental problems that have more serious consequences than sticky seats in movie theaters. Driving automobiles pollutes the air, some businesses dump their waste products into our water, and our modern life-styles, complete with automated gadgets that do everything from washing dishes to brushing teeth, are diminishing our supplies of natural resources. As a society we are wedded to our technology and it is unlikely that we will go back to the "good old days" when the environment was relatively safe from our ingenuity. Nevertheless, it seems that unless we change our behavior to some extent we will be in serious trouble. Already cities like Los Angeles and Denver have air pollution alerts, many people who lived in the Love Canal area of New York State have developed serious medical problems, and, in the early 1970s we experienced an energy crisis, which many experts predict will recur in the future.

In many cases people have an idea about what can be done to alleviate environmental problems. Some people carpool to work, some businesses are careful about how they dispose of waste, and many people are beginning to insulate their homes to save energy. Unfortunately, far more people seem to be unwilling to do their share. The major problem is one of convincing people that individual sacrifice is needed for the collective good and then getting those individuals to make the needed sacrifices. Hardin (1968) points out that the situation is analogous to the "tragedy of the commons." The commons tragedy is the ruin of common grazing land caused by the self-interest of individual shepherds. Land belonging to the community is set aside for grazing and all the shepherds have access to this common land. In the short run each shepherd's individual profits can be increased by placing more and more of his or her sheep in the commons. If everyone were to try to maximize their individual profits in this manner, however, the commons would be overgrazed so that, in the long run, all the shepherds would suffer. Hardin suggests that similar tragedies occur whenever individuals have uncontrolled access to inexpensive but finite resources. By analogy, current exploitations of the clean air, clean water, fossil fuels, and minerals can be considered commons tragedies.

While developing technological solutions to environmental problems may not be within the realm of the social sciences, social psychologists can apply their discipline to convincing and motivating people to use available conservation techniques. In this chapter we review social psychological research that may be relevant to dealing with environmental problems (applicable research) and some actual applications of social psychology to solving these problems.

Attitudes as Predictors of Proenvironmental Behaviors: Some Applicable Research

To understand much of the psychological research that is applicable and applied to solving environmental problems one should know about a controversy in social psychology. The controversy has to do with the relationship between attitudes and behavior. Simply put, an *attitude* may be defined as a feeling of liking or disliking for some thing or some person. One position in the controversy is that attitudes are predispositions to behavior. If, for example, you like science fiction novels, then you will be likely to read them. If you dislike spinach, then you will not be likely to eat it. To apply this position to solving real-world problems social psychologists might attempt to influence attitudes about the problem that in turn would influence relevant behaviors. Convince people that it is a good idea to conserve resources and perhaps they will be more likely to lower their thermostats in the winter or recycle old newspapers. Unfortunately, things may not be that simple. A great deal of empirical research indicates that the correspondence between attitudes and behavior is weak and unreliable (see Wicker, 1969 for a review). Hence, a second position in the controversy suggests that attitudes are not predispositions to behavior. To complicate matters further a third position suggests that the relationship between attitudes and behavior is exactly opposite of what had been originally proposed; that is, rather than attitudes determining behavior, it has been proposed that observations of our own behavior can help determine our attitudes (Bem, 1968). One infers the attitude "I like science fiction novels" from self-perceptions of having read them.

Despite the evidence that the relationship between attitudes and behavior is weak, some studies have shown a strong relationship (Heberlein & Black, 1976; Weigal & Newman, 1976). One way to reconcile these findings is to posit that attitudes influence behavior (or vice versa), but only under certain circumstances. In the absence of these circumstances we can expect very little correspondence between attitudes and behavior. Attitudes can conflict with one another, some are more important than others, and sometimes they do not seem relevant or salient in certain situations. I do not like the taste of spinach, but I might eat it because I think it is good for me (conflicting attitude) and my health is more important to me than taste. I think it is wrong to kill, but that attitude may seem irrelevant to swatting a fly. Also, it seems possible for an attitude to influence behavior and then for that behavior to influence my attitude. If I eat spinach because it is good for me, maybe I will eventually decide that I like the taste of it. We will see that much of the research that is applicable, or has been applied, to environmental problems is based on the assumptions that under certain conditions attitudes influence behavior and behavior influences attitudes.

Heberlein and Black (1976) demonstrated that attitudes can be good predictors of proenvironmental behavior provided that the attitudes and behavior are assessed at the same level of specificity. The behavior they were trying to predict was the use of lead-free gasoline. The lead in gasoline is a major air polluter and in 1973, when the research was actually carried out, the use of lead-free gasoline was largely voluntary. (Today it is dictated, for the most part, by the size of the nozzles at gasoline pumps). People who participated in the study responded to eight attitude scales that varied on four levels of specificity with regard to using lead-free gasoline. In increasing order of specificity, the four levels were general attitudes about proenvironmental behavior, beliefs about air pollution, beliefs about lead-free gasoline, and one's personal obligation to use lead-free gasoline. Observations made by gas station attendents were used to determine which of the research participants actually used lead-free gasoline. The results showed that general attitudes about proenvironmental behavior were not highly related to actual use of lead-free gasoline, but as the attitudes scale became more and more specific the attitude-behavior relationship became stronger. The two most specific scales, assessing obligations to use lead-free gasoline, were highly correlated to actual use. Thus, one condition that strengthens the correspondence between attitudes and behavior is the assessment of the attitudes and behavior at the same level of specificity.

Heberlein and Black's study is applicable to dealing with environmental problems because it suggests that to induce specific proenvironmental behavior, such as voluntary use of lead-free gasoline, it might be more effective to strengthen personal obligations to perform the specific behavior than to use the more typical approach of appealing to general environmental attitudes. It should be noted, however, that the study was correlational and was intended to clarify the attitude-behavior controversy rather than to suggest applications. It is possible that personal obligations to use lead-free gasoline caused people to use it, but it is also possible that using lead-free gasoline caused people to perceive that they were personally obligated to that behavior. It is also possible that there was no direct causal link between the obligation to use lead-free gasoline and its actual use. A third variable, like the kinds of cars people owned, might have determined both the type of gasoline people used and the perceived obligation to use lead-free gasoline. As is usually the case with a correlational study, the results are ambiguous with respect to cause and effect. In short, Heberlein and Black's study *suggests* applications involving manipulations of specific attitudes to induce specific behavior, but it did not involve an actual application, nor was it intended to do so.

Weigal and Newman (1976) approached the attitude-behavior controversy in a different way. Rather than assessing a specific attitude to predict a single behavior, they assessed a variety of environmental attitudes to predict multiple behaviors. They argue that their approach has the advantage of allowing the researcher to predict a wide variety of related behaviors rather than single acts. Beginning three months after the attitude survey each person was contacted and asked to participate in ecology projects. These requests were made over a five month period and the projects involved signing and circulating a petition opposing offshore drilling and nuclear power, picking up litter along roadsides, and recycling paper and bottles. As expected, the general measure of environmental attitudes was not a good predictor of participation in any specific one of the ecology projects, but the general measure was a good predictor of overall participation in the projects. People with generally proenvironmental attitudes participated in more ecology projects than those who were less environmentally concerned. Like Heberlein and Black's study, this research was correlational and was not intended to be an application dealing with environmental problems. Nevertheless, it seems to suggest that generally promoting proenvironmental attitudes may lead to many proenvironmental behaviors.

It is likely that most people already share the attitude that it would be nice to have a clean, healthy, and aesthetically pleasing environment that could also meet our needs. For some reason, however, many of us do not act according to this attitude. Heberlein (1972) points out that early in our history the population was sparse and natural resources were abundant and, therefore, people did not need to worry much about pollution and conservation. With the growth of the population and technology, however, many people are beginning to see the negative consequences of freely meeting our immediate needs without regard for the environment. Thus, culturally determined norms (or attitudes) that define acceptable and unacceptable behavior have emerged.

If we have norms that predispose us to conserve the environment, then why do we sometimes act to destroy it? Schwartz (1970) suggests that certain conditions must be met before norms are likely to be activated. We are likely to act in accord with a norm only if we are aware that noncompliance will result in negative consequences for others, and if we ascribe personal responsibility for the negative consequences to ourselves. This theory may be useful in understanding why people fail to comply with proenvironmental norms. The negative consequences of many environmentally detrimental behaviors are not immediately apparent. For example, if you run your air conditioner needlessly, you do not see the country's energy supply dwindling. Two common reasons for failing to ascribe personal responsibility for the negative consequences to others are feelings that "everyone does it" and "I had no other choice." For example, decisionmakers for one company, knowing that their competitors cut costs by dumping waste products into the environment, might feel that they have no choice but to do the same.

Supporting Schwartz's norm-activation model, Heberlein (1972) and Van Liere and Dunlap (1978) demonstrated that awareness of consequences and ascription of personal reponsibility are related to proenvironmental behavior. In Heberlein's study people who were walking down a street were given handbills urging them to register to vote. The researchers unobtrusively observed how the people disposed of the handbill. Subsequent interviews revealed that those people who littered with the handbill were less aware of the consequences of littering and were less likely to ascribe personal responsibility for those consequences than were nonlitterers. Providing additional support, Van Liere and Dunlap (1978) found that people who were least aware of the negative consequences of burning yard and garden wastes (it pollutes the air making it particularly difficult for people with respiratory diseases to breathe), and who were least willing to accept personal responsibility for the consequences, were the most likely to engage in yard burning.

Although both the Heberlein (1972) and Van Liere and Dunlap (1978) studies show that awareness of consequences and ascription of personal responsibility are good predictors of environmentally relevant behavior, neither study involved direct application of the norm-activation model to inducing proenvironmental behavior. To apply the model it would be necessary to manipulate awareness of consequences and ascription of responsibility. To the extent that both of these factors could be made salient, one would expect that people would behave according to proenvironmental norms.

The research discussed so far in this section has been guided by theory and a priori hypotheses about the conditions under which attitudes and norms are likely to predict behavior. The *specificity hypothesis* suggests that attitudes predict behavior when both are measured at the same level of specificity; a variation of this hypothesis proposes that general attitudes are good predictors of related multiple behaviors; and the norm-activation model posits that moral norms are likely to be activated when people are aware of negative consequences and ascribe personal responsibility. In contrast to the theoretically guided approach, it is sometimes useful to employ more empirically guided techniques. Whereas a certain hypothesis can be logically derived from a theory, the empirically guided approach allows the researcher to discover unexpected relationships. It should be noted, however, that both approaches ultimately rely on empirical research for verification. The distinction has to do with deciding what hypotheses to test. Using the theoretically guided approach, a small set of hypotheses are deduced from the theory; whereas, with the empirically guided techniques the generation of hypotheses is less constrained by theory and typically more hypotheses are tested.

Seligman and his colleagues (Seligman et al., 1979) used empirically guided techniques to identify factors that would predict summertime home energy use. First, they conducted a survey that involved a large number of questions regarding attitudes that might be related to energy consumption. The results of the survey were *factor analyzed,* which is a statistical technique that identifies survey items that are related to one another but unrelated to other items. Each group of related items is called a factor and is determined empirically rather than theoretically. Although the items that make up each factor often are theoretically related, they do not need to be. The purpose of this procedure is to reduce an unmanageably large number of items down to a small, manageable set of factors. In this case the factor analysis helped Seligman and his colleagues reduce their large set of attitude items down to six factors—personal comfort, belief that science will solve the energy crisis, the role of the individual in solving the energy crisis, perceived legitimacy of the energy crisis, and perceived effort required to conserve.

The next step was to determine which, if any, of the attitude factors was related to actual home energy consumption. With the homeowners' permission Seligman and his colleagues obtained records of energy use for all participants in the study. Then a statistical technique, called *multiple regression,* was used to empirically determine which, if any, of the attitude factors was a good predictor of actual energy consumption. Even though many or all of the factors seem like they would be related to energy use, the best and only reliable predictor of energy use was personal comfort. Seligman and his colleagues suggest that one way to apply this finding would be to provide information about ways to achieve personal comfort that do not involve the consumption of large amounts of energy. For example, at certain times of the day homes could be cooled by using window shades and opening windows rather than by indiscriminate use of air-conditioning.

The research reviewed in this section is applicable because it *suggests* possible solutions to environmental problems. Specific proenvironmental behaviors might be induced by appeals designed to influence obligations to perform those behaviors; broad persuasive appeals might elicit general activity in ecology projects; reminding people of negative consequences and personal responsibility may serve to activate moral norms regarding behavior that influences the environment; and informing people about alternative ways of achieving personal comfort may persuade them to use less energy in their homes. While suggesting solutions to environmental problems, none of these studies involved the testing of actual interventions. In the next section we examine some actual applications of social psychology to solving environmental problems.

Interventions Designed to Induce Proenvironmental Behaviors: Some Applied Research

Several social psychological principles and theories have actually been applied to solving environmental problems. Among the interventions that have been tested are those designed to reduce residential energy consumption, to control littering, and to promote recycling.

Reducing Residential Energy Consumption

As we have seen, Seligman and his colleagues (1979) found that personal comfort is a good predictor of summertime residential energy use, and they concluded that people should be better informed about how to cool their homes without air-conditioning. Becker and Seligman (1978) point out an interesting problem regarding the use of air-conditioning. To run an air conditioner properly all windows should be closed, which makes people less aware of when it cools down outside; therefore, people do not know when it would be best to turn off the air conditioner and open windows. Ironically, at certain times of the day, especially in morning and evening, it is possible for the air to be cooler outside than it is inside with the air conditioner on.

Given that there is a strong attitude-behavior correspondence between personal comfort and use of residential energy, and that people are unaware of the outside temperature when their air conditioners are being run, information about when it is cool outside might prompt people to reduce their use of air-conditioning and thus save energy. Becker and Seligman (1978) tested the effect of such information by supplying people with signaling devices in their homes. The signaling device was a blue light that flashed on and off when the outside temperature was below 68 degrees Fahrenheit and the air conditioner was on. In the same housing project other homeowners who lived in identical houses were not given the signaling device and were considered a control group. The assignment of homes to the signal or control condition was determined randomly. Meter readings for the month following installation of the signaling device showed that when it was cool outside homeowners who were signaled used significantly less electricity than did homeowners in the control condition. As might be expected there was no significant difference between conditions when it was hot outside. Overall, there was a 15.7 percent decrease in energy use by homeowners in the signaled conditon. Becker and Seligman point out that with such a large savings in utility bills the signaling device would pay for itself in two years. They suggest that the development of other "state-sensing information systems" might be useful in saving energy.

The link between attitudes and behavior becomes stronger when people publicly commit themselves to their attitudes (Kiesler, 1971). Telling others that you intend to do something apparently evokes a personal obligation to follow through with the promised behavior. Thus, commitment theory suggests that people will support publicly stated attitudes with relevant behaviors. If it is true, as Heberlein (1972) suggests, that there are developing proenvironmental norms, then most people probably feel some private commitment to conserve energy. Getting people to publicly commit themselves to these norms should increase the probability that they will actually conserve.

Pallak and Cummings (1976) applied commitment theory to conservation of residential energy. People were interviewed, told that the purpose of the study was to determine the degree to which personal efforts could influence home energy conservation, and were given some energy-conserving tips. The interviewer also made it clear that the researchers intended to share the results with the public through newspaper articles and other means. Some of the people were told that their names would be listed in the public presentation of the results and others were told that their names would not be used. Assignment of people to these conditons was done randomly. It was assumed that people who thought their names would appear in the newspapers would feel publicly committed to the project, whereas the people who were told that their names would not be revealed would only feel a private commitment. It is possible that the mere knowledge that one is participating in an energy study might induce energy conservation, and to control for such a possibility a third group of people were not interviewed. Thus there were three groups: public commitment, private commitment, and control.

The interviews were conducted shortly before peak usage seasons (i.e., summer cooling and winter heating). Meter readings during the peak seasons showed that the amount of increased natural gas and electricity consumption was significantly less for the public-commitment condition than for either the private-commitment or control conditions. The latter two conditions did not significantly differ, indicating that mere participation in an energy study is not sufficient to reduce energy consumption. It is interesting to note that the conservation demonstrated by the public-commitment condition persisted even after the people were told that their names would not appear in the paper as originally planned, which indicates that it was the commitment, and not the chance of recognition, that was important in activating the conservation attitude. Follow-up data showed that, relative to the private-commitment or control conditions, public commitment resulted in lower natural gas consumption for the entire six-month heating season and lower electricity consumption for the whole next year (Pallak, Cook, & Sullivan, 1980). In another study a formal commitment to reduce residential electricity consumption was even more effective in producing actual conservation than were attractive monetary incentives (Katzev & Johnson, 1984).

Using another approach, Pallak, Cook, and Sullivan (1980) applied social comparison theory to conservation of residential energy. *Social comparison theory*, first developed by Festinger (1954), posits that people have a need to evaluate themselves. Although there are times when performance can be compared to objective standards (like running against the clock), in many situations such standards are not available or, if available, they may not be meaningful. Therefore, we often compare ourselves to the performance of others. For example, a clock may not always be availble and, even if it were, running against time is not very meaningful unless we know the times of other runners. Festinger also suggests that, rather than comparing ourselves to anyone, we have a tendency to evaluate our performance compared to similar others. For example, a Sunday jogger probably would not compare his or her time to that of a world class marathoner, but might be likely to compare him- or herself to other part-time joggers. In their application of social comparison theory, Pallak and his colleagues attempted to induce energy conservation by giving homeowners feedback about their own energy consumption and that of comparable others. Homeowners were interviewed in much the same way as the private-commitment condition in the Pallak and Cummings (1976) study. In addition they signed an agreement allowing the researchers to read their meters every two weeks for a six-week period and following each meter reading a postcard was sent to each participant. Some homeowners were randomly assigned to a control condition and their postcards merely reported how much electricity they had used in a manner similar to that of their usual utility bills. For homeowners in the comparative-feedback condition the postcard indicated both the homeowner's own electricity usage and the average amount of usage by other homeowners in the study. It was expected that, given the chance to compare their own usage to that of comparable others, homeowners would be influenced to conserve. Supporting the hypothesis, the results indicated that as early as two weeks into the study homeowners in the comparative-feedback condition were using significantly less electricity than were those in the control condition, and the effect persisted for at least six weeks after the feedback had terminated (see Figure 4-1). What makes this technique particularly promising is that comparative feedback would be easy to provide as part of regular monthly utility bills.

In yet another social psychological approach to prompting residential energy conservation, Craig and McCann (1978) manipulated the credibility of the source of a message that contained energy saving tips for homeowners. Their research was based primarily on a line of social psychological inquiry that began with the Yale Communication and Attitude Change Program (e.g., Hovland & Weiss, 1951). Hovland and his associates engaged in a systematic program of research designed to determine the conditions under which people are likely to be persuaded to change their attitudes. As discussed in Chapter 3, the Yale school approach was to break the process of persuasive communication into its component parts—the communicator (or source), the message, and the audience—and to examine the effects of independent variations of each part. One reliable finding, first noted by Hovland and Weiss (1951) and later substantiated by others (Watts & McGuire, 1964; Miller & Baseheart, 1969), is that messages identified as

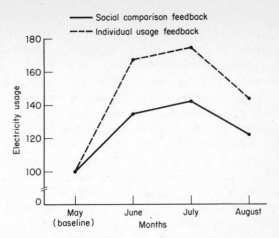

Figure 4-1. Electricity usage, measured by percentage of baseline average, for homes receiving social comparison or individual usage feedback. (Adapted from Pallak et al., 1980. Copyright © 1980 by Society for the Psychological Study of Social Issues, Inc. Reprinted by permission of Sage Publications, Inc.)

originating from a highly credible source (expert or trustworthy) induce more attitude change than the identical messages attributed to a less credible source. Subsequent research has shown that messages attributed to highly credible sources also are more likely to result in behavioral compliance (Crano, 1970; Crisci & Kassinove, 1973; Woodside & Davenport, 1974, 1976).

Applying the communicator credibility effect to energy conservation, Craig and McCann (1978) enclosed messages in the regular monthly bills of 1000 people. The messages, sent during the summer, suggested several ways to reduce electricity consumption associated with air-conditioning. In all cases the energy-saving messages were the same, but by random assignment half of the accompanying cover letters identified the tips as originating from the "Manager of Consumer Affairs" of the local utility company and the other half were supposedly from the state "Public Service Commission." It was assumed that a message from the utility company would have dubious credibility because the utility is a profit-making organization that might have ulterior motives, whereas the

"Public Service Commision" would have greater credibility because it is a nonprofit organization charged with the responsibility of serving the public. Also enclosed with the bills and messages was a stamped postcard that could be returned to get additional energy-saving information. People in a control condition received neither the energy-saving message nor the postcard. The results once again substantiated the communicator credibility effect. Significantly more people who received a message that ostensibly originated from the Public Service Commission returned postcards for additional energy-saving information than did customers receiving the message that was supposedly from the utility company. Of greater importance, when the consumption of kilowatt-hours was compared for the month subsequent to sending the messages, it was found that people in the high-credibility condition used significantly less electricity than people in the low-credibiltiy or control conditions. A two-month follow-up of energy consumption indicated that the difference between the two experimental conditions was no longer significant, but, as the researchers point out, the second month subsequent to the messages was in the fall rather than the summer and by that time the air-conditioning tips were less relevant.

Another social psychological approach to reducing residential energy consumption has been to model conservation strategies related to heating and cooling (Winett et al., 1982). In the winter, residents in electrically heated townhouses were shown a videotape that demonstrated how energy and money could be saved with minimal inconvenience or discomfort by using well-planned thermostat adjustments and alternative ways of keeping warm, such as dressing warmer and using heavy blankets. In the summer, residents in centrally air-conditioned apartments were shown a videotape that demonstrated planned thermostat adjustments and alternative ways to keep cool, including use of fans and natural ventilation, closing windows and drapes in the morning, and using the patio for meals and other activities. As with some of the interventions discussed in Chapters 2 and 3, this approach was based on social learning theory (Bandura, 1977). To enhance the likelihood that the energy-saving strategies would be imitated, the videotapes were filmed in homes similar to those of the subjects and a voice-over narration of the major points was used. Compared to control conditions, the modeling videotapes produced significant and substantial reductions (averaging about 15 percent) in electricity consumption. These reductions were especially large (over 30 percent in the summer) when combined with daily feedback of energy use.

Psychologists have tested several other interventions that are intended to prompt residential energy consumption, including individual feedback about consumption (e.g., Seligman & Darley, 1977), self-monitoring of energy use (Pallak & Cummings, 1976), and incentives for conserving (e.g., McClelland & Cook, 1980). These techniques are based more on behavioral psychology than on social psychology and therefore will not be elaborated on here (see Stern & Gardner, 1980, 1981 for a review).

In summary, home energy consumption has been reduced by signaling people that it is cool outside, eliciting public commitments to conserve, providing social comparison feedback about consumption, sending messages from highly credible sources, and presenting videotaped models. Whether there will be any wide-scale use of these techniques remains to be seen. The potential for general use of the social comparison and communicator credibility interventions seems promising because both techniques are easy to implement through slight modifications of regular billing procedures. However, it would be prudent to test the long-term effects of such billing procedures before implementing them on a wide scale. A broadly targeted application of the modeling approach, which has demonstrated long-term effects, could potentially be accomplished through a television campaign. A field test using that medium would be a prudent first step. State-sensing information systems, such as the cool-weather signaling device, also seem to have potential for general use, especially if people could be convinced that the devices would save them money in the long run. Although the public-commitment intervention has provided the most impressive long-term data, it is more difficult to imagine how it could be implemented on a wide scale. As a further note of caution, it should be kept in mind that in all the home energy studies the participants knew they were involved in projects designed to conserve energy. There is no assurance that the same reductions in energy use would be obtained if the interventions were implemented with people who did not feel that they were participating in a special project.

Is Reducing Residential Energy Consumption a Worthwhile Goal?

Suppose that a national media campaign could influence people across the country to reduce the use of electric lights in their homes by an average of 10 percent. Most social scientists would agree that a 10 percent change in behavior on such a large sample of people is an impressive effect and undoubtably the reduction would be statistically significant. Nevertheless, it could be argued that the campaign would not be worthwhile compared to other possible interventions. Lighting is responsible for only about 3 percent of energy used in households (Stern & Gardner, 1980). Thus, the media campaign would produce a net home energy savings of less than one-third of 1 percent (10% of 3% is 0.3%). Furthermore, the household sector accounts for only about a third of the total energy used in the United States (Stern & Gardner, 1980); therefore, the overall national energy savings of the hypothetical media campaign would be less than one-tenth of 1 percent.

While recognizing that psychological interventions have induced certain energy-conserving behaviors, Stern and Gardner (1980, 1981) make the criticism that more attention should be given to where, and for what purpose, the biggest portions of energy are used, and to the most efficient ways of reducing the large allocations. As we have seen, most of the social psychological research that has been applied to energy conservation has attempted to induce homeowners to curtail their use of space heating and air-conditioning. The potential for energy saving from this approach seems promising because heating and air conditioning account for the largest portions of household energy use. Stern and Gardner point out, however, that insulating and weatherizing homes saves twice as much energy as does reduction in the use of heating and cooling systems. In fact, they present estimates indicating that investing in energy-efficient equipment (e.g., insulation) generally saves far more energy than does curtailment of consumption (e.g., adjusting thermostats). Perhaps the most telling criticism they make is that the interventions are not directed at industry, commerce, and government, which collectively account for over two-thirds of the energy consumption in the United States. It might be wise, therefore, for social psychologists to coordinate their efforts with policymakers, engineers, economists, and other professionals who may have knowledge about how our energy system works.

Litter Control

Litter is a more important problem than most people probably realize. In 1973 an organization called Keep America Beautiful reported that people in the United States carelessly discard nearly 7 million tons of litter a year and that the annual cost to clean up the mess is about one billion dollars. Besides being unsightly and expensive, litter is wasteful of natural resources and causes health problems. The control of litter is therefore an important social problem. Although it may seem that littering can best be curtailed by posting warning signs, fining violators, and educating the public about the negative consequences of littering, social psychologists have found that such straightforward techniques may not be particuarly effective, and may in some cases backfire.

Written messages, usually in the form of signs, are commonly used to remind, or warn, people not to litter. Reich and Robertson (1979) analyzed the potential effects of such messages from a social psychological perspective and concluded that, unless carefully worded, antilittering messages could be counterproductive. Some messages simply tell people what to do (e.g., "Don't Litter") and may even be threatening (e.g., "$50 Fine for littering"). According to psychological reactance theory (Brehm, 1966), people react to threats to their freedom by acting in a manner that reestablishes their freedom. This might mean acting in direct opposition to the threat. It follows that a "Don't Litter" sign, especially one that involves a fine, may actually motivate people to litter. On the other hand, a friendly message (e.g., "Please don't litter") could produce positive results by serving as a nonthreatening reminder of a social norm. This idea is quite similar to Schwartz's (1970) norm activation theory, discussed earlier in this chapter. Thus, Reich and Robertson hypothesized that antilittering messages worded as commands would actually increase littering, whereas messages that focus on reminding people of antilitter norms would reduce littering.

As a test of the hypothesis, children patronizing a concession stand at a swimming pool were given antilitter handbills. Some of the children received messages that were worded as commands (e.g., "Don't litter"), while other children received messages reminding them of their social responsibility (e.g., "Keeping the Pool Clean Depends on You."). Messages that were irrelevant to littering were distributed in a control condition. The children were then observed to see how they would dispose of the handbills. Contrary to the prediction, over three experiments the norm appeals failed to produce less littering than in the control condition. Nevertheless, the reactance hypothesis was supported because the antilitter commands produced significant increases in littering. It should be noted, however, that Geller, Witmer, and Orebaugh (1976) found that handbills that demanded behavior ("You must dispose . . .") were just as effective in inducing compliance as were polite requests ("Please dispose . . ."), and Reiter and Samuel (1980) found that signs threatening fines were just as effective in reducing littering as were less threatening ("Pitch In") signs. Evidently the reactance effect is not very reliable.

Research by Bickman (1972) indicates that simple, one case exposure to a model is not enough to induce individuals to pick up other people's litter. In a field experiment two empty soft drink cans were placed in front of a college library. As a pedestrian approached the library a confederate picked up one of the cans and threw it in a trash receptacle, apparently not noticing the second can. In a control condition the confederate "unintentionally" kicked the first can and walked away leaving both cans on the ground. None of the 20 pedestrians tested, whether in the model or control condition, picked up a can. This occurred despite the fact that in a subsequent interview, with a similar sample of pedestrians, 94 percent of the people questioned said it was everyone's responsibility to pick up litter. Yet immediately after the interview only 1.4 percent of these same people picked up a crumpled piece of newspaper that was directly in their path. It appears that for the most part people do not really feel any personal responsibiltiy to pick up other people's litter, but will, when asked, say that they do. This apparent inconsistency may be explained by a tendency for people to respond to interviews in a socially desirable manner (Crowne & Marlowe, 1964).

The failure of Bickman's modeling manipulation should not be taken as a disconfirmation of social learning theory, which, as we have already seen in Chapters 2 and 3, has received consistent support in a wide variety of contexts. The manipulation in this case was quite weak. The target behavior was modeled only once and there is no assurance that the pedestrians even noticed the confederate.

In addition, the robustness of social learning is illustrated by an interesting application of the theory to the problem of littering. One of the modeling effects posited by the theory is disinhibition (Bandura, 1971). Observation of other people violating a social norm, especially when such behavior does not appear to result in negative consequences for the models, tends to free an observer to engage in similar antisocial behavior. Krauss, Freedman, and Whitcup (1978) reasoned that the presence of litter informs people that others have violated the social norm against littering, thus weakening the observers' inhibitions against the same behavior. It follows that people will be more likely to litter in littered places than in clean areas.

In a series of field studies in various locations (e.g., public streets and psychology laboratories), Krauss and his colleagues (1978) found that people littered more when the area was already littered than when it was clean. Similarly, Reiter and Samuel (1980) observed a higher littering rate in parking lots that had been previously littered than in clean lots. An implication of these findings is that cleaning up littered areas, which at first glance might seem to reinforce littering, should actually be effective in curtailing further littering. Another implication is that the movie theater cartoon showing a maintenance man getting buried in litter, while funny, might actually induce littering by increasing the viewers' awareness that other people litter.

Miller, Brickman, and Bolen (1975) found that an attribution strategy was successful in teaching fifth graders not to litter. The strategy is based on Kelley's (1967) *attribution theory,* which holds that a consistent pattern of information about oneself leads to a stable self-attribution. This new perception of oneself should, in turn, induce a corresponding pattern of behavior. Applying the theory to litter control, Miller and his associates provided students in a fifth grade class with consistent information that they were neat and tidy. Over an eight-day period, their teacher, the janitors, and even the principal commended the children for being ecologically minded in general and litter-conscious in particular. Over the same eight-day period, children in another fifth grade class were exposed to persuasive communications from their teacher, the janitors, and the principal. These communications were designed to convince the students that they should be ecologically minded and litter-conscious. A third class received no messages and served as a control group. The three classes were randomly assigned to the conditions.

To assess the effects of the treatments, students in all three classes were given candy shortly after the treatment period and Christmas presents two weeks later. The manner in which the candy and gift wrappers were disposed of was observed. As can be seen in Figure 4-2, children in the attribution condition were much more likely to dispose of the wrappers in a trash can than were the children in the persuasion and control groups. Apparently, telling children that they *are* neat is more effective in producing litter-conscious behavior than is telling them that they *should* be neat. Miller and his colleagues suggest that persuasive communications may even backfire. To the extent that trying to convince people to change their behavior implies that they typically do not do something that ought to be done, the recipients of a persuasive communication may make negative self-attributions.

In conclusion, the application of social psychology to litter control has had only limited success. The notion that threatening signs may backfire by causing psychological reactance has not been consistently supported by the data. An application of social learning theory, which involved modeling of the desired behavior, was not successful. On the other hand, social learning theory provides an explanation for the well-supported finding that people are more likely to litter in littered areas than in clean areas. Also, an application of attribution theory was successful in reducing littering in fifth graders.

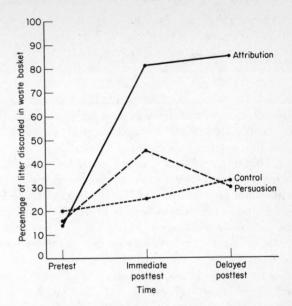

Figure 4-2. Nonlittering behavior of the attribution, persuasion, and control groups over time. (Adapted from Miller et al., 1975. Copyright © 1975 by the American Psychological Association. Reprinted by permission of the publisher and authors.)

Recycling

Collectively, we incur great costs, in terms of money and lost resources, because most individuals habitually throw away potentially reusable or recyclable materials such as old newpapers, aluminum cans, and glass bottles. In addition to perserving the reclyclable materials themselves, it has been estimated that by recycling newspapers and aluminum cans, 70 to 95 percent of the energy required to produce these products from raw materials could be conserved (Jacobs & Bailey, 1982-1983). Recycling could also greatly reduce the amount of land needed for disposal of garbage. Consider, for example, the extent of the problem in just one city. According to the San Diego Ecology Centre, about every 66 days San Diegans throw away enough recyclable materials to fill San Diego Stadium. If more people recycled, the land used as disposal areas for garbage could be put to some other use, or could be preserved for its natural beauty.

It is clear that great savings of money, energy, land, and other resources could be realized if large numbers of people would recycle. Of course, for most people this would mean a change of habit—a task for which applied psychology is well suited. To accomplish this task several attempts have been made to apply psychological techniques to induce recycling. While some of the approaches follow from other areas of psychology (e.g., Geller, Chaffee, & Ingram, 1975), some social psychological applications have also been attempted. We will concentrate on the latter.

Arbuthnot and his colleagues (1976-1977) applied the foot-in-the-door technique (Freedman & Fraser, 1966) to induce recycling. The technique is analagous to that used by people in door-to-door sales, who must get into a house before they can sell their products. In general, the technique relies on the fact that compliance with a small request (e.g., allowing the salesperson to enter the house) increases the likelihood of compliance with a susequent larger request (e.g., buying an expensive set of encyclopedias). Analyzed from the perspective of self-perception theory (Bem, 1972), the technique works because when people believe that they freely chose to engage in a behavior (i.e, comply with a small request) they tend to make inferences about themselves. In a sense we learn what kind of people we are by taking note of what we do. If I let an encyclopedia salesperson into my house, then it is logical for me to infer that I have some interest in encyclopedias.

It follows that if someone freely engaged in an activity that was intended to preserve the environment, then that person would be likely to perceive that he or she is concerned about ecological matters. Such a self-perception might then induce participation in more substantial conservation activities. Of course, this sequence of events would occur only if the person were to engage in the initial conservation activity. Applying the foot-in-the-door technique, this is accomplished by asking the person to engage in an activity that requires only minimal effort.

The application developed by Arbuthnot and his associates began with requests calling for behaviors that required minimal effort. The requests were to answer survey questions about environmental protection, to save aluminum cans for one week, and to send a postcard that urged government officials to expand a local recycling program. For comparison purposes, people were exposed to some, all, or none of the requests. As expected, self-report measures indicated that, for as long as 18 months after the requests were made, those people who were asked to perform the simple ecology tasks were more likely to subsequently recycle than were those people who had not been asked to comply with the simple requests. Furthermore, being asked to comply with multiple requests, which theoretically would provide more opportunities to self-perceive ecology consciousness, led to more recycling than did one or two requests (see Table 4-1).

To speculate a bit it seems that campaigns that make small conservation requests, like turning off unnecessary lights, may have beneficial effects beyond mere compliance with the specific requests. As we saw earlier in this chapter, turning off lights does not save much energy, but if in doing so people perceive themselves as concerned about conservation, then they might be more likely to engage in subsequent behaviors that are more effective in preserving natural resources.

It is interesting to note that while interventions that involve attractive monetary incentives for recycling typically have effects that last only as long as the incentives are offered (De Young, 1984), the foot-in-the-door technique had effects that lasted well past the treatment period. Arbuthnot and his colleagues suggest that self-perception theory can explain the difference. Bem (1972) posited that self-perceptions are based on observations of one's

Table 4-1. Short- and Long-Term Effects of Foot-in-the-Door Requests on Subsequent Recycling

	Percentage of people recycling	
Number of requests	1–2 months	18 months
0	0	0
1	4.9	3.7
2	23.7	21.6
3	32.1	33.3

Adapted from Arbuthnot et al., 1976–1977. Reprinted by permission.

own behavior and the circumstances under which that behavior occurs. To the extent that there is extrinsic motivation for a behavior, such as a monetary incentive, people will be unlikely to infer that their behavior reflects their attitudes. The incentives provide a sufficient explanation for the behavior. If, for example, you recycled cans for a dollar a can, then it is unlikely that you would perceive that you are concerned about the environment, because you could easily explain your behavior as motivated by wanting the money. When the monetary incentive is taken away or reduced (no one would pay you a dollar a can for long) you are likley to stop recycling. On the other hand, if you agreed to save aluminum cans for a week without a monetary incentive, then the most plausible explanation for your behavior is that you are concerned about the environment. This self-perception might then cause you to persist with further efforts to conserve the environment. In short, the argument is that money is an external incentive that will be effective as long as the money if offered; whereas, to the extent that the incentives for a behavior are minimal, performance of the behavior will lead to self-perceptions of internal motivation. Perception of internal motivation should lead to the persistence of the behavior over time.

The same basic principle of minimal justification was successfully applied to recycling in a different way by Pardini and Katzev (1983-1984). Rather than using the foot-in-the-door technique, recycling was induced through public commitment. As we saw earlier in this chapter, public commitment to an attitude tends to increase the probability of corresponding behavior. Pardini and Katzev point out that, since public commitment does not involve an external incentive, its application can be conceptualized as a minimal justification technique.

The experimenters went door-to-door to recruit people for a newspaper recycling program. Each recruit was randomly assigned to a verbal commitment, written commitment, or control condition. In the verbal-commitment condition the people were asked to verbally state that they were willing to participate in the program. People in the written-commitment condition were asked to sign a statement committing themselves to the program. It was assumed that the people would perceive themselves as more strongly committed in the written than in the verbal condition. In the control condition people received information about the program but were not asked to make any commitment to it. All the subjects were informed that the experimenters would return on certain dates to collect any newspapers the participants had collected.

The results strongly supported the efficacy of the public-commitment technique. During the two-week period of the project people in the two commitment conditions more frequently left newspapers for the experimenters, and left significatly more pounds of newspaper, than did people in the control condition. Two weeks after the program subjects in the written-commitment condition continued to recycle more newspapers than did the control subjects, whereas the positive effects initially observed in the verbal commitment condition dissipated in the follow-up. The fact that the written commitment condition led to more recycling even after the period of commitment provides further evidence that minimal incentive techniques can bring about long-term recycling. It should also be noted that in this study actual recycling, rather than self-reports, was measured. Nevertheless, since the experimenters picked up the newspapers, one still might question whether the same results would have been obtained if the subjects had to take the papers to a recycling center themselves. In a community where the city regularly picks up recyclable materials, which is rare, a public commitment technique was once again effective in inducing recycling (Burn & Oskamp, 1984). It would be of practical interest to find out, with a behavioral measure, whether the minimal justification techniques can induce people to bring materials to a recycling center. This would have practical significance because more commonly used monetary incentive programs sometimes cost more to implement than is saved by the recycling they induce (Jacobs & Bailey, 1982-1983).

In summary, there is evidence indicating that applications of the principle of minimal justification, which involve either the foot-in-the-door technique or public commitment, are effective in inducing recycling. There is even some indication that these techniques are more cost-effective and produce longer lasting effects than does the more common approach of offering monetary incentives. Since the measures in the supportive studies were either self-reports or involved pickup service of the recyclable materials, it remains to be seen whether the minimal justification techniques can actually get people to bring materials to a recycling center.

Summary and Conclusions

To a large extent the environmental problems addressed in this chapter can be conceptualized as tragedies of the commons. Unrestrained individual use of low-cost but finite resources can lead to depletion of those resources. The task for social psychologists is to convince and motivate people to conserve.

Some of the relevant social psychological research demonstrates conditions under which proenvironmental attitudes and norms are likely to be predictors of proenvironmental behaviors. Much of this research is correlational and does not clearly indicate cause-and-effect relationships, nor does it involve actual interventions designed to induce proenvironmental behaviors. Nevertheless, these studies are applicable in that they *suggest* interventions that may be useful in applying social psychology to dealing with environmental problems. The data seem to support the following suggestions:

1. If the goal is to induce a specific proenvironmental behavior, then it would be more effective to influence the intention to engage in that particular behavior than to influence general attitudes.
2. If the goal is to induce a wide variety of proenvironmental behaviors, then it would be more effective to influence general attitudes than to influence a specific intention.
3. To induce compliance with proenvironmental norms, people should be made aware of the negative consequences of noncompliance and of their personal responsibilty to comply.
4. Teach people that there are altenatives to air-conditioning for achieving personal comfort.

In addition to the applicable studies, there have been several attempts to apply social psychology to the solution of environmental problems. These applications are directed toward conservation of energy, litter control, and recycling.

The application of social psychology to litter control has been only moderately successful. A simple modeling approach failed to produce positive effects. The prediction that warning signs may backfire, which is based on reactance theory, has had mixed support. The disinhibition hypothesis, which suggests that seeing litter reduces inhibitions against littering, has been more consistently supported. A promising technique, derived from attribution theory, involves telling children that they *are* (rather than *should* be) ecologically conscious.

Applications of the principle of minimal justification, rather than extrinsic rewards (e.g., money), have been successful in inducing recycling. One such approach, the foot-in-the-door technique, involves gaining compliance with a moderate request in order to enhance the likelihood of gaining subsequent compliance to a larger request. Another approach involves getting people to publicly commit themselves to recycling.

The most impressive applications of social psychology to environmental problems are the interventions designed to reduce residential energy consumption. The successful interventions include signaling people when it is cool outside, getting people to publicly commit themselves to conservation efforts, providing social comparison feedback about the energy consumption of similar others, sending energy-saving messages from credible sources, and modeling energy-saving techniques. Most of these interventions are potentially quite useful, because they could be implemented on a wide scale. Since the signaling device is inexpensive and would quickly pay for itself with energy savings, people might be inclined to buy it. Social comparison feedback and credible energy-saving messages could easily be included with regular monthly utility bills. Widescale modeling of energy-saving techniques might be accomplished through public service media campaigns.

Despite impressive demonstrations of their effectiveness, the applications of social psychology to residential energy conservation have been criticized. The major problem centers on the target of the interventions. The goal has been to induce self-restraint, despite the fact that use of energy-efficient products has more potential to save energy. Also, the emphasis has been on influencing energy consumption in the household sector, which only accounts for about a third of all energy consumed. Thus, it might be more worthwhile to design interventions that would increase the use of energy-efficient products and decrease energy consumption by industry, commerce, and government, which are the biggest users.

5

Education

Although many of the memories I have about my early school years are vague, there are a few events and feelings that I can recall reasonably well. I remember that, at first, going to kindergarten was a somewhat overwhelming experience. The other children were strangers, the classroom and school grounds were unfamiliar, and the teacher was the first formal authority figure I was to encounter. The first grade was somewhat traumatic as well. I missed some critical time when I had the measles, or maybe it was the mumps. Before being absent I was in the first reading group, but afterwards I was demoted to the last. To this day I stll feel uncomfortable when reading out loud. In the third grade we learned to square dance and I discovered girls. Actually, they were there all the time, but the consensus among the boys was that girls had a mysterious affliction called "coodies," and were to be avoided at all costs. The feeling was probably mutual. Imagine my surprise when I actually enjoyed promenading with one of these contaminated individuals. By the fourth and fifth grades I was gaining confidence in myself, largely because I was a pretty good natural athlete and was usually picked early for teams. Overall, like most people I have both positive and negative memories of those years. As I begin to write this chapter I wonder how those early experiences with my teachers and classmates influenced who I am today.

Most of us begin school at an early age and continue going for many years. There is no doubt that these years have a major influence on our lives. Without a broad knowledge about the world around us, an appreciation of the arts, and the basic skills of reading, writing, and arithmetic it would be difficult to lead a happy and productive life. Perhaps less obvious, but nevertheless important, is the social psychological influence of our school years. In school our circle of acquaintances broadens dramatically, new friendships develop, and teachers and other school officials become new authority figures in our lives.

Although social psychologists have been writing about the social psychology of education for years (Backman & Secord, 1968; Getzels, 1969; Guskin & Guskin, 1970; Johnson, 1970), it has only been recently that specific social psychological interventions have been developed to solve problems in the classroom. As we will see in this chapter, interpersonal aspects of the classroom influence students' self-concepts, perceptions of others, social behaviors, and academic achievement. Some of the research described below is potentially applicable in that it describes problems, identified by social psychologists, that might be avoidable if people were aware of them. The primary focus, however, will be on social psychological interventions designed to induce positive self-concepts, to reduce prejudices, to promote accepting and mutually beneficial interactions, and to enhance academic achievement.

Expectation Effects

For a variety of reasons teachers will form expectations about the performance and other behavior of their students. Such expectations could be formed on the basis of records of prior performance, results of aptitude tests, or other intellectual measures. Teachers may also form expectations based on the sex, race, manner of dress, or other characteristics of their students. Some striking examples are a study in which the physical attractiveness of children influenced teachers' estimates of the children's intelligence (Clifford & Walster, 1973), and a study that showed that, for some teachers, there was an extremely high correlation (.90) between teacher ratings of students' potential and the quality of the students' clothing (Babad, Inbar, & Rosenthal, 1982). Can such expectations have an important influence on self-concepts and behavior? Social psychologist Robert Rosenthal and others suggest they can and have shown that, in a variety of settings, if others have expections of certain behavior, the likelihood that the expected behavior will occur increases (see Rosenthal, 1976, for a review). These effects are often called self-fulfilling prophecies.

In a classic study Rosenthal and Jacobson (1968) induced teacher expectations in order to determine what, if any, influence they might have on students. An IQ test was administered to elementary school students in several classrooms. Teachers were given the names of those students who, supposedly on the basis of the test, showed great potential for intellectual growth. Unknown to the teachers the selection of these intellectual "bloomers" was done randomly and had nothing to do with their test scores. Thus the teachers were given false expectations about some of their students.

After a year the teachers rated the bloomers as significantly happier, more curious, more interesting, and more likely to succeed than the other students. In addition, the teachers assigned reading grades to the bloomers that indicated significantly more improvement than did the grades assigned to the other students. Of course, all these assessments could reflect the teachers' own expectations rather than any real differences in the performance of the students. Therefore, the most impressive result was that after a year a readministration of the IQ test showed that the bloomers, especially in the early grades, had significanty greater gains in total and reasoning IQ than did the other students (see Figure 5-1). Since the teachers were involved in neither the administration nor the scoring of the IQ test, it was concluded that the teachers must have somehow communicated their expectations to the students and that self-fulfilling prophecies resulted.

It should be noted that not all studies of expectancy have resulted in self-fulfilling prophecies (see Cooper, 1979, for a review). Nevertheless, in more than a third of the 311 studies reviewed by Rosenthal (1976), subjects were affected by expectancies and the percentage of supportive studies was slightly higher (38 percent) when only those studies done in real-life settings, like classrooms, were considered. Therefore, although expectancy effects do not always occur, they have been observed well beyond

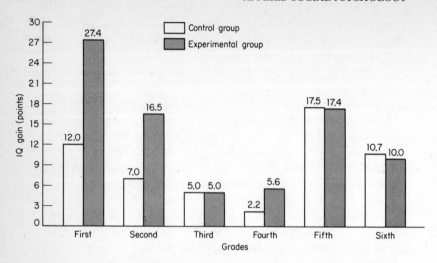

Figure 5-1. Comparison of gains in total IQ between the expectation (treatment) and control groups for each of six grade levels. (Adapted from *Pygmalion in the Classroom* by R. Rosenthal & L. Jacobson. Copyright © 1968 by Holt, Rinehart and Winston, Inc. Reprinted by permission of CBS College Publishing.)

a chance level. In addition, there is substantial evidence that, while not always *changing* the level of student performance, teacher expectations can *sustain* low levels of performance by students who have the potential to improve (Cooper, 1979). Caught in a vicious cycle, the student who starts slowly can induce low teacher expectations that, in turn, can impede improvement on the part of the student.

How do teacher expectations get communicated to students? Rosenthal (1974) suggests four general ways. One factor is an atmosphere where teachers are especially warm in their interactions with bright students. For example, a study by Chaikin, Sigler, and Derlega (1974) found that tutors smiled more, maintained more eye contact, and nodded their heads more when they were with supposedly bright students than with supposedly dull students. The second factor, called *input,* is that teachers are more likely to present bright students with new and challenging materials. Another means of communicaton is output that is manifest in the tendency for teachers to interact more with bright students.

The final factor is feedback where bright students are praised and those who are not so bright are criticized.

Given that there are numerous studies indicating that expectancies might bias teachers in their interactions with students and that these biases can influence student performance, it is surprising that there is very little research investigating ways to induce more egalitarian treatment of students. One might expect that making teachers aware of expectation effects and how they get communicated would help. Along these lines Rosenthal and Jacobson wrote a book entilted *Pygmalion in the Classroom* (1968), which was intended, in part, to help teachers become aware of the subtle, but potentially powerful, influence that their expectations can have on their students. In addition, most textbooks on educational psychology describe expectancy effects. It remains to be demonstrated, however, whether such readings have any affect on teacher expectations or on the communication of expectations to students.

The strategy of educating teachers about expectation effects seems to be based on the assumption that teachers can monitor their interactions with students. Research has shown, however, that teachers are not generally aware of their patterns of interaction with students (Brophy & Good, 1974). To remedy this situation Good and Brophy (1972) developed a treatment intervention that provides teachers with feedback. The feedback is presented in a single one-hour interview, but is based on behavioral evidence that is collected by an observer who spends 40 hours in the classroom prior to the interview. During the interview the teacher is shown how he or she interacts inappropriately with some students and appropriately with others. The two basic kinds of inappropriate teacher behaviors that are discussed are infrequent interactions with certain students and "giving up" too easily when certain students fail to come up with a correct answer. To guard against the teachers becoming defensive about the feedback, whenever it is pointed out that the teacher is interacting inappropriately with one student it is also noted that he or she is interacting appropriately on the same dimension with another student.

Good and Brophy tested their intervention in several first grade classrooms. Subsequent to the interviews, behavioral evidence, collected by observers who were unaware of what was said in the interviews, showed that teachers increased their interactions with students who they had previously interacted with infrequently and were more persistent in trying to elicit correct answers from students who they previously had a tendency to give up on. Brophy and Good (1974) conclude that their intervention is beneficial in inducing more egalitarian teaching and, because the interview only takes an hour, is practical. It should be noted, however, that since no control conditions were used, the reason for the improved pattern of teacher–student interactions is open to alternative explanations.

The Cooperative Classroom

Typically, the American classroom has a competitive structure. While in the classroom students interact directly with the teacher and interaction among students is limited and usually forbidden. Grades are based on individual work; it is up to the student to get the teacher's attention and to demonstrate that he or she knows more than the other students.

Although there may be some advantages to the competitive structure, there may be disadvantages as well. On the positive side competition may motivate some students to excell. In addition, grades based on individual work may most directly reflect each student's achievement. On the other hand, competition may serve as a disincentive for the slower student, who sees classmates get more praise and higher grades. Competition might also cause hostility among students, because they realize that one student's gain is another student's loss.

Beginning in the late 1940s and continuing today, several social psychologists have suggested that, while not completely abolishing competition, more emphasis should be placed on promoting cooperative learning experiences in the classroom. For example, Deutsch (1949) demonstrated that a cooperative goal structure, in which grades depended on group performance, induced introductory psychology students to be more mutually helpful and productive than did the more traditional competitive grading system. In light of these results, Deutsch questioned the wisdom of the predominate use of competitive grading systems. Subsequent studies have shown similar advantages to cooperative grading schemes over competitive systems (e.g., Haines & McKeachie, 1967).

While demonstrations of the benefits of cooperative classroom structures are important, the development of specific techniques that can be readily implemented in the classroom should be most persuasive in motivating teachers to adopt cooperative classroom structures. Fortunately, such interventions have been developed and successfully field tested. Let us examine these techniques.

The Jigsaw Classroom

Mandatory busing of children to achieve racial balance in our school systems has been one of the most controversial policies of recent times. Rather than promoting greater understanding and acceptance of members of other races, forced desegregation of schools has, it seems, often led to increases in interracial prejudices and hostilities. Despite numerous attempts, most of the curricula that have been designed to teach positive racial attitudes and to dispel myths about ethnic differences have been unsuccessful in reducing racial prejudice (see Westphal, 1977, for a review). Aronson and his colleagues suggest that the reason desegregation of schools has not been successful is that classrooms are structured for competition rather than for cooperation (Aronson, Stephan, Sikes, Blaney, & Snapp, 1978), and they developed a cooperative classroom structure, called the *jigsaw classroom,* to remedy the situation.

Before discussing the jigsaw technique, it should be pointed out that the rationale behind court-ordered desegregation of schools was based in part on social psychological principles. In 1954 the Supreme Court of the United States made a landmark decision in the the case of *Brown* v. *Board of Education of Topeka* (1954). The Court ruled that the doctrine of "separate but equal" educational facilities for blacks and whites was fundamentally in error because the mere fact that the facilities are separate implies that there is a difference. Some of the testimony in the case and a nonlegal brief were provided by social scientists. For example, social psychologist Kenneth Clark testified that his research (Clark & Clark, 1947) indicated that blacks from segregated schools had particularly poor self-concepts that could impair their ability to learn. The social science brief was unique because, as Clark (1979) notes, "this was probably the first time that a separate non-legal brief dealing with the social and psychological aspects of a constitutional issue was submitted to *and accepted by* the United States Supreme Court" (p. 477).

The social science testimony and brief led to a promising social psychological theory about the probable outcomes of desegregation of schools (Stephan, 1978). Interracial contact would expose whites to evidence that would dispel their prejudicial attitudes toward blacks. Whites would begin to accept blacks and blacks would gain in self-esteem. Aided by gains in self-esteem blacks would achieve more, causing them to feel less frustrated. Feeling less frustrated, blacks would become less prejudiced toward whites. More than 20 years after the *Brown* decision, Stephan (1978) reviewed the evidence on the effects of desegregation and concluded that the promise of the social science theory was not realized.

What went wrong? Aronson and his associates (Aronson, Stephan, Sikes, Blaney, & Snapp, 1978) point out that a more careful examination of the social psychological knowledge about racial prejudice in 1954 indicates that racial contact will reduce prejudice only under certain conditions. In his classic book *The Nature of Prejudice* (1954), Allport states three facilitating factors. These conditions are equal status, common goals, and sanction by authorities. The jigsaw technique was developed with these factors in mind.

In the 1970s, Aronson and his colleagues were contacted by officials of a local school district who were having problems with a new school busing program (Aronson et al., 1978). To deal with the problems the jigsaw technique was developed and implemented. Following Allport's suggestions, the overall stategy was to structure the classroom so that, for at least some portion of the day, students would interact as equals pursuing common goals.

The jigsaw technique involves dividing the class into small groups of usually about five to six students each. Each child in a group is given information about one part of a total lesson. For example, a lesson on Spanish and Portuguese explorers might be divided such that one child in the group is given information about Magellan, another student receives information about Balboa, another about Ponce de Leon, etc. The members of the group then proceed to teach their part to the group. Afterwards the students are tested individually on the entire lesson. Just as all the pieces of a jigsaw puzzle must be put into place to get the whole picture, the only way any one student can master the entire lesson is to learn all the pieces of information from his or her peers. Equal status is attained because every student has an equally important part. The common goal is to put together the entire lesson.

In a field test volunteer teachers used the jigsaw technique in their fifth grade classrooms for about 45 minutes a day, three times a week, for six weeks (Blaney, Stephen, Rosenfield, Aronson, & Sikes, 1977). Anglos, Blacks, and Mexican-Americans were purposely mixed together within jigsaw groups. In a control condition other teachers used traditional methods of instruction. To assure that the jigsaw technique was put to a challenging test the teachers in the control condition were chosen on the basis of their high level of competence. The results were very encouraging. A comparison of pre- and postmeasures indicated that, unlike the control students, the jigsaw students showed significant increases in liking for their classmates, in a belief that they could learn from their classmates, and in self-esteem. Subsequent studies have shown that, when compared to traditional instruction, the jigsaw technique leads to higher achievement by minority students while not reducing the performance of majority students, more positive interracial attitudes, more positive attitudes toward school, and greater empathy for the viewpoint of others (Bridgeman, 1981; Geffner, 1978; Gonzalez, 1979; Lucker, Rosenfield, Sikes, & Aronson, 1976). These results are in line with the original intent of desegregation. It also should be noted that the benefits were obtained without a major disruption of regular classroom procedure, but rather with just a few hours of jigsawing a week.

In addition to the impressive outcomes of the field experiments, there are several other notable aspects of the jigsaw technique that should be pointed out. In their book *The Jigsaw Classroom*, Aronson and his colleagues provide instructions about how to implement the jigsaw technique (Aronson et al., 1978). These instructions include suggestions for group selection, "teambuilding" exercises designed to promote interaction, a description of the role of the teacher as a facilitator, ways to deal with "squabbles" among group members, some examples of actual jigsaw lesson plans, and methods to help slower students learn their parts. For example, to help students learn their parts, counterpart groups could be formed. Counterpart groups are composed of all the students in a class who have a similar part in their jigsaw groups. In the Spanish and Portuguese explorer lesson, for example, all the students assigned to learn about Balboa would get together to practice their part so that later they could make a good presentation to their jigsaw group. Using the counterpart technique it is likely that even the slower learners would make a competent contribution to their jigsaw group.

Aronson and Yates (1983) also suggest that the jigsaw technique is applicable to a wide variety of classroom situations. One example is the trend toward mainstreaming. Rather than segregating handicapped children in special classrooms, *mainstreaming* is the integration of such children into regular classrooms. With the jigsaw technique the integration should be smoother because the handicapped and the nonhandicapped would interact toward common goals on an equal-status basis. As we have seen these conditions are likely to induce mutual attraction, empathy, and increases in self-esteem.

In conclusion, the jigsaw technique is a good blend of science and practicality, and could serve as a model for applied social psychology. It combines a "meticulous assessment, rigorous enough to pass the scrutiny of our scientific colleagues" with "techniques that teachers could readily apply to their classrooms" (Aronson & Osherow, 1980, p. 177). The research has shown that the technique helps reduce prejudices and enhance the self-esteem and achievement of minorities. At the same time, jigsawing is practical because it requires very little classroom time, good information about how to use it is available, and ways to handle problems are provided.

Student Teams

Members of teams usually need to cooperate in order to succeed. In football the quarterback drops back to pass, the line blocks, and the receivers run previously arranged routes. If anyone fails to do his or her job, it would be unlikely that the play would succeed, whereas the cooperation of everyone involved would maximize the chance of success. We might also expect that such cooperation would induce feelings of mutual respect and attraction among the team members.

As discussed earlier, in the traditional classroom students compete with one another individually and there is no incentive to cooperate. But what if students were members of academic teams? To explore this possibility social psychologists DeVries and Slavin have developed and field-tested classroom techniques involving student teams (DeVries & Slavin, 1978; Slavin, 1978).

One team method is called the *Teams-Games-Tournament* (TGT). Students are put into teams of four to five members. Each team is a heterogeneous mixture of students including both sexes, various ethnic groups, and different levels of ability. The teacher makes an initial presentation of a lesson and then the team members help each other learn the material by a process of peer tutoring. A week later there is a class tournament. In the tournament students compete individually as representatitives of their teams. To give everyone a reasonable chance to succeed students compete against members of other teams who are similar in ability. The performance of each team member is added together to arrive at a team score. To provide an incentive to perform well in the tournament team scores are reported in a newsletter.

A variation of TGT, called *Student Teams and Achievement Divisions* (STAD), was developed to simplify the procedure in hopes that teachers would be more likely to use it. STAD is basically the same as TGT, except that there are no tournaments. Instead, student quiz scores are converted into team points on the basis of achievement levels of the individuals on a team. Conceptually the achievement division system is similar to handicapping in golf. High achievers need to perform at a very high level to score points, whereas low achievers can score points while performing at a lower level. To avoid embarrasment students are not told which achievement level they are in. As in TGT, a newsletter reports team scores.

In some respects the team approach is similar to the jigsaw technique, but there are some fundamental differences. Both methods are designed to promote cooperation among group members, both involve small groups of mixed composition, and

both employ the technique of peer tutoring. One fundamental difference is that the team techniques purposely promote competition *between* groups. This is based in part on the social psychological finding that a superordinate goal, in this case winning,
increases cooperation (Sherif & Sherif, 1953), and in part on the
observation that students have great enthusiasm for competitive
games. A second fundamental difference is that with the jigsaw
technique peer tutoring is necessary for any one student to master
a lesson, whereas with the team methods peer tutoring is encouraged but not necessary to learn the material.

Numerous field experiments have been conducted to assess the
effects of the team approach (for reviews, see DeVries & Slavin,
1978; Slavin, 1978). These studies were done in public schools
with regular classroom teachers. Teachers, and sometimes even
students, were randomly assigned to team or control conditions.
And in most of the studies teachers in both the team and control
conditions were given the same curriculum objectives and materials. In general, the results showed that compared to traditional
classrooms the team approach induced greater academic achievement, more mutual concern, and increases in cross-racial friendships. As with the jigsaw technique, these results are supportive of
desegregation under carefully structured conditions. One unanswered question, however, is whether competition between teams
leads to better or worse relations among students from different
teams. The possibility of antagonisms between teams is suggested
by the research of Sherif and Sherif (1953).

Cooperative Goal Structures

Both the jigsaw and the student-team methods are highly structured techniques, and each involves specific procedures. For
example, the jigsaw technique requires division of a lesson into
component parts, peer tutoring, and small heterogeneous groups
of students. Student teams require between group competition,
heterogeneous teams, and feedback about team scores. The structure of these techniques are part of their strength. A teacher who
wishes to employ jigsawing or student teams knows just what to do
and can be assured that the specific techniques have been successfully field-tested.

For some teachers, however, the structure of the jigsaw or student-team techniques may not be appealing. They might prefer more general guidelines for promoting a cooperative atmosphere in the classroom. In a book entitled *Learning Together and Alone,* Johnson and Johnson (1975) provide such guidelines.

Based on social psychological research conducted in the classroom, Johnson and Johnson (1975) concluded that traditional classrooms are too often structured for competition among individual students. One student's gain is usually another student's loss. What is needed, they suggest, is a greater use of cooperative goal structures, where a student can achieve a goal only if other students obtain their goals. Their review of the relevant research indicates that such cooperative goal structures create a classroom climate where students learn interpersonal skills, reduce their prejudices, develop positive attitudes about school and themselves, and, on most academic tasks, perform at a higher level.

The general guidelines to achieve these benefits include dividing classes into small heterogeneous groups, setting group goals, encouraging division of labor, making it clear that students should look at each other as resources, and providing group rewards. These guidelines are quite similar to what is done with jigsaw groups and student teams, but rather than providing a specific program for implementation Johnson and Johnson suggest to educators that "implementing ideas is your profession" (p. viii).

Compared to the jigsaw and student-team approaches, the general guidelines for cooperative goal structures suggested by Johnson and Johnson have the advantage of being flexible, but such flexibility may also be a weakness. A teacher using the general guidelines will be less certain how to proceed. Improvisation may lead to creative new techniques, but may also produce undesirable effects. It is important to note that, since Johnson and Johnson do not provide a specific program for implementation of their ideas, any application will be new and untested.

Cooperative Classrooms in Israel

Since the United States is not the only country to experience racial and ethnic tensions and poor academic performance in it desegregated schools, it is of interest to know whether cooperative classroom structures can also be beneficial in other countries. Recently, Sharan and his colleagues (1984) investigated the impact of cooperative learning techniques in Israel, where tensions between two ethnic groups, Western and Middle Eastern Jews, have had deleterious effects on academic achievement and social relations. In a comprehensive field experiment a comparison was made between two small group, cooperative classroom teaching techniques and the traditional, whole-group method. One of the cooperative classroom techniques was student teams and academic divisions (STAD), which, as we have seen, was originally developed by Slavin (1978) in the United States. The other cooperative learning procedure, *groups-investigation,* was developed by Sharan and his colleagues (1984). Similar to other cooperative teaching techniques, groups-investigation involves small multiethnic groups of students working interdependently. The unique aspect of this approach is that each group exercises some autonomy in selecting a topic for investigation and in dividing the labor. The end product is a presentation to the whole class. Supporting the findings obtained in the United States, the cooperative techniques generally resulted in higher academic achievement and better social relations among the students than did the traditional classroom.

Summary and Conclusions

Many social psychologists agree that the individualistic, competitive goal structure that is typical in classrooms may have undesirable effects, such as increased hostilities, undeveloped social skills, and poor academic performance. Classroom techniques that involve structured cooperation in heterogeneous groups of students have been shown to reduce prejudices, increase empathy, raise self-esteem, and, in many cases, improve academic performance. The jigsaw technique is particularly noteworthy because, as well as being well supported by research, it requires very little classroom time and its method of implementation has been clearly specified.

Enhancing Motivation

A common problem in school is the child who does not work to his or her potential. These underachievers have the ability to succeed, but lack the motivation to consistently apply themselves to their work. Besides being terribly frustrating for teachers, such underachievement is a great waste of talent. To deal with this problem some social psychological techniques have been developed to induce persistent achievement striving in students. These interventions range from complex training programs (e.g., Kolb, 1965) to much simpler manipulations (e.g., Dweck, 1975).

Achievement Motivation Training

Kolb (1965) developed and tested a special training program to increase the achievement motivation of underachieving high school boys. All the boys had IQs above 120 but were doing below average work at school. In addition to regular summer school classes some boys participated in the motivation training program. A control group did not receive any special training.

The motivation training program, which was based primarily on research by McClelland and his associates (e.g., McClelland, Atkinson, Clark, Lowell, 1953), was quite complex. Over a series of several sessions the boys were taught about the characteristics of people with a high need for achievement. Basically, these characteristics are taking personal responsibility for one's own actions, taking moderate risks, and seeking feedback about the results of one's actions. The boys were asked to think about these characteristics, discuss them, and incorporate them while participating in specially designed games. In one of the games, for example, the boys were to manufacture products with tinker toys. As manufacturers they had to take personal responsibility to negotiate contracts, to contract for an attainable but profitable amount of production, and to produce the products. It was hypothesized that the boys would begin to identify with the characteristics of high achievers, set realistic but challenging goals, expect to achieve their goals, and actually achieve more.

Overall the motivation program was a limited success. Although a six-month follow-up revealed no positive results, in an 18-month follow-up the grade point average of the boys who had participated in the training program improved significantly more than did the grades of the boys in the control condition. Further analyses showed, however, that the improvement in grades occurred only for boys from high socioeconomic backgrounds; there was no improvement for boys from lower class backgrounds. Another drawback to this technique is that it could be costly in terms of time, facilities, and personnel.

Personal Causation Training

DeCharms (1972, 1976) makes an interesting distinction between two types of people that he calls *Pawns* and *Origins*. One type seems to have a tendency to let other people determine their behavior. They are indecisive and easily manipulated by other people. Like pawns on a chessboard, they are weak and often "pushed around" by others. In contrast, Origins are much more likely to initiate their own behavior. They make their own decisions and are more internally motivated. In the traditional classroom, teachers usually treat students like Pawns. This is unfortunate, deCharms argues, because people are happiest and most productive when they actively initiate their own behavior rather than reacting to the dictates of others. He hypothesized, therefore, that if teachers were trained to treat students as Origins rather than as Pawns, then the students would perceive themselves as causal agents and would perform more competently.

To test his hypothesis, deCharms (1972) developed and implemented a personal causation training program for teachers. Prior to the fall semester elementary school teachers attended a week of residential training. The training was designed to encourage independence, achievement motivation, realistic goal setting, and Origin rather than Pawn behavior. In addition, during the following school year these teachers were supplied with classroom exercises designed to promote Origin motivations and behaviors in their students. Other teachers were randomly assigned to a control condition and therefore did not receive the personal causation training nor were they supplied with the special classroom exercises.

Data were collected for three years and it was found that the training had beneficial effects for both the teachers and the students. Two years after the training, significantly more of the trained teachers had been promoted (e.g., became principal) than had the control teachers. Students rated trained teachers as significantly more encouraging of Origin behavior than control teachers. Students of trained teachers more often wrote stories exhibiting Origin behavior, such as realistic goal setting and taking personal responsibility, which suggests that they internalized Origin characteristics. These students also became more responsible. For example, they were less often absent than were students of the control teachers. There were academic benefits as well, as students of trained teachers scored higher on standardized tests of achievement than did students of control teachers. Therefore, the personal causation training program was a success. However, as deCharms points out, since the Origin-Pawn concept is multidimensional, it could not be determined which part, or parts, of the training was responsible for its overall success.

Attribution Retraining for the Helpless Student

As we have seen, despite having sufficient mental competence many students have difficulties mastering school tasks. Sometimes the student might aggravate the problem by developing increasingly pessimistic thoughts about the causes of his or her poor performance. For whatever reason, a child may initially perform poorly on a task. Such failure tends to lower expectations of future success, and, for children with high anxiety, impairs subsequent performance (Weiner, 1974). With continued failure the child might begin to think "I am stupid." At this point the child begins to experience what is known as *learned helplessness* (Seligman, 1975).

According to Seligman experiencing conditions under which there seems to be no control over one's outcomes can cause cognitive, motivational, and even emotional disturbances. The cognitive disturbance manifests itself in the failure to learn how to control outcomes when, in subsequent situations, control is possible. Since there appears to be no connection between one's efforts and one's outcomes, there is no incentive to try, hence the motivational disturbance. With no apparent control over one's environment and no motivation to try, the emotional result is depression. This syndrome of learned helplessness has been demonstrated with both animals and humans (see Seligman, 1975).

Dweck and her associates (e.g., Dweck, 1975; Dweck & Licht, 1980; Dweck & Repucci, 1973) have shown that many school children experience the learned helplessness syndrome with regard to their school work. Helpless children give up rather than persist on intellectual tasks, and they tend to attribute their failures to factors beyond their control, such as lack of ability or the difficulty of the tasks, rather than to lack of effort, which they could control. Similar to the Pawns described by deCharms (1976), helpless children do not perceive themselves as causal agents. If, as the helpless attributions suggest, failure is beyond one's control, then there would be no incentive to try. For example, if I believe that I am "no good at math," then I would perceive no good reason to apply myself on tasks that require mathematical skills.

To cure the learned helplessness syndrome, Dweck (1975) applied a social psychological technique called *attribution therapy* (cf. Valins & Nisbett, 1971). As we saw in Chapter 2, attribution therapy involves teaching new attributions to replace those that produce debilitating or undesirable consequences. Dweck's strategy was to change helpless students' attributions of failure from uncontrollable factors to lack of effort. The hypothesis was that if children were to perceive that failure could be avoided by trying harder, then they would become more persevering and ultimately more successful. Pretests were used to distinguish helpless children from similar others who were more persistent when faced with failure. The helpless children were assigned to two treatment conditions. In one condition the children were given math problems that they could easily solve within the time limit given. This success-only treatment, which Dweck points out is the typical behavior modification approach, was repeated for 25 sessions. Children in the attribution-retraining condition participated in the same number of sessions, but for them some programmed failures were included. In about 20 percent of the trials the required number of problems exceeded the amount the children could solve in the given time limit. Whenever these "failures" occurred, the trainer made an attribution to lack of effort by saying "you should have tried harder." Since helpless children usually attribute failures to lack of ability or other factors beyond their control, the trainer's attribution was used as a means of retraining.

Posttests revealed that children in the attribution-retraining conditon made significant increases in the number of problems they could solve per minute, whereas the success-only children did not improve (see Figure 5-2). In addition, children in the attribu-

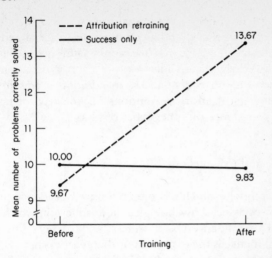

Figure 5-2. Mean number of problems correctly solved before and after attribution retraining or a success-only treatment. (Adapted from Dweck, 1975. Copyright © 1975 by the American Psychological Association. Reprinted by permission of the publisher and authors.)

tion-retraining condition attributed their failures to lack of effort rather than to lack of ability significantly more than they had prior to training. Therefore, attribution therapy involving programmed failures accompanied by attribution retraining was more effective in changing helpless students into persistent, successful problem solvers than was the behavior modification technique.

Subsequent research has provided further empirical support for the effectiveness of attribution retraining. Chapin and Dyck (1976) found that children who were poor readers became more persistent in attempting to read difficult sentences after reattribution training. As in Dweck's method the reattribution training involved programmed failures followed by verbal comments attributing failures to insufficient effort.

Using an interesting variation of the attribution-retraining technique, Andrews and Dubus (1978) asked children to attribute programmed successes and failures to one of four possible determinants—ability, task difficulty, luck, or effort. Rather than providing attributions for the children, the trainer would reinforce the children's own attributions to effort. Both social reinforcements (e.g., the trainer saying "that's good" after the child made an attribution to effort) and a combination of social and tangible reinforcements (i.e., tokens that could later be exchanged for gifts) induced significant increases in effort attributions and in persistence on subsequent tasks. In addition it was found that reinforcements of effort attributions on one type of task would increase persistence on other types of tasks.

Summary and Conclusions

Going to school is much more than a purely academic process. It also involves a social psychological atmosphere in which students meet and are influenced by classmates and teachers. One example of such influence is the expectations that teachers have about their students. Although research has shown that these expectations can have undesirable effects on students, surprisingly little has been done to help teachers control the communication of their expectations. One technique that has been effective is to provide teachers with objective feedback about how they interact with students.

Many social psychologists agree that there is too much emphasis on competition in traditional classrooms. They argue that the competitive structure fosters hostilities, especially those based on interethnic prejudices, and can impair the self-concepts and intellectual achievement of slow learners and minorities. Techniques that provide students with cooperative experiences, like the jigsaw classroom and student teams, have been shown to increase interracial friendships, liking for school, empathy for others, self-esteem, and academic achievement.

The talents of some students are wasted because they do not work to their potential. These underachievers usually lack the motivation and persistence needed to succeed. Special motivation programs and attribution-retraining techniques have been used to induce motivation and persistence in underachievers.

6

Organizations

In modern society we often rely on complex organizations to produce goods and to provide services. From various telephone services, to textile factories, to the protection of citizens by local police forces, organizations provide us with conveniences, necessities, and security. Ideally, it would be nice if such businesses, industries, and service organizations would efficiently provide goods and services for the public and, at the same time, would be gainful and satisfying for the people who work for them. The achievement or lack of achievement of these two goals—productivity and worker satisfaction—have been the main focal point of research on organizations.

For those studying organizations it is important to realize that the productivity and worker satisfaction of an organization are influenced by both its formal and informal structures (Tannenbaum, 1966). The formal structure is planned by the designers or administrators of an organization. It specifies things like purpose, procedures, authority, rules, and standards. Formal structure is how, from the administration's point of view, the organization is supposed to work. As Tannenbaum points out, however, these formal plans and the behavior of the members of an organization never match perfectly. Invariably, an unplanned, or informal, structure develops. Far from being merely cogs in the grand design of formal structure, the members of an organization develop their own attitudes, affiliations, friendships, and standards of behavior that greatly influence the organization. It is the informal groups and rules and how they influence productivity and worker satisfaction that are the main subject matter of the social psychology of organizations.

It should be noted that the field of organizational, or industrial, psychology and disciplines other than psychology have provided many applications to organizations. Rather than attempting to present all of these approaches, the current chapter focuses on social psychology applied to organizations. Given the social psychological emphasis on informal structure in organizations, these applications usually involve the manipulation of informal structure to increase productivity and worker satisfaction.

The Hawthorne Studies

In 1754 Horace Walpole, a British scholar, coined the term *serendipity*, by which he meant a gift for accidentally but sagaciously discovering something other than what was being looked for (Reimer, 1965). Since that time it has been noted that many scientific discoveries have been made serendipitously. An example is the discovery of penicillin. Having no idea that he was about to discover a wonder drug, British bacteriologist Dr. Alexander Fleming noticed something very peculiar about a contaminated petri dish he had been using. There was a remarkably clean area on the dish. Further examination under a microscope revealed that the mold from the dish would dissolve microorganisims. This perceptive observation led to the eventual use of penicillin as a means of combating germs.

Serendipity also was responsible for the discovery that social psychological factors have a powerful influence on the productivity and satisfaction of workers (Tannenbaum, 1966). Beginning in the 1920s a series of studies was conducted in Western Electric's Hawthorne plant. Later to become known as the Hawthorne studies, this research was designed to examine how changes in the formal operating procedures of the plant, such as amount of lighting, length and frequency of rest periods, and length of work weeks, would influence productivity. Many of the results were as expected. For example, increased lighting led to increased productivity. Many of the results were quite surprising and seemingly contradictory, however. Decreased lighting also led to increased productivity. In fact, it seemed that almost any change—for example, longer rest periods or shorter rest periods—was associated with higher productivity.

Upon further examination of the situation the Hawthorne researchers arrived at a perceptive conclusion. Rather than being caused directly by the planned changes in lighting and rest periods, the increases in productivity were the result of unplanned improvements in human relations that were a byproduct of the changes. These unplanned changes in human relations took many forms (Tannenbaum, 1966). For example, after the introduction of planned changes supervisors tended to be more friendly and attentive toward the workers. In addition, to implement the changes the workers, who were used to working in the large impersonal plant, were sometimes asked to work in a small test room. In the small test room an informal structure quickly developed. Friendships formed, leaders emerged, and the group informally developed and enforced standards of acceptable behavior. Enforcement of these standards included encouragement of high productivity and pressure on slow workers to improve their performance. It was also observed that the morale in the test rooms was usually quite high. Thus, by accident it was discovered that the informal interpersonal and group relations in an organization are powerful determinants of productivity and worker satisfaction.

It should be apparent that the Hawthorne studies were not an application of social psychology. In fact, the researchers had intended to manipulate such nonsocial psychological variables as lighting and rest periods. The surprising findings, however, led to a new human relations emphasis in organizational research, which paved the way for social psychological interventions.

Worker Participation

In the 1940s Lewin and his associates (Lewin, 1947a) did the pioneering work in group dynamics. This research focused on how people influence, and are inluenced by other people, especially groups of people. Besides becoming a classic area of social psychological inquiry, the study of group dynamics has had a profound impact on the development of human relations in organizations.

Perhaps the most important aspect of the work on group dynamics was the study of the value of group decisions as a means of facilitating social change (Lewin, 1947b). Getting people to change how they do things often is quite difficult. Lewin reasoned that part of the difficulty is that most individual patterns of behavior are maintained by social pressures, or as he called it, the *social field*. This social field is similar to the informal structure found in the Hawthorne studies. Strategies to induce individual changes will inevitably meet with resistance when the changed individual interacts with the unchanged group. Suppose, for example, a salesperson convinces you that red striped shoes were going to be the fashion this year. How would your uninformed friends react to your new red striped shoes? Would you continue to wear them if they did not react favorably? Even presenting information to a group as a whole, as in a lecture, can meet with resistance because, although the lecture might arouse some interest, the group as a passive audience might not be sufficiently motivated to change. Hearing a lecture on the new fashions might not move you and your friends to wear red striped shoes. Lewin argued that the act of decision serves as a transition from interest to action. Therefore, the least resistance to change would come from a process of group decision. With such decisions the social field can be altered to be compatible to change, and involvement in the decision process can provide motivation to actually change behaviors. Accordingly, you and your friends would be most likely to wear red striped shoes if you talked it over and made a group decision to wear them.

Several experiments supported Lewin's theorizing about group decisions (Lewin, 1947b). For example, as discussed in Chapter 1 of the present volume, attempts were made to change food habits of American families during World War II. Supporting Lewin's theory, women who were involved in a group discussion about serving visceral meats to their families were more likely to do so than were women who merely heard a lecture advocating that course of action.

The classic application of Lewin's group decision technique to organizational change was done by Coch and French (1948). A small town pajama factory was having great difficulty initiating changes in operating procedures that management thought were necessary in order to remain competitive. The changes usually involved transferring workers within the factory to jobs that involved new machinery or that required different techniques. Initiating these changes was particularly frustrating to the workers because the plant operated on a piece rate of pay, which means that the amount of pay for any one worker was contingent on the amount that he or she produced. As expected, working a new job after a transfer led to an initial relearning period that decreased productivity. Management expected that after a reasonable period of relearning the rate of production would recover and even exceed the pretransfer levels. This did not happen. Instead, resistance to the change came in many forms, such as grievances, high turnover, intentional decreases in output, and aggression against the management. Management made many attempts to deal with these difficulties. For example, to reduce the frustration for the workers a transfer allowance was provided to offset any decrease in wages that would result from the decreased productivity during the relearning period. Other attempted solutions involved trying to gain the cooperation of the union and the laying off of slow workers. None of these attempts was successful. Thus, Coch and French were called in to analyze the problem and develop an effective intervention.

Generalizing from Lewin's field theory, Coch and French reasoned that the resistance to change was rooted in the informal group dynamics of the workers. Although the resistance seemed to be initiated by personal frustrations, it appeared to be maintained by standards and accepted ways of doing things that the workers had informally developed for themselves. In fact, the more cohesive the workers, or as Coch and French put it, the more "we-feeling," the more resistance there was to changes initiated by management. An effective strategy for introducing innovation would therefore need to focus on gaining group acceptance of the changes. Applying Lewin's work, Coch and French developed and tested a technique of group participation in decisions to facilitate changes in the workplace.

In a study conducted in the pajama factory two variations of worker participation were compared with a control group. In one condition worker participation was accomplished through representatives. After the workers met with management and heard about the need for changes they agreed to select representatives to help design the new jobs and to set the new piece rates. In a second condition, total participation, all of the involved workers were allowed to participate in designing the new jobs and setting the piece rates. In the control condition the changes were introduced in the usual way. Management met with the workers, explained the need for change, described the changes, and answered questions raised by the workers. Although workers were not randomly assigned to these conditions, an attempt was made to match them on efficiency before the new jobs, degree of change required on the new jobs, and their amount of we-feeling.

As shown in Figure 6-1, the results clearly supported the effectiveness of employing worker participation to reduce resistance to change. A comparison of pre- and postchange productivity showed that the control group did not noticeably improve by 32 days after the change. In addition, these workers were aggressive toward management and seemed to deliberately restrict their production. Within 40 days 17 percent of the workers in the control group quit their jobs. In contrast, the workers who participated through representatives relearned quickly after the changes and by 32 days after the changes were producing at a higher level than before the changes. Also, none of this group quit and there was only one instance of aggression toward management. The best results were obtained in the total participation group. Their production increased by 14 percent over their prechange rate, they showed no aggression, and none of them quit. It should be noted that the control group was later allowed to participate in a subsequent change and, as a result, their production increased to a new high level.

The technique of worker participation has evolved so that it now generally refers to allowing employees to take part in decisions that affect their roles in an organization (Katz & Kahn, 1978). The purpose is to increase worker satisfaction and productivity. Sometimes the technique involves allowing workers to participate in specific decisions, as in the Coch and French study. In another form, workers are given additional power and responsiblity more generally. For example, in a study by Morse and Reimer (1956) rank-and-file clerical workers were allowed to make decisions usually made by supervisors. Although in some cases worker

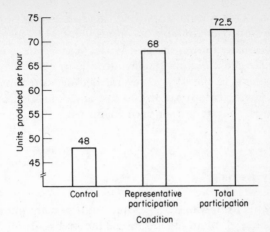

Figure 6-1. Productivity by pajama factory workers 32 days after a change in operating procedures under various conditions of change. (Adapted from Coch & French, 1948. Copyright © 1948 by Plenum Publishing Corporation. Reprinted by permission of the publisher and authors.)

participation has not led to positive results (e.g., French, Israel, & As, 1960), carefully assessed applications successfully increased productivity (Coch & French, 1948; Seashore & Bowers, 1963), improved relations between workers and supervisors (Morse & Reimer, 1956), increased worker satisfaction (Seashore & Bowers, 1963), and reduced absenteeism (Lawler & Hackman, 1969).

In light of the encouraging findings it is interesting to note that, although the theoretical basis and systematic empirical support for worker participation originated in the United States, the technique has flourished more in other parts of the world, especially in Japan and Europe (Tornatzky & Soloman, 1982; Whyte, 1983). Whyte, a frustrated early advocate of worker participation, describes the situation during the post World War II era as follows:

> While we behavioral scientists were trying in vain to get the attention of leaders of management, the Japanese picked up the ideas provided to them by early human relations researchers and returned to their country to rebuild their organizations more along the lines of the vision they picked up in the United States . . . particularly emphasizing participative leadership. (1983, p. 402).

He attributes the resistance of U.S. managers to what was then an innovative approach to the tremendous success of American business and industry during the post World War II era, which led to a "Don't change a winning game" attitude (p. 397). Whyte notes that beginning in the 1970s, several decades after the original research, General Motors, Ford, Xerox, and other U.S. companies began to incorporate worker participation into their management procedures.

Sensitivity Training

Working effectively with other people requires many interpersonal skills. At all levels of an organizational hierarchy—from the workers on up to the president—the individual who knows how his or her behavior affects others, who is sensitive to the needs of others, and who can adjust his or her behavior according to these perceptions will be more likely to make a productive contribution than will someone who lacks these skills. The development of such sensitivity, therefore, can be of critical importance for an organization. To improve interpersonal sensitivity, the Lewinian principles of group dynamics have been applied through a technique called *sensitivity training* (Katz & Kahn, 1978).

Although there are various forms of sensitivity training, the basic procedure and goals are the same. Approximately 10 to 16 individuals meet together in what are called *T-groups* (*training groups*). The overall goal is for each member to become more aware of how he or she influences, and is influenced by, others. It is also expected that the individuals will learn how a group can function to meet the needs of its members. The groups are unstructured, usual roles are abandoned, and all members interact as peers. A trainer is present but does not take a leadership role. Instead, the trainer encourages the group members to talk about themselves, especially about their present feelings. At first the group members often feel anxious and hesitant because of the lack of structure. It is hypothesized that this period of uncertainty helps facilitate changes in interpersonal behaviors by a process that Lewin called "unfreezing" (Tannenbaum, 1966). Old ways of interacting become less set, or unfrozen, allowing for new behaviors to develop. To further promote change, the trainer attempts to foster an atmosphere of acceptance and openness. Group members are encouraged to give each other honest, and sometimes blunt, feedback about how their behaviors are perceived by others. After receiving this feedback an individual can experiment with new ways of interacting. If these experimental interpersonal behaviors are successful in the group, they will tend to become more permanent, or frozen.

The potential benefit for an organization is that the sensitivity gained in the T-group would help people work together more effectively. In the prototypical form, employees participate in T-groups with total strangers. With strangers they can more easily put aside their usual roles and experiment with new ways of interacting. However, the individual may experience resistance when he or she tries to use these new ways of interacting at work. As we have seen, it is difficult to change the informal behavior patterns of a group without addressing the change strategy to the whole group. To avoid this problem some organizations now use *family groups* for sensitivity training. A family group consists of a manager and the people who immediately report to him or her. Family groups can be formed at many levels. Rank-and-file workers could meet with their supervisor and supervisors could meet with their superior. Changes in means of interpersonal interacting in such family groups should carry over into the workplace more readily than those learned in stranger groups.

Although the use of stranger and family T-groups by organizations is widespread (Katz & Kahn, 1978), the benefits of such training to the organizations has been questioned. For example, in a comprehensive review of research studies that have investigated the effectiveness of T-groups in organizations, Campbell and Dunnette (1968) concluded that a positive influence of the training on the performance of individuals in their organizational roles has not been adequately demonstrated. Part of the problem is that T-groups are difficult to research scientifically. There are many facets to a T-group—lack of structure, open communication, emphasis on feelings, feedback, and a focus on the present— that are expected to influence the individuals in several ways: their self-concepts, empathy, and modes of behavior. Because a combination of all the facets of a T-group are considered to be important, an attempt to isolate precisely what facet causes what result typically has not been done and may not be desirable. Campbell and Dunnette also question whether interpersonal sensitivity can be measured. As they put it: "People who have been in a T-group do apparently use more interpersonally oriented words to describe certain situations, but this says nothing about their general level of 'sensitivity' or the relative accuracy of their interpersonal perceptions" (p. 99). Most of the supportive studies have used a *perceived change* measure, which means that a coworker, superior, or subordinate was asked to report any change in the trained person's behavior. Often the observers knew that the individuals that they were rating had received sensitivity training. Such knowledge could have biased their perceptions. Campbell and Dunnette suggest that more objective measures of performance that are directly relevant to the organization would be more appropriate and convincing.

Leadership Training

Most organizations have a hierarchy. Some people lead and others follow. The type of leadership in an organization can greatly influence productivity and worker satisfaction. It is difficult to work for a boss who is incompetent or insensitive to the needs of the workers. On the other hand, some leaders have great success in motivating workers. Some people might argue that there are "born leaders" who naturally possess the appropriate skills, whereas the social psychologist is more inclined to believe that people can learn to become effective leaders. In this section we look at two social psychological approaches to leadership training—*leader match* and *social learning*.

Leader Match

Would someone who is a good leader in one situation tend to be a good leader in other situations? According to Fiedler and his associates (Fiedler, 1978) the answer to this question is not necessarily. In fact, Fiedler's contingency model of leadership *predicts* that in many cases a good leader in one situation will be a poor leader in another situation. Also, a poor leader is likely to be a good leader in other circumstances. How can this be so? The reason centers on Fiedler's observation that there is no one best leadership style and that in any given case the most effective way of leading depends on the circumstances.

The contingency model contrasts greatly with earlier theories of leadership. The early theories suggested that there are certain personality characteristics that are generally associated with leadership effectiveness. For example, according to some theories a good leader is sensitive to the needs of the workers. Other theories suggest that a more businesslike, task-oriented approach is more effective. Fiedler and his associates (Fiedler & Mahar, 1979a) contend that selection of leaders on the basis of such personality theories or attempts to change personality characteristics of leaders have not been generally successful in providing effective leadership. Taking a more social psychological position, Fiedler and Mahar (1979a) argue that "it is considerably easier for a leader to modify the leadership situation than to change his personality, motivational structure" (p. 46).

According to Fiedler's (1978) contingency model there are two basic leadership styles. The style that a leader will adopt depends on his or her goals, needs, and motivational structure. One type of leader is most concerned with maintaining good personal relations with others. These *relationship-oriented leaders* are concerned about what others think and feel and are likely to seek feedback and suggestions. In contrast, *task-oriented leaders* are mainly concerned with getting things done. Task-oriented leaders tend to take a more structured, less personal approach. Although most leaders have some concern for both relationships and getting things done, Fiedler maintains that for any given leader one or the other of these motivations is likely to dominate.

A great deal of research has shown that neither the relationship-oriented nor the task-oriented style of leadership is superior across situations. Indeed, Fiedler and others (Fiedler, 1978) have found that the effectiveness of leadership style is *contingent* on the situation. Three aspects of the situation—leader-member relations, task structure, and the position power of the leader—are most important.

Leader-member relations refers to the extent to which the group supports the leader. *Task structure* is the degree to which goals and procedures are clearly determined. *Positon power* refers to how much authority the leader has to reward and punish subordinates. The combination of these dimensions serves as a general index of situational control for the leader. For example, strong leader-member relations, high task structure, and a great deal of position power characterizes a situation with high control. Research has consistently shown that when situational control is either high or low a task-oriented leadership style is more effective than a rela-tionship-oriented style, whereas a relationship-oriented style is more effective when there is a moderate level of situational control.

To improve leadership effectiveness Fiedler and his associates have developed and field-tested a self-help technique called *leader match* (Fiedler, Chemers, & Mahar, 1976). With a self-teaching manual, entitled *Improving Leadership Effectiveness: The Leader Match Concept,* the average person can complete the training in about five hours. The first step in leader match is to determine one's own leadership style. This is accomplished by completing the Least Preferred Coworker (LPC) Scale. The LPC scale involves making a series of personality judgments about the person with whom the leader works least well. Assigning high personality rat-ings to one's LPC indicates a relationship-oriented leader, whereas low ratings indicate a task-oriented leader. The next step is to com-plete scales to assess situational control, which is accomplished by completing a scale for each of the three major dimensions. Having completed the scales, the trainee is prepared to assess how well his or her leadership style matches the situation.

If one's leadership style is appropriate for the situation (e.g., a personal relation orientation and a moderate degree of situational control), the trainee can expect to be successful as a leader. A mis-match of leadership style and situational control requires some adjustment of the situation. The manual suggests several tech-niques for adjusting each of the three major components of situ-ational control. For example, leader-member relations can be changed by spending more or less informal time with the mem-bers. Again it should be stressed that the strategy is to change the situation because it is assumed that one's leadership style is based on enduring personality characteristics that are not likely to change.

The effectiveness of the leader match technique has been demonstrated in numerous studies (see Fielder & Mahar, 1979a, for a review). In most of the studies leaders were randomly assigned to leader match self-training or to a control condition. Such studies have been conducted in a wide variety of settings, including county government, local police, public health organizations, and the military. Measurements of performance, usually taken one to four months after the training, have consistently shown that the training increases leadership performance. For example, in one study ROTC cadets who had taken leader match training received higher leadership ratings from both their advisers and their peers than did cadets in a control condition (Fiedler & Mahar, 1979b). The ratings covered many aspects of leadership, such as planning and organizing, initiative, interaction with others, setting an example, sound decision making, supervision, communication, and confidence. In addition, the cadets in the training condition performed better on practical and simulated tests of tactics.

Overall, there are many reasons to support the conclusion that leader match is a useful and practical method for enhancing leadership effectivness. The training takes very little time and no special equipment, besides the manual, is needed. It can be effectively self-taught. The underlying theory has been well articulated and there is much research, in a variety of settings, that supports the effectiveness of the training.

Social learning

Surely there is wisdom in the saying "A picture is worth a thousand words." Similarly, in the realm of behavior a demonstration of how to carry out a task can be an especially useful means of instruction. But some demonstrations have more influence than others. In articulating social learning theory, Bandura (1977) has described four processes—attention, retention, motor reproduction, and motivation—that enhance learning from a behavioral model. Accordingly, learning from a behavioral model is likely under conditions where the observer (a) attends to the model, (b) retains what he or she observes, (c) has an opportunity to mentally or behaviorally reproduce the observed behavior, and (d) feels that the observed behavior would be rewarding.

Applying social learning theory, Goldstein & Sorcher (1974) developed a behavioral modeling program to help supervisors deal more effectively with employees. The attention of the supervisors is gained by showing them a series of films. Each film depicts a model supervisor effectively interacting with an employee in a particular situation, such as orienting a new employee, giving a worker recognition, correcting poor work habits, or dealing with an employee's complaint. To enhance retention the major points about how to handle each situation are presented at both the beginning and end of each film. After each film the trainees discuss it, role-play the appropriate behaviors by improvising similar situations, and provide each other with feedback. These activities are designed to further enhance retention, to allow opportunities for motor reproduction of the observed behaviors, and to provide mutual reinforcements for demonstrating the desired actions.

The effectiveness of Goldstein and Sorcher's program was demonstrated by Latham and Saari (1979). Supervisors employed by an international company were randomly assigned to the behavioral modeling program or to a no-treatment control group. Members of the control group were told that they would receive the training at a later date. The training sessions only took two hours a week and lasted for nine weeks. Although there was some initial resistance and lack of cooperation, several follow-up measures indicated that the training was quite successful. For example, three months after the training supervisors who had received the training outperformed supervisors in the control condition in a behavioral test that involved resolving supervisor-employee problems (see Figure 6-2). To assure that the test was fair none of the problems presented in the test were the same as those given in the training. Also, the test was tape-recorded and the performance of the supervisors was judged by superintendents who did not know who was in the training or control conditions. The trained supervisors also performed better than the controls on a written test of how to handle supervisory problems that was given six months after the training. In addition to the tests of hypothetical situations, superintendents gave the trained supervisors higher evalu-

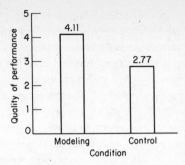

Figure 6-2. Quality of performance on a behavioral supervisory test three months after either a modeling or control treatment. High scores indicate good performance. (Adapted from Latham & Saari, 1971. Copyright © 1971 by the American Psychological Association. Reprinted by permission of the publisher and authors.)

ations than controls on behavioral observations of actual work one year after the training. Finally, a year after the initial training the control group was given the training, and subsequently the quality of their supervisory performance was no different than that of the original training group.

Of course, the ultimate goal of supervisory training is not merely to change the behavior of the supervisors but to effect improvements in the overall functioning of the organization. With this in mind, Porras and his associates (1982) extended the work of Latham and Saari (1979) by assessing the broader organizational impact of supervisory training. In a field study, comparisons were made between a plant in which a program of modeling-based supervisory training was implemented and similar plants in which no special training was given. The results showed that, in addition to improving the supervisors' leadership skills, the modeling program produced improved employee perceptions of the organizational climate, actual increases in productivity, and reductions in absenteeism and turnover rates. These effects were observed shortly after the training and six months later.

Inequity

Are workers in a capitalistic society primarily concerned with maximizing their own individual outcomes, or are they more concerned with being treated fairly? To the surprise of many, Adams and others (Adams, 1965) developed a theory and collected data that suggest the latter. Although the theory has not led to the development of an intervention that has been formally tested, the data it has generated do seem to be applicable.

According to the theory, which Adams originally called *inequity* but which is now commonly called *equity* (Walster, Walster, & Berscheid, 1978), each worker compares his or her inputs and outcomes with those of others. *Inputs* are anything that an individual feels adds to his or her value as an employee. Examples are effort, competence, and experience; however, from the employee's perspective less generally accepted factors, such as sex or social class, also may have an influence. Adams provides an example of Paris-born bank clerks who, because of their birthplace, considered their inputs to be greater than that of non-Parisian clerks. Although others may question the relevance of, or fail to recognize, certain inputs, it is the perception of the individual that will determine whether he or she feels fairly treated. *Outcomes* include such benefits as wages, prestige, and power, and, like inputs, the individual and others may disagree about the relevance or recognition of certain outcomes. To the extent that an individual perceives that his or her ratio of inputs to outcomes is equal to those of others, he or she will feel equitably treated and satisfied. On the other hand, if one perceives that these ratios are not equal, then he or she would experience cognitive dissonance (Festinger, 1957) and would feel dissatisfied.

An important aspect to understanding the concept of equity is that it is the comparison of *ratios* of inputs to outcomes that determines perceptions of equity. For example, even though Jones might make less money than Smith, Jones may perceive the situation as equitable because of the long hours Smith works. A second key factor to understanding equity is the subjective nature of perceived inputs and outcomes. For example, Brown may not consider her large office as an important outcome, while Fisher does. Or Green may feel that his years of experience are an important input, whereas Jenkins might not consider experience relevant.

According to equity theory the experience of inequity is unpleasant. For example, the cognitions "I contribute greater inputs than Jones" and "Jones makes more money than I do" are inconsistent or dissonant (Festinger, 1957). In the workplace such dissonance may affect job satisfaction and performance. Such reactions may occur even when the inequity favors the individual. For example, in a classic experiment Adams and Rosenbaum (1962) demonstrated how being inequitably overpaid influenced job performance.

College students were hired to conduct interviews. By design some of the students were led to believe that they were being overpaid because they were inadequately qualified for the job. Students in a control group were led to believe that they were qualified and would receive fair wages. Adams and Rosenbaum predicted that the students who thought they were being overpaid would try to compensate for the inequity by increasing their inputs. They also predicted that the way of increasing inputs would vary according to the method of pay. Their predictions were confirmed. Overpaid students who were paid by the hour conducted more interviews than did the control subjects who were paid by the hour. When the students were paid on a piecework basis, which in this case meant by the number of completed interviews, the results were different. As predicted, with piecework pay the overpaid students conducted fewer interviews than did control subjects, but they produced higher quality interviews. These results follow from equity theory because by completing fewer interviews the overpaid students reduced their outcomes and by taking the time to conduct quality interviews they increased their inputs.

Subsequent studies, conducted in both laboratory and field settings, have shown that inequity can have an important impact on workers (see Adams & Freedman, 1976, for a review). Whereas overpaid workers may try to compensate by increasing their inputs and decreasing their outcomes, underpaid workers tend to be dissatisfied, reduce productivity, and may even quit. In one study both underpaid and overpaid workers felt more negatively than did equitably paid workers (Austin & Walster, 1974). Thus, in general, it seems that workers are happier and more productive when they perceive that they are being treated equitably. Although no published interventions have been based on equity theory, the potential for utilization seems promising. For example, since it has been found that an organization runs most efficiently when workers are treated equitably (Clark, 1958), it would seem wise for employers to consider equity when trying to solve organizational problems. But actually achieving equity may not be enough. The workers must perceive that they are being treated equitably. This suggests that employers should talk to workers to find out how they perceive various situations. If workers express feelings of inequity, then the employer could either change the working conditions or try to persuade the workers to perceive their inputs and outcomes differently.

Summary and Conclusions

As the Hawthorne studies have shown, organizations are greatly influenced by informal structure, which is the unplanned social atmosphere that inevitably develops. Applications of social psychology to organizations have, for the most part, involved manipulations of the informal structure to increase productivity and worker satisfaction. For example, worker participation allows employees to have a greater input into how the organization is run. Theoretically, group participation in decisions creates a "we-feeling" and greater acceptance of the decisions by the group members. In support of the theory, early field studies demonstrated that worker participation could reduce resistance to change, increase productivity, improve supervisor-employee relationships, increase worker satisfaction, and reduce absenteeism. More recently, various forms of worker participation have been used quite widely, although most of the applications have taken place outside of the Unitied States.

Another intervention designed to positively influence the informal structure of organizations is sensitivity training. The assumption underlying this technique is that working effectively with others requires certain interpersonal skills. Such skills include sensitivity to the needs of others, knowledge of how one's behavior affects others, and the ability to adapt one's own behavior to meet the needs of others and the organization. To promote the development of these interpersonal skills training groups are formed. In an open, permissive atmosphere the group members are encouraged to express their true feelings, to provide honest feedback to other group members, and to experiment with new ways of interacting with others. Although there have been many studies that seem to demonstrate the effectiveness of sensitivity training, the supportive data have been criticized as being biased and subjective.

Organizations typically have a hierarchy, in which some people lead and others follow. Good leadership can greatly enhance productivity and worker satisfaction. Based on the assumption that effective leadership can be learned, two social psychological interventions have been developed. One technique, called leader match, involves identifying one's own leadership style, assessing the leadership situation, and manipulating the situation to match one's style. The leader match technique can be self-taught very quickly and there is much data that demonstrate that it produces effective leadership. The other social psychological intervention is based on social learning. Trainees observe model leaders effectively dealing with employees in various situations. Afterward the trainees discuss the situation, role-play similar situations, and provide each other with feedback. Follow-up research demonstrated that the social learning technique improved leadership performance and that the effect was long term.

Research has shown that workers compare their relative inputs and outcomes to others. To the extent that the ratio of one's perceived inputs to outcomes are equal to the ratios of others, the individual experiences equity and is happy and productive. If, however, the worker perceives that his or her ratio of inputs to outcomes does not equal that of others, then inequity will be experienced and satisfaction and productivity are likely to be adversely influenced. Although research on equity has not led to systematic applications, the implications for possible interventions seem clear.

7

Consumer Behavior

Imagine that it is Saturday morning and you have the day to yourself. Maybe you would like to do something outside, perhaps ride a bicycle or go on a picnic. You click on the radio to hear the weather report. To your annoyance you are greeted by a commercial for a certain kind of chewing tobacco. When the weather report comes on the forecast is for rain. Determined not to let this minor frustration ruin your free day, you check the television listings and notice that one of your favorite movies will be aired beginning in a few minutes. As you go to turn on the television set, the doorbell rings. A representative for a charity is at the door and asks you for a donation. You contribute a dollar and then settle down to watch the movie. During the next couple of hours you are engrossed in a dramatic depiction of injustice, violence, and revenge. Periodically, the movie is interrupted by commercials for anything from toilet paper to a new car. Afterwards you decide to go shopping, perhaps for a camera that you just saw advertised on television.

Most people would readily identify the last activity in the preceding paragraph, shopping for a camera, as *consumer behavior*. We are consumers when we buy goods and services. A broader definition of consumer behavior, however, might include all of the above activities. That is, consumer behavior could include listening to the radio, donating money to charity, and watching television, as well as shopping. Simply put, in this chapter the term consumer behavior will refer to the way people choose to use their personal resources, particularly money and leisure time. Such a broad definition is not without precedent and indeed in a social psychological analysis of consumer psychology Jacoby (1975) defined consumer behavior quite generally as "the acquisition, consumption, and disposition of goods, services, time, and ideas" (p. 979). Here the focus is on the use, or consumption, of time and money.

Social psychological applications designed to influence how people use money and leisure time may be divided into two general categories. One approach involves inducing *socially conscious* consumption. Webster (1975) defines the socially conscious consumer as one "who takes into account the consequences of his or her private consumption or who attempts to use his or her purchasing power to bring about social change" (p. 188). Examples might include using nonphosphate detergents to avoid polluting water supplies or donating money to support medical research. In this chapter we see how social psychological principles can be applied to induce socially conscious consumption.

A second area of social psychological applications to consumer behavior centers on the influence of television. A report by the National Institute of Mental Health (1982) refers to a survey indicating that Americans spend more time watching television than engaging in any other activity, except for working and sleeping. Since the latter two activities are essential uses of time, it could be argued that watching television is the most prevalent consumer behavior in America. Later in this chapter we examine social psychological techniques that have been designed to mitigate the effects of television's antisocial content and to enhance the effects of its prosocial content. We also see how social psychological principles may be applied to televised public service campaigns.

Since the main theme of this book is the use of social psychological principles for societal benefit, applications of social psychology to induce people to buy one brand of a product rather than another, which would mainly benefit the producer, will be reviewed only briefly.

Inducing Socially Conscious Consumption

Although some evidence exists that certain combinations of personality, attitude, and socioeconomic characteristics can help identify socially conscious consumers, the relationships are weak (Webster, 1975). Even if the correlations were strong, such findings may not be helpful in devising applications. It is difficult enough to change a person's personality, attitudes, and socioeconomic status, without having to target such changes to an optimum configuration for a particular kind of behavior. Therefore, a social psychological approach that relies on creating situations to stimulate socially conscious behavior might be more fruitful. Such applications have been designed to elicit two forms of socially conscious behavior, environmentally conscious consumption and charitable behavior.

Environmentally Conscious Consumption

As discussed in the chapter on the environment, individual consumption without regard to the consequences for others can be detrimental to all. To put the problem in a consumer perspective, a "tragedy of the commons" can occur when the self-interest of individual consumers destroys or depletes a resource for everyone. For example, irresponsibly high levels of individual consumption of energy could result in the depletion of energy supplies and pollution of air and water. Thus from the consumer perspective many of the applications in the environment chapter can be viewed as means of inducing socially conscious consumption. To avoid repetition, only two applications, which were specifically developed with the concept of socially conscious consumption in mind, will be discussed here.

Reviewing research on the prevalence of socially conscious consumption, Scott (1977) notes that only a small segment of society actively guides their individual consumption by considerations of the societal consequences. Nevertheless, she also contends that there is great potential for such behavior because people generally express favorable attitudes about socially conscious behavior. Since people already have the supportive attitudes, Scott argues

that traditional attitude change approaches will be relatively ineffective in inducing socially conscious consumption. Instead the
key to a successful strategy would be to "convert the potential
responsiveness into actual behavior" (p. 156). Taking a social psychological perspective, she suggests that the foot-in-the-door technique (Freedman & Fraser, 1966) is particularly well suited for this
task. Existing favorable attitudes should assure compliance with
small requests to engage in environmentally conscious consumption, and the self-perception (Bem, 1965) of carrying out such
behavior should convince the person that he or she is a socially
conscious consumer. This technique should be most effective
when there are no ulterior motives for complying with the initial
request, because an ulterior motive, such as a monetary incentive,
will detract from the self-perception that it was social consciousness that caused the compliant behavior. The idea is to get people
to perceive themselves as socially conscious, not as motivated to
obtain money or some other extrinsic goal.

Scott tested her ideas in a field experiment. People were contacted at their homes and were asked to display a sign that said
"Conserve Resources—Recycle." Compliance with this small
request, which was quite high and did not differ across conditions,
served as the "foot in the door." By random assignment some of
the people were offered one dollar to display the sign, others were
offered three dollars, and others were not offered an incentive.
Afterward, the same people were asked to address either 25 or 75
envelopes for letters publicizing local recycling programs. Receiving partial support for the hypothesis it was found that, when the
second request was moderate (address 25 envelopes), a significantly higher percentage of people who were given no incentive
to comply with the first request (displaying the sign) addressed the
envelopes than did the people in the incentive conditions. The no
incentive condition even led to more compliance to the second
request than did a double incentive condition in which people
were offered three dollars for the second request after having
received three dollars for the first request. Oddly enough, there
were no significant differences in compliance between the experimental conditions when the second request involved addressing
75 letters.

Building on the work of Scott and others, Allen (1982) suggests that special television advertisements designed to influence self-perceptions (Bem, 1972) can stimulate socially conscious consumption. Whereas Scott used the foot-in-the-door technique to influence self-perceptions, Allen's approach involves labeling people. The assumption is that a label provides a person with an interpretation of his or her motivations and behavior; therefore, if you tell people that they are environmentally conscious, then they will perceive themselves as such and act accordingly. The typical persuasive appeal advocating environmentally conscious behavior may backfire because such appeals usually point out how neglectful people are, which could lead to self-perceptions of not caring. The key is to tell people they do care. Supporting the labeling hypothesis, Allen (1982) found that a television commercial that labeled American consumers as active in solving the nation's energy problem was more effective than a traditional persuasive appeal on a variety of consumer measures, including self-perceptions of being energy conscious when purchasing products and choosing an energy-efficient refrigerator for a possible lottery prize. It should be pointed out, however, that Allen's experiment involved a highly contrived situation in which groups of subjects who thought they were in a study about political opinions viewed programs that were supposedly videotaped from a a local network. Further research would be needed to determine whether the labeling effects would be effective in a more naturalistic setting.

In conclusion, two studies have demonstrated that application of Bem's self-perception theory (1965, 1972) can be useful in inducing environmentally conscious consumption. One application of the theory involves the foot-in-the-door technique in which compliance with a small conservation request is used to induce self-perceptions of social consciousness. A second approach is to create self-perceptions of social consciousness by providing that label for people. The latter technique has the advantage of being easily incorporated into mass-media compaigns. Although these applications are promising, further testing seems warranted. It would be particularly interesting to determine whether such techniques could stimulate people to buy products that help conserve the environment, such as nonphosphate detergents.

Charitable Behavior

In the classic tale *A Christmas Carol* by Charles Dickens, visits from several ghosts changed Ebenezer Scrooge from a miserable, self-serving miser to a generous benefactor of the poor. Scrooge's subsequent penchant for donating money to the needy exemplifies socially conscious consumption because he was using his purchasing power to bring about social change (cf. Webster, 1975). Social psychologists have not employed ghosts to stimulate such behavior nor have their results been so dramatic, but they have had some modest success in inducing charitable donations.

Kraut (1973) successfully manipulated social labeling to induce donations. In a door-to-door campaign a canvasser for the Heart Association verbally labeled some of those who donated as "charitable" but made no such comments to other donators. Labeling or not labeling an individual was determined at random. A couple of weeks later a second canvasser, collecting for Multiple Sclerosis, had better luck soliciting donations from those who had been labeled than those who had not. It was also found that labeling people who did not contribute to the Heart Association as "uncharitable" reduced the likelihood that they would subsequently donate to Multiple Sclerosis.

Although Kraut's study provided empirical support for labeling theory in an applied setting, practical use of the technique seems unlikely. Each potential contributor would have to be contacted twice by independent charities in order to induce greater giving to the second charity. To be fair to Kraut, however, it should be noted that his main purpose was to test the social labeling hypothesis rather than to provide a practical means of inducing donations.

As discussed earlier in this chapter, the foot-in-the-door technique can be used to induce self-perceptions of social consciousness (Scott, 1977), which in turn can influence behavior. A similar approach has been applied to inducing charitable donations. In general, the strategy involves asking a person to comply with a small request that is somehow related to a charitable cause and subsequently asking the person to donate money to the same charity. The small request is used as a foot-in-the-door (Freedman & Fraser, 1966) in that compliance with it (which is likely if it is small enough) should lead the person to self-perceive (Bem, 1972) that he or she is concerned about the charitable cause. This concern should increase the likelihood of making a donation.

Pliner, Hart, Kohl, and Saari (1974) used the foot-in-the-door-technique to induce donations to the Cancer Society in suburban Toronto. Residents were randomly assigned to either of two treatment conditions or to a control group. The night before a door-to-door fund-raising drive residents in one of the treatment conditions (small request) were contacted and asked to wear a plastic lapel pin to publicize the Cancer Society's campaign. Residents in the other treatment condition (moderate request) were asked to wear the pin and to persuade a family member to do the same. All the people complied with these initial requests, thus providing a foot-in-the-door. A control group was not contacted about the pins. The next day canvassers, who did not know which condition each subject was in, went door-to-door asking for doantions to the Cancer Society. As indicated in Figure 7-1, the foot-in-the-door requests significantly increased the percentage of residents who contributed. Over an entire fund-raising campaign the increased likelihood of donating achieved with the foot-in-the-door technique could greatly increase the total amount of money contributed. A more recent study indicates that the average size of individual donations can also be increased by combining the foot-in-the-door technique with specific requests for somewhat larger than usual contributions (Schwarzwald, Bizman, & Raz, 1983).

As with the labeling technique, practical use of the foot-in-the-door applications developed by Pliner and her associates and by Schwarzwald and his associates would suffer from the fact that both techniques involve two visits to each house. Inspection of the data indicates that more money could be raised by visiting twice as many houses once without the foot-in-the-door manipulation. Providing a solution to this problem, a more practical application of the foot-in-the-door technique was developed by Reingen (1978). The small initial request and the the request for a donation were combined in the same visit to each house. Upon answering the door residents were first asked to answer a few simple questions about heart disease and then were asked to make a contribution to the Heart Association. It was hypothesized that by taking the time to answer the questions people would self-perceive that

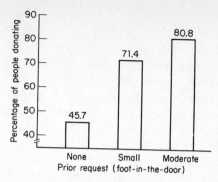

Figure 7-1. Percentage of people donating money in small, moderate, or no-prior-request conditions. (Adapted from Pliner et al. 1974. Copyright © 1974 by Academic Press. Reprinted by permission of the publisher and authors.)

they were concerned about heart disease and, therefore, would be more likley to donate money to the Heart Association. The hypothesis was supported. Compared to a control group, who were merely asked to make a contribution, a significantly higher percentage of the residents who were first asked the foot-in-the-door questions made a contribution.

In the same study Reingen was also successful in applying virtually the opposite strategy. Instead of beginning with a small appeal and ending with a large request, the alternative strategy involves an initial large request followed by a more moderate appeal. First developed by Cialdini and his associates (1975), this alternative approach is called the *door-in-the-face technique,* because the initial large request is likely to be refused. The underlying principle behind this madness is reciprocal concessions. The initial request is designed to be somewhat unreasonable and, therefore, is easily declined. In contrast, the more moderate appeal that follows should appear to be a reasonable concession on the part of the requester. Now that the requester seems to be more reasonable, an appropriate reciprocal concession would be to comply with the second request. In Reingen's study some residents were first asked to donate three dollars a month, which they all refused to do, and then were asked to make a single contribution of any amount. As predicted, this door-in-the-face manipulation signicantly increased the percentage of people who contributed compared to a control condition in which no prior request was made.

Using yet another social psychological approach, Reingen (1982) was again successful in inducing door-to-door donations to charity. This time the technique was based on the theory of *informational social influence*, which was first developed by Deutsch and Gerard (1955). According to this notion, when people are uncertain about how to act in a given situation, they will tend to define appropriate behaviors by observing the actions of others. Capitalizing on this tendency, Reingen found that the probability and size of donations could be influenced by reading a fictitious list of other contributors and their supposed contributions.

Another practical, successful, and cleverly simple means of inducing charitable contributions was developed and empirically tested by Cialdini and Schroeder (1976). Their technique involves adding the words "even a penny will help" to a standard request for contributions. By legitimizing small donations, commonly used excuses about being short of money lose credibility and, therefore, people should be likely to contribute. Field experiments involving door-to-door solicitations for the American Cancer Society demonstrated that the even-a-penny technique significantly increased the probability that people would contribute without reducing the size of donations. These findings have been replicated by other researchers (Reingen, 1978; Weyant, 1984). The consistency of the even-a-penny effect is illustrated in Figure 7-2. Since legitimizing small donations increases the probability of receiving contributions, it is reasonable to expect that asking for large donations may backfire by reducing the probability of receiving a contribution. Supporting this expectation, Weyant and Smith (in press) found that asking for a "generous contribution," which is suggested in some of the American Cancer Society's training films and pamphlets, significantly decreased the probability of getting a donation and did not increase the size of contributions.

People might question whether it is ethical to manipulate people into donating to charity. One might argue that it would be best to rely on nonmanipulative requests, so that people could decide whether to donate on the basis of the need and merits of the charity. Also it is possible that unscrupulous individuals could use such techniques for their own personal gain. Such arguments should

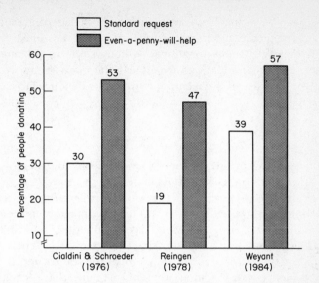

Figure 7-2. Comparison of the "Even-a-penny-will-help" request with a standard request for donations in three studies. (Adapted from Cialdini & Schroeder, 1976; Reingen, 1978; Weyant, 1984. Reprinted by permission of the publishers.)

not be dismissed too easily, but there are strong counterarguments. While the individual contributions induced by the techniques reviewed in this chapter are small and should pose no financial hardship on those who donate, the collective benefit to the charities could be great. Second, it is undoubtably the case that most solicitors for charities already try to phrase their requests in a manner that will induce donations, and thus the motivation behind the techniques reviewed here is no less worthy than it is in any fund-raising drive. Third, while unscrupulous people can use virtually any scientific advancement for their own self-serving needs, the emphasis here is to benefit society. Perhaps most importantly, although somewhat manipulative, the techniques reviewed here clearly give people the opportunity to refuse to donate and are not based on misrepresentations of the charities. For these reasons the applications appear to be honest and effective means of benefiting society.

In conclusion, several applications of social psychological principles have been successful in inducing charitable contributions. Most of the techniques are very practical in that they fit easily into standard requests for donations. Although one might question whether such manipulations are ethical, there are several reasons to believe that use of the techniques would be beneficial to society.

Television

In the United States consumers spend a tremendous amount of time and money on television. As incredible as it may seem, "More Americans have television than have refrigerators or indoor plumbing" (NIMH, 1982, p. 1) and in the average household the television set is on over six hours a day (Steinberg, 1980). Children spend more time watching television than they do in school (Liebert, Sprafkin, & Davidson, 1982) and, as we said earlier, there is some evidence that for adults the only activities that exceed television viewing are working and sleeping (NIMH, 1982). Because of its prevalence and its potential as a socializing agent, the influence of television on viewers, especially on children, has been the topic of considerable attention and research. Much of the initial concern centered on whether the prevalence of violence on television would cause children to act in a similar manner. The concern was so great that in the late 1960s the Surgeon General of the United States organized a scientific inquiry to determine any harmful effects that violent programs might have on children. Several research projects were funded, and in 1972 the results were published in a report entitled *Television and growing up: The impact of televised violence*. A ten-year follow-up report by the National Institute of Mental Health (1982) indicates that since the Surgeon General's report the amount of research on the social implications of television has increased considerably and over the years the concern has expanded beyond the influence of televised violence to a myriad of other potentially important social issues, such as the potential positive effects of prosocial programs, the influence of advertising on children, and the depiction of women and minorities on television.

The vast majority of social science research on television has focused on the content of programs and advertisements and the influence of that content on viewers. In contrast, there has been a relative paucity of applications aimed at mitigating the negative effects, or stimulating the positive effects, of television. Nevertheless, the emphasis here will be on the applications. A broader review of the research on the social implications of television is beyond the scope of this book and those readers who are interested should read other sources (e.g., Liebert, Sprafkin, & Davidson, 1982; NIMH, 1982).

Television Violence

On several occasions there have been unusual real-life acts of violence that occurred shortly after the airing of television shows that depicted similar incidents. For example, Wrightsman and Deaux (1981) cite a case in which a young girl was raped with a beer bottle in a manner quite like that shown a few days earlier in the television movie *Born Innocent*. The televised and real rapes were so similar that the mother of the real victim sued the network, contending that the movie prompted the attack.

Although social scientists are greatly influenced by incidents like the rape case described above, they must rely on more systematic evidence before drawing causal conclusions. To fill this need a great deal of evidence on the topic has been amassed using laboratory and field studies. In 1972 the Surgeon General's report tentatively concluded that for some children in certain environments televised violence may have a causal influence on aggression. Since then the evidence has been even more compelling. Although a few social scientists are not convinced (e.g., Kaplan & Singer, 1976), the NIMH ten-year follow-up report (1982) more strongly concludes that "the consensus among most of the research community is that violence on television does lead to aggressive behavior by children and teenagers who watch the programs" (p. 6). Perhaps even more impressive the same report states "television violence is as strongly correlated with aggressive behavior as any other behavioral variable that has been measured" (p. 6).

Several sources (e.g., Liebert, Sprafkin, & Davidson, 1982; NIMH, 1982) suggest that one of the most convincing and well-supported explanations of why televised violence causes aggression is provided by social learning theory (cf. Bandura, 1977). The basic assumption of the theory is that, although direct rewards and punishments have some influence, children develop their personalities primarily through observation and imitation of others. This process is often referred to as observational learning. Since most everyone agrees that violence is a predominant behavior on television and that children watch many of the most violent shows, it follows that young viewers will learn to become aggressive. Both laboratory and field studies support this prediction (NIMH, 1982). Adding to the assumption that observational learning is the primary means of socialization, the development of social learning theory has led to the discovery of several variables that determine whether it is likely that any particular observation of behavior will result in acquisition and performance of the observed behavior. We will see that most of the attempts to mitigate the effects of viewing violent television are based on social learning theory and involve manipulating the variables that mediate between observation on one hand and acquisition and performance on the other hand.

Despite the fact that for at least 30 years there has been evidence that violence on television may induce aggression in viewers, careful monitoring indicates that the amount of aggression depicted on television, especially on children's shows, has remained at a very high level (NIMH, 1982). An often cited reason for the prevalence of violence on television is that, as a commercial enterprise, the television industry is merely responding to the demands of the marketplace. The networks maintain that violent shows tend to attract the largest audiences. There is, however, some social psychological evidence that the popularity of adventure shows may be independent of their violent content. In a field study, Diener & DeFour (1978) found no significant correlation between an objective measure of the amount of violence depicted in episodes of prime time television programs and the subsequent popularity of the programs, as determined by Nielson ratings. Similarly, in a laboratory experiment the same researchers found that college students did not prefer an unedited episode of *Police Woman* to a version with the violent content edited out. From these results Diener and DeFour suggest that the networks "could reduce the incidence of portrayed violence substantially and lose few or no viewers" (p. 339).

Given the evidence for a causal link between violence on television and aggression by the viewers and the networks' reluctance to reduce the amount of violence in their programs, some social psychologists, albeit only a few, have made attempts to lessen the effects of violent programs. For example, based on experimental findings that supported the hypothesis that televised violence leads to social learning of aggression (e.g., Bandura, Ross, & Ross, 1963), Bandura (1963) wrote an article for *Look* magazine entitled "What TV violence can do to your child." In the article Bandura warned parents that their children were "being raised on a heavy dose of televised aggression and violence" in the form of "Western gunslingers, hopped-up psychopaths, deranged sadists, slapstick buffoons and the like" (p. 46). The article goes on to describe his research in layperson's terms and he clearly draws the conclusion that viewing televised violence reduces inhibitions against aggression and teaches children how to be aggressive. Obviously, by writing such an article in a popular magazine Bandura was attempting to persuade parents to monitor and modify their children's television viewing. Whether parents were successfully persuaded is not known because the impact of the article was not assessed.

Even if parents were persuaded that television violence could be harmful to their children, they might not know how to deal with the problem. One possibility is for parents to talk to their children about the violence portrayed on television. Using a social learning perspective, several researchers have investigated whether comments made by adults about televised aggression can mitigate the effects of violent programs (Grusec, 1973; Hicks, 1968; Horton & Santogrossi, 1978). In developing social learning theory Bandura and his associates (Bandura, 1965; Bandura, Ross, & Ross, 1963) have shown that imitation of modeled behavior is influenced by vicarious consequences. That is, observation of a model who was rewarded for being aggressive tended to induce imitative behaviors; whereas, observing a model being punished inhibited imitation. Presumably the child would expect consequences similar to those of the model. It should be noted that Bandura (1963) maintains that overall the influence of television programs probably increases aggression in children because, although some vague punishment may occur at the end of a show, the immediate consequences for aggressors on television is usually some kind of reward, such as obtaining power or money.

Hicks (1968) set out to determine whether inhibitions similar to those induced by vicarious punishments would occur if, instead of the model being punished for aggressing, an adult watching a program with a child would make negative comments about the model's aggressive behavior. Presumably the child would then expect disapproval from adults if he or she would engage in the modeled behavior. In a special laboratory school, children ranging in age from five to eight years viewed a brief film on a television console. In the film an adult model attacked a large inflatable "bobo" doll in a number of highly specific ways, such as striking the doll with a baton. During the presentation of the film another adult, who was present in the room with the child, made positive comments about the aggressive model (e.g., "He sure is tough."), negative comments (e.g., "That's wrong."), or made no comments. Each child was randomly assigned to one of the comment conditions. After viewing the film each child was observed while playing with some toys, which included a bobo doll. By random determination half of the children were alone while playing with the toys and half played while in the presence of the adult with whom they had watched the film. It was found that the positive and negative comments produced corresponding disinhibition and inhibition of imitative aggression, but only when the adult who made the comments was present while the children were being observed. Hicks concludes that "during such initial socialization trials such cues would modify behavior only in the presence of a socializing agent" (p 309). This limitation greatly reduces the usefulness of the technique. Using essentially the same procedure, Grusec (1973) found, however, that negative comments made by an adult inhibited imitative aggression of ten year olds even when the adult was no longer present. Thus, negative comments about televised aggression appear to be particularly effective in inhibiting imitative aggression for older children.

In addition to imitating aggression shown on television, it has often been suggested that by watching a steady diet of violence on television children will become indifferent to actual instances of aggression. Citing evidence for this effect (Drabman & Thomas, 1975), Horton and Santogrossi (1978) set out to see if adult commentary about aggressive actions on television could be used to influence children's responsiveness to "real life" aggression. Second through fifth grade boys were shown a violent excerpt from the television program "S.W.A.T.," while an adult made comments. By random assignment the adult comments were antiaggressive (e.g., "Shooting at that policeman is so disgusting."), nonaggressive (e.g., "There are other ways instead of shooting.") or neutral (e.g., "That policeman has a big rifle."). In a control condition the boys watched an excerpt from a televised volleyball game that did not involve violence. Subsequent to viewing the television excerpt each boy was asked to watch some younger children via a television monitor to make sure they did not "get into trouble" while the experimenter left the room to make a telephone call. Although they were led to believe that the children were in a nearby room, the boys actually saw a videotape in which the children to be watched argued and fought. The dependent measure was the amount of time it took the boys to seek the help of the adult when the younger children began to fight. As expected, the boys in the antiaggressive and nonaggressive commentary conditions were quicker to respond to the subsequent "real" aggression than were the boys in the neutral commentary condition (see Figure 7-3). Contrary to expectations the boys in the control group were no less responsive to the "real" aggression than were the boys in the nonaggressive and antiaggressive conditions. Thus, there was partial support for the notion that negative comments made by adults about the aggressive content of television shows can mitigate indifference on the part of young viewers when they subsequently encounter real instances of aggression.

Taken together the three studies that investigated the effects of adults making negative comments about the aggressive content of television shows indicate that this technique may help mitigate some of the negative effects that violent shows have on children. These results, however, should be interpreted with caution. In two studies adult comments reduced imitative aggression, but the dependent measure involved aggression toward an inanimate object (i.e., a bobo doll) when the children were immediately

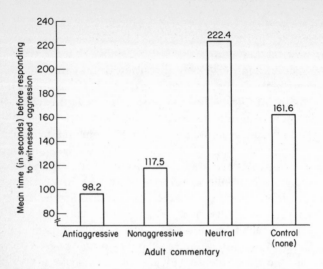

Figure 7-3. Comparison of elapsed time before responding to witnessed aggression by children previously exposed to antiaggressive, nonaggressive, neutral, or no adult commentary about TV violence. (Adapted from Horton & Santogrossi, 1978. Copyright © 1978 by The Society for Personality and Social Psychology, Inc.. Reprinted by permission of Sage Publications, Inc.)

placed in a setting that was similar to that depicted on the television monitor. Whether the inhibitions would generalize to interpersonal aggression over a long term in a variety of settings has not been determined. Also these two studies used films that were created for research rather than actual television shows and the films were viewed in school rather than at home. Although the study on the effect of adult comments on reponsiveness to "real" aggression involved excerpts from an actual television program, there were many aspects of the study that were somewhat contrived, such as viewing "live" aggression on a television monitor. Therefore, it seems that, although adult commentary is a promising technique for mitigating the negative effects of television violence, it should be tested in more naturalistic settings and with more realistic measures.

More recently, Huesmann and his colleagues have developed a particularly noteworthy technique to mitigate the negative effects of viewing violent television shows (Huesmann, Eron, Klein, Brice,

& Fischer, 1983). Their approach is of practical value because it can be applied in an elementary school curriculum and it has been shown to be effective with measures of real-life aggression. The technique involves a multifaceted intervention that is based primarily on cognitive theories and principles of social psychology, especially Bandura's social learning theory, Berkowitz's (1974) theory of aggression facilitating stimuli, and the technique of counterattitudinal advocacy (Cook & Flay, 1978). Basically, the strategy is to change children's cognitions, or how they think, about televised aggression and its relation to the real world. Toward this end attempts are made to persuade children that the violence portrayed on television is unrealistic, unacceptable in real life, and should not be emulated. Presumably, such cognitions would reduce the likelihood that children would imitate the aggression they see on television, and indeed there is evidence that children who believe that television violence is unrealistic and who do not identify with aggressive television characters are less aggressive than are children who do believe that television violence is realistic and who do identify with aggressive characters (Eron, 1982).

To test their intervention Huesmann and his colleagues selected a sample of first and third grade boys and girls who typically watched a great deal of violent television shows. After selecting the sample, the children were randomly assigned to either the treatment or a control condition, both of which were conducted in three sessions that were spaced over a period of about two months. In each treatment session small groups of children were shown a violent television program (e.g., "The Six Million Dollar Man") and afterward participated in a structured interview. During the interview the experimenter explained how people would ordinarily deal with the problems in the story without resorting to violence. Then the children were introduced to a new story line and were asked to think of realistic ways to solve the problems that the new story posed. The experimenter asked leading questions to prompt realistic, nonviolent solutions and made sure that all the children participated in the discussions. In the control condition the children watched nonviolent shows (e.g., "Happy Days") and discussed topics that were relevant to the show they had watched (e.g., nicknames).

It was expected that the children in the treatment condition would develop the attitude that televised violence is unrealistic and undesirable and, therefore, would watch it less and would become less aggressive themselves. None of these expectations were confirmed. Three month follow-up measures indicated that the children in the treatment condition did not change their attitudes about the realism of televised violence and exhibited no reduction in the amount of televised violence they watched, their tendency to identify with violent television characters, or their own aggressive behavior. Huesmann and his colleagues speculated about several reasons why their intervention did not work: perhaps the treatment was too weak; the follow-up may have been conducted too early for the effects to have taken place; or maybe the violent shows in the treatment condition provided models of aggression that, because of the weak treatment, may have offset any beneficial effects of the intervention. Of course, speculation about the weakness of the treatment begs the questions *why* it was weak and *how* it could be strengthened.

Focusing on the weakness of their original treatment Huesmann and his colleagues decided that it probably did not motivate the children to change. To remedy the situation they extended the intervention by applying additional social psychological techniques that have been shown to motivate attitude and behavioral change. Several social psychological theories, for example cognitive dissonance (Festinger, 1957), suggest that the act of delivering a message that is counter to one's own attitude can lead to a change in attitude toward the advocated position. Such counter-attitudinal advocacy is especially likely to lead to lasting attitude and behavioral change when a person writes his or her own counterattitudinal message and has an opportunity to observe him- or herself deliver the message (cf. Cook & Flay, 1978). Huesmann and his colleagues decided to apply these principles in their extended intervention. Nine months after the initial intervention children who were in the original treatment group were asked to develop their own arguments advocating three related issues— that television violence is unrealistic, that it is bad to imitate television aggression, and that it is bad to watch too much television. These children subsequently delivered their messages to other children and saw a videotape of themselves presenting the arguments. Children who were in the original control group went through a similar procedure except that their topic—why people should have hobbies—had nothing to do with television violence.

Results obtained after the extended treatment were quite encouraging. Two to three months after the intervention children in the treatment condition showed a significant change in their attitudes about television aggression, rating it as more unrealistic and potentially harmful for viewers. The control group showed no significant change in attitude. Moreover, four months after the intervention children in the treatment condition were rated as significantly less aggressive by their peers than were the control children. Although the intervention did not reduce the number of hours that the children watched violent television shows, viewing television violence and one's own aggression became unrelated for the children in the treatment condition; whereas, the television viewing-aggression correlation remained significant for the children in the control group.

In evaluating the Huesmann intervention there are two reasons to be optimistic about its usefulness and one reason to be cautious. On the positive side the intervention was accomplished in a few brief sessions in an elementary school setting and, therefore, can be practically applied. Also, since the major dependent variable was peer ratings of aggression taken four months after the treatment, there is evidence that the intervention is effective in reducing *real* aggression over a relatively long time period, as opposed to the immediate reduction of aggressive play toward a bobo doll that was found in the adult commentary studies. One reason for caution, however, as Huesmann and his colleagues admit, is that since the same children were used in the initial and extended treatments it is not clear which aspects of the intervention were effective. Therefore, it seems that the intervention is worthwhile, although further research to refine the technique would be advisable.

Prosocial Television

Although television programs generally overrepresent violence, there are shows that have prosocial themes. Whereas violence and aggression may be defined as behaviors that are intended to harm other people, a behavior is *prosocial* when it is intended to benefit others. Helping, cooperation, and friendliness are general forms of prosocial behavior. These kinds of behavior have been regularly exhibited in only a few commercial television programs (e.g., "The Waltons"), and also can be reliably seen on public television shows that are produced for children (e.g., "Mister Rogers' Neighborhood"). The influence of prosocial television on children and ways to enhance the positive effects have been assessed scientifically and, as Siegal (1982) points out in the NIMH report, "this research is closely articulated with current theories in social psychology" (p. 178).

Just as the social learning perspective suggests that viewing television violence induces aggression, it also leads to the prediction that viewing prosocial programs would stimulate learning of beneficial interpersonal behaviors. Supporting this hypothesis, there is some evidence that by merely watching prosocial television children learn the prosocial content and generalize the learning to new situations (Friedrich & Stein, 1973, 1975). Moreover, children assigned to watch prosocial programs were subsequently more helpful, gave more positive reinforcement to others, and initiated more social contacts than did children who were shown either neutral or violent programs (Coates, Pusser, & Goodman, 1976; Friedrich & Stein, 1973, 1975).

Although the mere viewing of prosocial television programs has been shown to influence the learning and actual behavior of children, many of the observed effects were weak and sometimes were obtained only for children with certain backgrounds or in certain situations (Friedrich & Stein, 1973, 1975; Friedrich-Cofer, Huston-Stein, Kipnis, Susman, & Clewett, 1979). To enhance the beneficial effects of prosocial television Friedrich-Cofer and her associates have developed and tested applications of social learning theory. According to the theory, learning and imitation of new behavior are enhanced when a person verbally labels and rehearses observed behavior (Bandura, 1969b, 1977). Applying these principles, Friedrich-Cofer and her associates hypothesized that the acquisition and performance of prosocial behavior would be enhanced if children were provided with verbal labels for behavior shown on prosocial television programs and opportunities to role-play this behavior.

Friedrich and Stein (1975) first tested their applications with middle-class kindergarten children in a school setting. Each child was randomly assigned to one of five conditions. In four of the conditions the children were shown several episodes of "Mr. Rogers' Neighborhood" and in a control condition the children saw neutral programs. After viewing each program the children engaged in activities that were designed by the experimenters. In the verbal-labeling condition the activity involved looking at storybooks that depicted and labeled prosocial themes from the programs. For each program there were two storybooks. The characters (mostly puppets) and themes in the first book were the same as those seen in the program and, to induce generalizations to real-life situations, the characters in the second book were children engaged in prosocial activities similar to those shown in the program. In the role-playing condition the children and the adult trainer reenacted prosocial themes from the programs with hand puppets. As in the verbal-labeling condition, the role-playing condition was designed to enhance learning of the prosocial content of the programs and generalizations of that learning to real-life situations. Therefore, each role-playing session involved reenacting scenes from the program with puppets of Mr. Rogers' characters followed by practicing similar prosocial themes with puppets that looked like children. In a third condition the children received both verbal-labeling and role-playing training. Children in a fourth condition engaged in activities that were irrelevant to the programs. Finally, in the control condition the children saw neutral programs (e.g, about going to the post office) and engaged in activities irrelevant to prosocial behavior.

A particularly noteworthy aspect of this research was that the effects of the five conditions were carefully assessed with three kinds of measures. In one measure experimenters, who were blind to the treatment experienced by each child, administered a content test that consisted of numerous items. Each item confronted the children with two alternatives, one of which was a prosocial response. For example, one item was "Tom loses Sam's ball," and the children were asked if Mr. Rogers would tell Tom to find it or help Tom find it. To assess both specific and generalized learning the test included items about particular scenes from the program and new situations similar to, but not the same as, those in the program. For the second measure an experimenter and each child would act out several scenes with puppets. To begin each scene the experimenter manipulated a puppet in a manner that confronted the child with an opportunity to behave prosocially. To assess both specific and general learning, sometimes the puppets and scenes were the same as those shown on the program and sometimes they were different. In all cases the children's play was recorded and the later content was analyzed for prosocial, neutral, and hostile behaviors. Finally, as a more direct assessment of prosocial behavior, each child was placed in a situation where he or she could help another child by either helping to repair the other child's broken collage or by giving the other child some stars. By using these multiple measures the researchers were able to assess specific and general verbal learning of prosocial themes, specific and general fantasy helping, and actual helping behavior.

Several interesting results were obtained. Even without training, the children who watched "Mr. Rogers'" learned the prosocial content of the programs, were able to generalize this learning to other situations, and were more helpful on the behavioral measure than were the children who watched the neutral programs. Nevertheless, both the verbal-labeling and role-playing interventions enhanced the positive effects, but in different ways. Training with verbal-labeling enhanced the verbal *learning* of specific and generalized prosocial content, especially for girls; whereas, role-playing enhanced imitative and novel prosocial *behavior*, especially for boys. Those children who received both kinds of training learned the most and were the most helpful. Thus either kind of training was useful and a combination of the two was particularly beneficial.

To further assess the practical usefulness of their techniques, Friedrich-Cofer and her associates (1979) later tested the combined verbal-labeling and role-playing treatment in a quasi-experimental field study. In the context of a Head Start Program, whole classes of underprivileged two to five year olds, matched on demographic and classroom variables, were assigned to various conditions. Rather than having experimenters train the children directly, which would not be likely in a widespread application of the technique, the training condition was conducted by Head Start teachers who received 12 hours of instruction in the verbal-labeling and role-playing techniques from the experimenters. Naturalistic observations of the children in the various conditions indicated that, whereas the mere viewing of prosocial programs had little or no effect on the children's behavior, those children whose teachers were trained in the enhancement techniques increased their spontaneous positive contacts with others while showing no increase in aggression. A condition in which the children were provided with play materials relevant to the prosocial programs (e.g., the puppets) but no training also showed an increase in positive social contacts; however, these same children increased their aggression. Therefore, both the relevant play materials and training were needed to increase prosocial behavior without increasing aggression.

In summary, it appears that viewing prosocial television can induce similar behavior in young viewers; however, the effects seem to be weak and unreliable. Applications of social learning theory, involving verbal-labeling and role-playing, have been shown to enhance the positive effects of prosocial television. There is evidence that these enhancing techniques may be practically applied on a widescale basis.

Public Service Campaigns

In addition to special children's programs, another form of prosocial television is the public service campaign. Such campaigns, which seem to be increasing in recent years (Hennigan, Flay, & Cook, 1980), most often deliver messages promoting preventive health care measures, such as wearing seat belts or quitting smoking (see Soloman, 1982, for a review). Relatively few of the campaigns have been formally evaluated and, of those in which the outcomes have been adequately assessed, only a small number appear to have been successful. It has been suggested, however, that many of the failures may have been avoided if, among other things, the designers of the messages had applied existing social psychological knowledge (Hennigan et al., 1980; Soloman, 1982).

One "successful" project provides a good illustration of the potential usefulness of social psychological theory in designing public service campaigns. Behavioral and medical scientists in Finland and the United States worked together to design a health campaign that was delivered on Finnish television (McAlister,

Puska, Koskela, Pallonen, & Maccoby, 1980). The basic treatment consisted of broadcasting a series of actual group therapy sessions in which counselors helped smokers to quit smoking and to avoid relapses. These therapy sessions were shown nationwide on public television. Except for rehearsal and role-playing of situations that are likely to cause relapses, most of what was depicted on the programs was not social psychological. Instead, useful information was given about such things as diet control and stress management, and behavioral techniques, such as aversive rapid smoking, were demonstrated. The major social psychological component of the intervention, which was administered in only one province, was the organization of volunteer community self-help groups that were intended to provide a supportive environment for watching the broadcasts. Based on social learning theory (Bandura, 1977), it was predicted that, whereas all viewers might acquire *cognitive learning* by watching the broadcasts, *performance* of the modeled behaviors would be more likely for people who viewed the shows while in a supportive social environment than when alone. Providing at least partial support for this hypothesis, a significantly higher percentage of people in the province where community support groups were organized viewed the programs and attempted to quit smoking than did people in a comparison province. In addition, one- and six-month follow-up surveys indicated that a higher percentage of people in the province that received community support had quit smoking than in the comparison province; however, this difference was not statistically significant and the data are somewhat suspect because they consisted of self-reports.

Given the great amount of social psychological research and theory on attitude and behavior change, it is surprising that social psychologists have not played a major role in public service campaigns. Hennigan and his colleagues (1980) suggest that social scientists are missing an important opportunity. Although, as with any social science application, it would be naïve to expect that laboratory findings would always directly translate into useful intervention strategies, it seems equally foolish to ignore this vast store of relevant information (Soloman, 1982). It seems that social psychologists could play a valuable role, along with professionals from other disciplines, in both the planning and evaluation of public service campaigns.

Advertising

Advertising is perhaps the most obvious means of attempting to influence consumer behavior. The goal of most advertising is to persuade people to buy one brand of a product rather than another. Given that social influence is a major content area of social psychology, it should come as no surprise that advertisers could benefit from applications of social psychology. Indeed, a great deal of marketing and advertising research is based on social psychological knowledge, especially attribution theory (e.g., Settle & Golden, 1974; Smith & Hunt, 1978; Sparkman & Locander, 1980) and principles of persuasive communication (e.g., Burnett & Wilkes, 1980; Etgar & Goodwin, 1982; Smith, Gier, & Willis, 1982).

Of all of the applied areas of social psychology, applications to advertising raise perhaps the most serious ethical questions. From a societal standpoint, compared to such laudable goals as promoting good health, improving education, and reducing aggression, convincing people to drink Coca-Cola rather than Pepsi-Cola seems quite trivial. In addition, unlike other applications, many of those designed to improve advertising might not even increase our knowledge about human behavior, because, given the competitive nature of the business, advertising agencies may not always be willing to share the results of their studies (Hennigan, Flay, & Cook, 1980). It is therefore doubtful whether applying social psychology to advertising would help the discipline reach its traditional Lewinian goals of contributing to science and benefiting society.

Summary and Conclusions

Broadly defining consumer behavior as the way people choose to use their personal resources, especially money and leisure time, applications of social psychology to consumer behavior can be divided into two major categories. One category involves inducing "socially conscious consumption," which may be defined as considering the societal consequences of one's private consumption or attempting to use one's purchasing power to benefit society. The other category involves the societal implications of viewing television, which evidently is America's most prevalent leisure-time activity.

Research on inducing socially conscious consumptions indicates that applications of self-perception theory, either by the foot-in-the-door technique or by social labeling, may be useful in getting people to consider the environmental consequences of their individual consumption. Much more research has been done to prompt people to use their purchasing power for societal benefit by donating to charities, and several social psychological techniques have been used to increase the likelihood of charitable donations. Many of these techniques can be practically applied to door-to-door campaigns.

Although the vast majority of the social scientists who have studied the social implications of viewing television have focused on identifying problems rather than providing solutions, some social psychological principles, especially social learning, have been applied to mitigating the negative effects of violent television programs and enhancing the effects of prosocial programs. In general, the applications seem to be practical for widespread use, and evaluations of their effectiveness have provided some positive results. Some of the evaluations, however, especially the assessments of techniques designed to mitigate the negative effects of television violence, involved questionable outcome measures or methodological flaws. With promising techniques, sometimes supported with questionable data, there is a need for more research on the effectiveness of these applications.

8

Law

During the Vietnam War era a Catholic priest and antiwar activist named Phillip Berrigan and several of his associates were arrested and charged with conspiracy to raid draft boards, to blow up heating tunnels in Washington, D.C., and to kidnap presidential advisor Henry Kissinger. These accusations were dramatically revealed to the press and media by J. Edgar Hoover, who was then director of the FBI. As the facts of this highly publicized case became known, the defense attorneys learned that evidence against their clients was obtained by an FBI informant. The informant, posing as an antiwar activist, smuggled letters out of prison for Berrigan, who was already serving a sentence for disrupting draft boards. To make matters worse for Berrigan and his associates, the government chose to try the case in Harrisburg, Pennsylvania, which is a politically conservative community. Given the FBI's role in producing dramatic publicity and in using paid informants and the fact that antiwar activists were to be tried in a politically conservative community, defense attorneys were concerned about receiving a fair trial for their clients. In an effort to balance matters, the defense enlisted the services of a group of social scientists, including two social psychologists. These social scientists applied some of their knowledge and data-gathering techniques to help select the jury (Schulman, Shaver, Colman, Emrick, & Christie, 1973). We will return to the case of the Harrisburg Seven, as the defendants came to be known, and to the topic of systematic jury selection later in this chapter. First, let us look at the relevance of social psychology to the legal system more generally.

The Applicability of Social Psychology to the Legal System

In their book *Social Psychology in Court,* Saks and Hastie (1978) observe that there is "a strikingly good fit between many of the behavioral questions with which lawyers, judges, and litigants must deal, and knowledge uncovered by social psychological research" (p. v). What they are referring to is the potential applicability of social psychological findings to the legal process. Persuasive communication, for example, is a traditional and well-researched topic in social psychology. Perhaps the findings of such research could be helpful to a lawyer in trying to persuade a judge or jury about the merits of his or her case. Group dynamics, including group decision making, is another traditional area of inquiry in social psychology and it seems reasonable that such knowledge may be useful in developing procedures concerning juries, which are groups that must select a leader, deliberate, and make decisions. Indeed one would be hard-pressed to find any aspect of the legal system, from the entry point of a citizen reporting a crime to the end point of a parole board deciding whether to let someone out of prison, that does not involve some basic issue of human behavior that has been studied by social psychologists (Greenberg & Ruback, 1982).

In addition to the general observation that much of social psychology is potentially relevant to the legal system, social psychologists have made the connection more explicitly by conducting experiments that are designed to simulate aspects of the legal system. In a common form of simulation, subjects are asked to judge the guilt or innocence of a defendant on the basis of a written transcript or summary of a trial. Some aspect of the trial can be systematically manipulated as an independent variable. For example, Pyszczynski and Wrightsman (1981) systematically varied the extensiveness of opening statements by both defense and prosecution attorneys. Sometimes in order to enhance realism, audio- or videotapes of a staged trial are used instead of written descriptions (e.g., Wells, Lindsay, & Tousignant, 1980). If variation of the independent variable influences the verdict rendered by simulated jurors, then there may be reason to believe that similar cause-and-effect relationships might occur in real courtrooms. To a lesser extent social psychologists have gathered nonexperimental data through direct observation or by obtaining records from actual legal proceedings (e.g., Ebbesen & Konečni, 1975).

The relevance of basic research and simulations to the legal system has not gone unquestioned. Variables that have statistically significant effects in basic research, or even in simulations, will not necessarily have practical effects in real-world settings. Despite numerous attempts to simulate aspects of the legal system, there is little or no assurance that the findings of such studies are applicable to real-world settings, and some social psychologists have expressed serious doubts about their practical value (Konečni & Ebbesen, 1979). This skepticism is based somewhat on the argument that, knowing that their behavior will have no real consequences, subjects in simulations may not take the situation seriously. In addition, some research indicates that the results of simulations do not match data gathered from the records of actual legal proceedings (e.g., Ebbesen & Konečni, 1975). Konečni and Ebbesen suggest, therefore, that to study the legal system social psychologists should only use field research in real-world settings.

On the other hand, Bray and Kerr (1982) defend the applicability of simulation studies for several reasons. They argue that laboratory simulations allow for greater control of variables and therefore increase the likelihood of uncovering unambiguous cause-and-effect relationships. They note that in many cases laboratory and field studies have obtained similar results. Sometimes, they suggest, simulations offer the only ethical means of studying legal issues. As an example of this last point, the process of jury deliberation is of great interest, but observation of the deliberation room is not permitted and any surreptitious means of observation, such as bugging the deliberation room, presents ethical and legal problems. An alternative solution might be to conduct retrospective interviews with jurors after a verdict has been rendered, but the accuracy of such interview data would be subject to the fallibilities of memory. A simulation, on the other hand, could provide data on the deliberation process in a controlled situation without ethical problems.

There probably is no right answer to the debate. It is prudent to realize that simulations may not capture all the dynamics of the actual legal system. Blind faith in the applicability of the results of such studies would be unwise. On the other hand, to categorically dismiss the results of simulation studies may be equally unwise. The results of such studies may provide some practical insights, especially if care is taken to create simulations that are as practically and ethically realistic as possible. Two ways of achieving such realism have been suggested. Dillehay and Nietzel (1980) recommend that researchers begin by making careful field observations in order to diagnose the essential dynamics of legal proceedings and then use this information to design simulations. Saks (1980) suggests an interdisciplinary approach in which social scientists would enlist the help of judges and lawyers in all aspects of research projects, including the initial planning and design.

Applications of Social Psychology to the Legal System

Although social psychologists have produced a great deal of research that was intended to have practical value in the legal system (Haney, 1980), there have been relatively few actual uses of social psychology to solve legal problems. Several factors may be responsible for this paucity of applications. One inhibiting factor is the questionable relevance of basic research and simulations, especially when studies seem to be based on naïve conceptualizations of the legal system. Another factor is that, as scientists, social psychologists feel some obligation to be impartial and that impartiality may be fundamentally incompatible with a legal system that is based on advocacy (Haney, 1980). We will see that the partiality issue has led to criticism of systematic jury selection and the use of research psychologists as expert witnesses. Perhaps the greatest inhibitory factor is that people in the legal system know very little about social psychology. Indeed Saks (1974) criticized the legal profession by arguing that legal practitioners often make decisions that are based on naïve assumptions about human behavior that could be avoided by learning more about the social sciences. The consequences of such decisions, according to Saks, are ineffective laws, injustices, and incompetent legal counsel. Although Saks blames the legal profession for its ignorance of social science, some of the blame could be put on social scientists for not communicating their findings, and the relevance of those findings, to the legal profession (Tanke & Tanke, 1979). It is interesting to note that Saks published his criticism in *Trial,* which is a widely read legal journal. It appears that recently social scientists are becoming more active in publishing their findings and viewpoints in legal journals and hybrid journals, such as *Law and Human Behavior.* Perhaps with this input into the legal literature legal practitioners will learn about, and be influenced by, social science.

The few instances in which social psychology has influenced the legal system have come in two general forms. One form is direct participation by social psychologists in legal procedures. Examples are serving as an expert witness on the reliability of eyewitness identifications and assisting lawyers in the selection of jurors. These kinds of interventions by psychologists have the potential for a direct impact on a particular case, but have the limitation that they are not likely to bring about fundamental legal change (Haney, 1980). The second form of influence is utilization of social psychological knowledge by legal policymakers. For example, as described in the chapter on education, the Supreme Court made use of social psychological knowledge in deciding to desegregate public schools. Haney points out that, while such utilizations are relatively rare, they can bring about fundamental legal changes. We examine both of these general forms of influence.

Social Psychological Interventions in the Legal System

Systematic Jury Selection

Recall that in the case of the Harrisburg Seven, the antiwar activists, charged with conspiracy, were to be tried in a conservative community. Concerned about whether the defendants would receive a fair trial, a team of social scientists decided to intervene by assisting defense counsel in the process of jury selection. The trial ended in a hung jury—ten for acquittal and two for conviction—and the conspiracy charges were dropped. Subsequent to this intervention the techniques employed by the social scientists have been used, and refined (Bonora & Krauss, 1983), in a number of other cases. In fact, a number of consulting organizations specializing in systematic jury selection have arisen. For example, some of the social scientists involved in the Harrisburg Seven case helped found the National Jury Project with a commitment to assist in the "defense of progressive political movements" (Bonora & Krauss, 1979, p. 1), which now includes civil disobedience cases (e.g., antinuclear activists) and civil rights cases (e.g., battered women) (Bonora & Krauss, 1983). The political right, on the other hand, seems to be represented by organizations such as Litigation Sciences, which specializes in assisting corporate defendants in product liability and antitrust disputes (Andrews, 1982). As we will see, there is considerable debate about both the impact and ethics of systematic jury selection. Before discussing the controversy we examine the social science techniques and how they fit into the legal process of a jury trial.

The selection of a jury is a multifaceted process. There are three ways in which lawyers can intervene in the process in order to secure a jury that is not prejudiced against their clients (Kairys, Schulman, & Harring, 1975). First there is the matter of venue, or where the trial is to be held. As with most trial decisions, the place of trial is a matter of judicial discretion; however, if defense counsel has reason to believe that potential jurors in the selected trial district are likely to be prejudiced against the defendant, then the defense may attempt to persuade the judge to move the trial to another district. The usual grounds for a *change of venue* motion are damaging pretrial publicity or unfavorable attitudes toward the defendant in the district. The next step is selection of the jury panel, which serves as a pool of potential jurors. The panel is supposed to be representative of the community in which the case is to be tried. A common procedure for selecting the panel is to take a random sample of registered voters. If there is reason to believe that the panel is not representative of the district, the defense counsel may make a *composition challenge*. If the challenge is successful (the judge decides), a new panel of jurors is selected. Finally, each potential juror is interviewed during a process called *voir dire*. The purpose of the voir dire is to determine whether potential jurors are competent and impartial. The voir dire questions are asked by the judge or by the opposing counsel. The judge decides who asks the questions and what questions are permitted. After the questioning either counsel may challenge any potential juror either for cause or peremptorily. There is no limit to the number of challenges for cause that an attorney may make, but to be successful such challenges must be supported by reasons that are convincing to the judge. On the other hand, peremptory challenges are limited in number (the defense usually gets more than the prosecution), but result in the dismissal of challenged jurors with no questions asked. It is by assisting in these three processes—change of venue motions, composition challenges, and voir dire—that social scientists have become involved in jury selection.

For all three jury selection processes the primary technique used by the social scientists is a community survey (Kairys et al., 1975). A representative sample of the community in which the trial is to take place is interviewed either by phone or in person. The sample, which does not include the actual jury panel, is typically selected at random from people who would be legally eligible for jury duty. The survey instrument usually involves four sections. First, there is a brief introduction that vaguely informs the respondent that the survey deals with attitudes about crime and the criminal justice system. The respondents are not told that the ultimate purpose of the survey is to assist defense counsel in an upcoming case. If such a disclosure were made, it is doubtful that a representative sample of the community would agree to be interviewed. The second section of the survey involves general attitude questions. These questions might concern attitudes about politics, religion, race, or any other topic that may be indicators of prejudice. In the third section respondents are asked questions about the specific case. These questions are designed to assess knowledge and biases about the defendants and their case. For example, Kairys and his associates (1975) report that in a survey designed to assist in the defense of dissidents who were involved in the Wounded Knee uprising the following question was asked: "In the Wounded Knee dispute with whom did you sympathize more—the federal government or the Militant American Indians?" (p. 77). The final section involves gathering demographic data, such as race, sex, age, education, and occupation of the respondent.

To help support a motion for change of venue, surveys should be conducted in the district where the trial is scheduled to be held and in at least one other district (McConahay, Mullin, & Frederick, 1977). Surveying in more than one district serves two purposes.

First, a comparison between the trial district and other districts may reveal that on specific questions about the case citizens in the trial district may be relatively more prejudiced against the defendant or may have been exposed to relatively more pretrial publicity. Second, if less prejudice or publicity is found in another district, then defense counsel may recommend the trial be moved there. Using this strategy, McConahay and his colleagues were successful in assisting the defense counsel for Joan Little, a black woman charged with the murder of a white man, to secure a change of venue from a conservative North Carolina district to a less conservative district.

Remember that the jury panel is supposed to be representative of the general population in the trial district. If it appears that certain segments of the community are under- or overrepresented in the jury panel, then a challenge may be made with the goal of securing a new, and hopefully more representative, panel. Demographic data, either from a community survey or from census data, can help support a composition challenge. For example, in the Harrisburg Seven case Schulman and his associates (1973) compared the demographic results of their community survey with the jury panel and found that young people were underrepresented in the panel. A composition challenge was made and a new panel was selected before a jury was chosen. It should be pointed out, however, that even with the clear support of social science data, composition challenges may be denied. In the case of Joan Little, McConahay and his associates were able to determine that in the original trial district 30 percent of the community who were legally qualified for jury service were black, but only 13.5 percent of the jury panel were black. Despite this discrepancy a composition challenge was denied, but fortunately for Little the trial site was later moved to another district.

After issues concerning the venue (location of the trial) and jury panel have been settled, the final step in jury selection is the voir dire. The jury panel is interviewed by the judge and/or opposing counsel, and those prospective jurors who seem to be unsuitable may be dismissed by the judge or challenged by either counsel. Deciding which jurors to challenge may not be easy. The process of voir dire is not generally conducive to honest self-disclosure, especially with regard to revealing any prejudices the prospective jurors may have (Suggs & Sales, 1981). Since the prospective jurors are likely to be less than candid about their prejudices, it is difficult for attorneys to determine who may or may not be biased against their clients. Ironically, information that is less directly related to prejudices may be most accurate. Demographic information, such as one's sex, race, or age, is hard to conceal and prospective jurors may be relatively more self-disclosing about past experiences than about specific attitudes. It becomes important, therefore, to know if any of the prospective jurors' demographic characteristics or experiences would serve as good indicators of specific attitudes.

Once again analysis of the community surveys can be helpful. Since both the respondents in the community survey and the jury panel are selected to be representative samples of people in the trial district, the survey sample can be used as a model of the jury panel. Relationships that hold between demographic characteristics and attitudes in the survey sample should also hold in the jury panel. A potential advantage of the survey data is that since there is no threat of being dismissed from a jury, the respondents may be more self-disclosing about their biases. Therefore, the survey data can be used to determine profiles of demographics and experiences that are likely to be associated with favorable or unfavorable attitudes toward the defendants. Often statistical procedures, such as regression analysis, are used to derive a mathematical model that weights and combines demographics and other characteristics to predict specific attitudes about the defendant (e.g., Christie, 1976). Then demographic and other information obtained in the voir dire can be plugged into the mathematical model to predict each prospective juror's attitudes about the defendant's case. These predictions can be useful in deciding which propective jurors to pass and which to challenge. Given that prospective jurors are reluctant to admit prejudices that might serve as the basis for challenges for cause, the survey predictions are usually used in planning peremptory challenges.

Predicting prejudices based on survey data is by no means the only social science technique used to guide voir dire challenges. Indeed, those social scientists who have developed the techniques of systematic jury selection dismiss the idea that formulas provide foolproof predictions about who will be a "good" or "bad" juror

(Bonora, Linder, Christie, & Schulman, 1983). They claim that the survey predictions are useful only in conjunction with other techniques. These other techniques include observations of potential jurors' behavior during voir dire, consideration of group dynamics, and consultation with attorneys, the defendants, or any other interested party.

Observation of behavior during voir dire usually centers on the potential jurors' body language (e.g., McConahay, Mullin, & Frederick, 1977) and how each potential juror relates to others during the interview (e.g., Christie, 1976). Body language is used primarily as an indicator of the honesty of a potential juror's responses, especially for those questions dealing with prejudices. While people may consciously monitor what they say, they may be less aware of what their bodies communicate. Interpretations are made on the basis of body posture, hand movements, facial expressions, and eye contact (Bonora et al., 1983). Signs of possible deception include the folding of arms or legs, shifts in posture, touching the face, and quick changes of facial expression. Also, failing to look at the defendant is taken as a sign of distaste. Many of these interpretations are based on social psychological research (e.g., Ekman & Friesen, 1974; McClintock & Hunt, 1975). It should be noted, however, that in general people can detect deception from nonverbal cues at only slightly better than a chance level (Zuckerman, De Paulo, & Rosenthal, 1981), and there is no evidence that psychologists can do any better.

The case of the Gainesville Eight provides an example of how observation of interactions of prospective jurors with others is used to help guide voir dire challenges (Christie, 1976). The defendants were Vietnam Veterans Against the War. Since the authoritarian personality is characterized by a virtually unquestioned respect for authority (Adorno, Frenkel-Brunswik, Levinson, & Sanford, 1950), it was feared that authoritarian jurors would be intolerant of the defendants' antiestablishment views. During the voir dire two observers noted how prospective jurors reacted to the judge as an authority figure. The social scientists advised the defense attorneys to challenge some prospective jurors who appeared to be markedly deferential to the judge.

Of course, observations made during the voir dire can be combined with survey data to make predictions about the biases of each prospective juror. Having used such a method in the case of Joan Little, McConahay and his colleagues (1977) concluded:

> Regardless of what a juror might say during the voir dire by observing or obtaining his or her demographics (age, education, etc.) and social-psychological characteristics (politics, reading habits, etc.), the mathematical model enabled us to predict how predisposed he or she was to side with the prosecution or the defense. Potential jurors might lie about their preconceptions of guilt or innocence, but they were much less likely to lie about their age or education. (p. 216)

Although the jury consists of individuals, it will ultimately deliberate as a group. Therefore, in addition to ratings of individual prospective jurors, systematic jury selection typically involves some consideration of how the individuals will fit together as a group. Relevant theoretical and empirical information about group dynamics has been available in the social psychological literature ever since the the pioneering work of Lewin (1947a). The jury's task of making a group decision virtually assures that at least some jurors will be influenced by others in the group. Besides being asked to select a foreperson, juries are given very little formal structure. The potential for the development of an informal structure is quite high and certain roles are likely to develop (Bonora et al., 1983). Although the foreperson is usually recognized as the leader, other people who may be particularly likeable or articulate might emerge as leaders. Other jurors will fill roles of follower, negotiator, and holdout. Social scientists integrate their knowledge of group dynamics with survey data and observations of prospective jurors in order to recommend challenges by the defense.

A clear example of the group dynamics approach to voir dire challenges is provided by the case of the Gainesville Eight (Christie, 1976). Recall that the defense wanted to avoid jurors who were highly authoritarian. Observations of a particular member of the jury panel suggested that she might be an ideal foreperson as far as the defense was concerned. She was low on the dimension of authoritarianism and her self-assurance made her a likely candidate for leadership. To further enhance her chances for being chosen as foreperson, the social scientists advised the defense attorneys to challenge high status males. Another bit of strategy provides an interesting twist. The defense actually passed two jurors who were high authoritarians, but who also appeared to be of low status. The reason for this seemingly paradoxical decision was that the low status of these two individuals would probably prevent them from assuming leadership roles and their authoritarianism, characterized by deference to authority figures, might lead them to be persuaded by the views of the foreperson.

Although the focus here has been on the role of social scientists in the voir dire, it is important to realize that this input is only part of a team approach (Bonora et al., 1983). In addition to the social scientists' suggestions, challenges of prospective jurors are made on the basis of the attorneys' experience, observations, and intuitions. Oftentimes, the opinion of the defendants is also considered. Finally, it should be noted that organizations, such as the National Jury Project, train attorneys to use the techniques of systematic jury selection (Bonora & Krauss, 1983).

The role of social scientists as specialists in jury selection has been controversial ever since the first published accounts of such interventions. When Schulman and his associates (1973) introduced the techniques that were used in the Harrisburg Seven case, they defended their involvement by stating that they were merely trying to secure an impartial jury for the defendants. They felt that the publicity surrounding the case and the conservative district in which the trial was to be held were biasing factors that needed to be offset. On the other hand, soon thereafter, Etzioni (1974), a fellow social scientist, warned, "The impartiality of the jury is threatened because defense attorneys have recently discovered that they can manipulate the composition of the jury by the use of social science techniques, so as to significantly increase the likelihood that the defendants will be acquitted" (p. 28). Etzioni went on to suggest that the average defendant would not be able to afford systematic jury selection; therefore, the technique would unfairly benefit defendants who are wealthy or who have loyal supporters. Futhermore, Etzioni argued that the government would soon begin to use the techniques and would have a decided advantage because of its superior resources. Hence, techniques that may at first have been developed to help the downtrodden might eventually backfire. Etzioni recommends the adoption of legal measures that would curtail the involvement of social scientists in jury selection.

Responding to the criticisms, Saks (1976a, 1976b) both defends the ethics of systematic jury selection and contends that Etzioni has overestimated the impact of the techniques. With regard to the ethical questions, Saks points out that the social scientists' involvement in jury selection has been both legal and in keeping with the spirit of our adversary legal system. A basic assumption of this system is that if opposing counsel work diligently for their sides a fair trial will emerge. Consistent with this assumption the goal of voir dire is for both sides to discern bias in prospective jurors to the best of their ability. Systematic jury selection is designed to facilitate this ability. This led Saks (1976a) to ask, "If the goal was good, why has the ability to achieve it become bad?" (p. 11). As for the wealthy, the well supported, and the government having an unfair advantage with regard to systematic jury selection, Saks points out that similar advantages already exist for other legal resources. He contends, therefore, that unfair allocation of resources is a fundamental problem in our legal system that should not be blamed on social scientists. Moreover, he argues that to ban systematic jury selection because some people have superior resources would logically lead to a ban on any technology that is designed to improve a litigant's case.

As for the impact of systematic jury selection, Saks (1976a) points out that "No evidence exists to support the apparently widely held belief that scientific jury selection is a powerful tool" (p. 13). An adequate assessment of impact would require a comparison of cases in which systematic jury selection was used to a control group of cases in which the techniques were not used. McConahay and his colleagues (1977) suggest an additional placebo control group of cases in which the lawyers would be led to believe that they were receiving social science assistance, but would actually only receive support for their own intuitions. For obvious ethical reasons McConahay and his colleagues suggest that such an experiment be conducted as a simulation rather than in actual courtroom cases.

At the present time the overall impact of systematic jury selection remains a matter of speculation. The fact that in a high percentage of cases in which the techniques were used the defendants were acquitted could be accounted for by the nature of the cases. For instance, Saks (1976b) points out that the techniques were first used to help defendants who were accused of political conspiracy, which is a difficult charge to prove.

There are at least two reasons to believe that systematic jury selection has only a limited impact on the outcomes of trials. First, it should be realized that scientific predictions are probabilistic and not absolute. With regard to systematic jury selection, Zeisel and Diamond (1976) draw an analogy to batting averages in baseball. Selecting a right-handed batter to face a left-handed pitcher increases the chances of a hit, but by no means guarantees that outcome. Similarly, using survey data and observations might increase the probability of identifying a sympathetic juror, but does not guarantee that outcome. Second, it is likely that the presentation of a convincing case will override the biases of jurors. Supporting this notion Saks (1976a, 1976b) points out that social psychologists have generally found that situations (e.g., presentation of strong evidence) are more potent determinants of behavior (e.g., deciding on a verdict) than are personality factors (e.g., the characteristics of the jurors). Many social scientists agree that the impact of systematic jury selection is limited and that it will have its greatest impact in cases where the evidence is ambiguous (Berk, 1976; Christie, 1976; McConahay et al., 1977; Saks, 1976a, 1976b).

In summary, social scientists, including several social psychologists, have become involved in jury selection. The techniques employed include community surveys, observations of prospective jurors, and applications of group dynamics. Those who have become involved in this process claim that they are merely trying to secure impartial jurors, whereas critics charge that the interventions constitute jury tampering that is likely to give an unfair advantage to those who can best afford to hire the social scientists. From both a scientific and practical viewpoint, a great shortcoming of systematic jury selection is that the impact of the techniques has not been adequately evaluated.

Expert Testimony about Eyewitness Reliability

Most people are probably aware that psychiatrists and clinical psychologists are called upon to give expert testimony on the mental competence of defendants in cases involving the "insanity plea." In a newer and less well-known role psychologists are being called on to testify about the reliability of eyewitness testimony. The basis of such testimony is a great deal of research by both cognitive and social psychologists that indicates that eyewitnesses quite often make mistakes when trying to recall events or when trying to identify someone they saw only briefly (Buckhout, 1974; Loftus, 1979; Yarmey, 1979). Besides describing the general unreliability of eyewitness testimony, the expert can testify about research that is relevant to the circumstances of a particular case. For example, social psychological research has shown that people are generally more accurate in identifying members of their own race than they are in identifying members of other races (Brigham & Barkowitz, 1978; Malpass & Kravitz, 1969). In actual cases involving cross-racial identification psychologists have testified about the research findings on this issue (Loftus & Monahan, 1980). Since faulty eyewitness identification can lead to the conviction of innocent people, the role of psychologists as expert witnesses is potentially very important (Loftus, 1979).

Loftus and Monahan (1980) describe the legal criteria for the admissibility of expert testimony and make recommendations about how psychologists should handle the role. For example, the law requires that only qualified experts can give such testimony. Loftus and Monahan suggest that the relevant qualifications for expert testimony about eyewitness accuracy are an advanced degree in perception and memory and publications in that area. Since much of the evidence presented by these experts is social psychological, it would seem reasonable to expand these qualifications to include social psychologists. A second legal criterion is that the testimony must concern a proper subject matter. To be proper expert testimony must provide information that is beyond the knowledge of the typical layperson. Although it has been argued that factors that influence the reliability of eyewitness identifications are a matter of common sense (McCloskey & Egeth,

1983a), there is evidence that much of what researchers have discovered about eyewitness accuracy is not commonly known (Brigham & Bothwell, 1983). Besides needing to be beyond common knowledge, proper expert testimony cannot infringe on the jury's task of deciding on the credibility of a particular eyewitness. Here Loftus and Monahan recommend that, rather than giving an opinion about the credibility of a particular witness, the expert should merely review the relevant research findings. That way the jury is still allowed to decide whether they believe the eyewitness testimony, but hopefully will be better able to do so. Loftus and Monahan also recommend that during their testimony expert witnesses should be frank about the generalizability of research findings, the probabilistic nature of psychological findings, and one's own personal values. In short, the jury should be allowed to decide about the credibility not only of the eyewitness but also of the expert testimony.

With any application an important issue is whether it produces the intended effect. The intended effect of expert testimony about eyewitness accuracy is to induce greater and more sophisticated scrutiny of eyewitness testimony and to help avoid unfair convictions. Unfortunately, the impact of such expert testimony is difficult to assess. A comparison of actual cases in which such testimony was either given or not given would be fraught with confoundings of the expert testimony with other aspects of the cases, such as the strength of circumstantial evidence or whether the judge was inclined to allow such expert testimony. If, for example, defense counsel typically decides to use an expert to testify about eyewitness accuracy only when circumstantial evidence against the defendant is weak, then higher rates of acquittal in cases involving such expert testimony could be attributed either to the effect of the expert testimony or to the weakness of the circumstantial evidence. Simulation studies, on the other hand, offer greater control and clearer conclusions about cause and effect. Three simulation experiments indicate that expert testimony can produce the intended effects (Hosch, Beck, & McIntyre, 1980; Loftus, 1980; Wells, Lindsay, & Tousignant, 1980). In general, these studies indicate that expert testimony leads jurors to deliberate much longer, to be more skeptical about eyewitness testimony, and to be slightly less likely to judge a defendant guilty (Hosch, 1980).

The simulation experiment by Hosch et al. (1980) is particularly noteworthy because of its realism. Four juries were exposed to what they were told was a real burglary trial involving an eyewitness identification of the defendant. The setting was a real courtroom and the jurors were citizens who were demographically similar to those that would serve on a real jury. Actually the trial was staged by lawyers, a judge, and some actors. Two of the juries heard all of the evidence, including expert testimony about eyewitness accuracy, and the other two juries heard all the evidence except the expert testimony. After the trial each jury was taken to a separate room and was videotaped during its deliberation. Although all the juries acquitted the defendant (possibly because of a weak overall case), it was found that the expert testimony significantly increased the length of deliberation and significantly lowered the jurors' general belief in the reliability of eyewitness testimony. Four student juries, who watched the trial on videotape, produced similar results.

Although some support for the use of expert testimony about eyewitness reliability has appeared in the legal literature (e.g., Woocher, 1977), the legal profession as a whole seems to have mixed opinions. A survey of legal practitioners in Florida reveals that attitudes about this issue are strongly related to one's position in the advocacy system (Brigham & Wolfskeil, 1983) (see Table 8-1). Since eyewitness identifications are so often used by the prosecution as evidence against defendants, it seems reasonable to expect that prosecutors would have favorable opinions about eyewitness testimony and unfavorable opinions about expert testimony that might undermine the impact of the eyewitness; defense attorneys would be expected to have opposite opinions. In the Florida survey the vast majority of prosecutors felt that judges and juries already placed the right amount of emphasis on eyewitness identifications, whereas the vast majority of defense attorneys thought that judges and juries placed too much emphasis on such evidence. As for the propriety of expert testimony about eyewitness identifications, 59 percent of the defense attorneys thought such experts should be called on fairly often or routinely, whereas

Table 8-1. Defense and Prosecuting Attorneys' Opinions about the Amount of Emphasis That Judges and Jurors Place on Eyewitness Evidence

		Emphasis on eyewitness evidence		
Opinion of		Too much (%)	Right amount (%)	Too little (%)
Defense attorneys	Judges	88.7	11.2	0
	Jurors	89.3	10.1	0.6
Prosecuting attorneys	Judges	7.4	86.8	5.1
	Jurors	23.5	54.4	22.1

Adapted from Brigham & Wolfskeil, 1983. Reprinted by permission of Plenum Publishing Corporation and the authors.

none of the prosecutors agreed with such frequent use of these experts.

There is also considerable disagreement about the appropriateness of expert testimony on eyewitness accuracy in the psychological literature. For example, in a series of articles appearing in the *American Psychologist,* McCloskey and Egeth (1983a, 1983b) argued against such interventions, while Loftus (1983a, 1983b) argued for them. McCloskey and Egeth's criticisms center on three main issues. One problem, they argue, is the lack of a sufficient empirical basis for expert testimony. They contend that it has not been shown that jurors' "overbelieve" eyewitnesses. In addition, they charge that the experts sometimes testify about how certain factors influence eyewitness accuracy on the basis of very little data. The second major issue is the impact of the expert testimony. McCloskey and Egeth point out that, while expert testimony may induce skepticism about eyewitness testimony, there is no empirical evidence indicating that expert testimony can help jurors discriminate accurate from inaccuarate eyewitnesses. They suggest that the expert testimony may even have the detrimental effect of creating more skepticism about eyewitness testimony than is warranted. Given the uncertain nature of knowledge about eyewitness accuracy, another possible side effect would be the use of psychologists by the prosecution to try to refute the expert testimony presented by the defense. Such a "battle of the experts" might,

according to McCloskey and Egeth, confuse jurors and damage
the image of psychology as a science. The third major criticism is
that advocates of expert testimony seem to be concerned about
acquittal of the innocent at the expense of not convicting the
guilty. McCloskey and Egeth suggest that by creating skepticism
about eyewitness testimony the experts may actually help guilty
defendants be acquitted.

Loftus views these issues quite differently. She contends that
the empirical basis for expert testimony on eyewitness accuracy is
sound. Besides the large amount of relevant research about perception and memory in general and about eyewitness accuracy in
particular, Loftus points out that survey data (Yarmey & Jones,
1983) indicate that there is a strong consensus among the experts
about eyewitness phenomena. With regard to the impact of expert
testimony Loftus agrees that the effects of such testimony have not
been adequately assessed; however, rather than abandoning the
practice, she suggests that further research be done to evaluate
the impact empirically. As for being more concerned about the
acquittal of the innocent than the conviction of the guilty, Loftus
admits that she views the former as more important but also points
out that whenever an innocent person is convicted a guilty person
goes free.

An additional problem with expert testimony on eyewitness
accuracy is that widespread use of such experts is not practical.
The testimony can be time-consuming and it depends on the availability of a small pool of qualified experts. Wells and Murray
(1983) suggest that a more practical alternative would be to
develop a standard set of instructions that could be routinely given
to jurors in cases involving eyewitness testimony. Expert testimony
would be reserved for a smaller number of cases in which more
specific information would be useful. It is interesting to note that,
in a precedent-setting case (*Neil* v. *Biggers,* 1972), the Supreme
Court developed five criteria for judging eyewitness accuracy. The
criteria were, however, based on judicial intuition rather than on
research. Wells and Murray point out that while the Court's criteria may seem reasonable, they are not consistent with research
findings. For example, one of the Court's criteria suggests that
confident eyewitnesses are more likely to be accurate than less
confident eyewitnesses. Although this criterion is intuitively

appealing, research generally indicates that there is little or no relationship between eyewitness confidence and eyewitness accuracy (e.g, Wells, Lindsay, & Ferguson, 1979). Wells and Murray conclude that it would be important to use the findings of psychological research as the basis for general instructions concerning eyewitness accuracy.

In summary, in recent years psychologists have testified as expert witnesses on the accuracy of eyewitness testimony. Those who have served in this capacity suggest that by hearing testimony about a well-established body of relevant research findings judges and juries will be better able to evaluate the accuracy of eyewitness testimony. Critics charge that such interventions are scientifically premature and may bias jurors against convictions. As a more practical, and perhaps more evenhanded, alternative it has been suggested that jurors be routinely given standard, research-based intructions about eyewitness phenomena in cases involving eyewitness testimony.

Utilization of Social Psychology by the Legal System

Although interventions by social psychologists in criminal and civil trials may have consequences for litigants involved in those cases, utilization of social psychological findings by legal policy setters may have a broader impact. For example, in Chapter 5 we saw that the Supreme Court's decision to desegregate public schools may have been based, in part, on a social science brief. Since that time there have been a few additional instances in which the Court has considered social psychological findings when making decisions with far-reaching consequences. Two such important issues are the size of juries and the way in which juries are chosen in capital cases.

Jury Size and Decision Rules

From a precedent dating back to fourteenth century England, a jury in the United States is traditionally comprised of 12 people who are required to reach a unanimous verdict. This tradition was maintained, virtually unquestioned, until a series of Supreme

Court decisions in the early 1970s allowed for juries with as few as six members and for nonunanimous verdicts. Unfortunately, these decisions have been based, in part, on a misuse of social science data.

Criticisms of the Court's decisions regarding jury size and decision rules have been most eloquently stated by social psychologist Saks (1977). In *Williams* v. *Florida* (1970) the Court ruled that six-person juries were acceptable because such juries would be sufficient in size to promote group deliberation, to resist outside intimidation, and to be representative of the community. This decision was based, in part, on six "experiments" that were cited in the Court's majority opinion. As Saks points out, however, these "experiments" were nothing more than "expressions of opinion based, if on any evidence at all, upon uncontrolled observations that might be likened to clinical case studies" (p. 9). In a subsequent decision (*Colgrove* v. *Battin,* 1973) the Supreme Court again ruled in favor of six-person juries, citing four empirical studies that indicated no discernible difference between the performance of 6- and 12-person juries. Although the studies cited in *Colgrove* were empirical, Saks argues that they were misinterpreted and methodologically flawed. Three of the studies were correlational, yet the Court seemed to draw causal conclusions. The fourth study was a simulation experiment that showed no difference in the verdicts rendered by 6- and 12-person juries (Kessler, 1973); however, the evidence presented in the simulation was so weak that none of the juries voted to convict. Subsequent research has shown that stronger prosecution evidence leads to significant differences in the verdicts rendered by 6- and 12-person juries (Valenti & Downing, 1975). Saks makes similar criticisms about the Supreme Court decisions to allow nonunanimous verdicts.

Dissatisfaction with the Court's misinterpretations of flawed data has prompted social scientists to attempt better studies of the effects of 6- versus 12-person juries and unanimous versus quorum juries. Perhaps the most carefully designed and comprehensive of these studies was done by Saks (1977). Subject-jurors were randomly assigned to 6- and 12-person juries and were shown a videotape of a staged trial. To enhance realism the trial was performed by experienced professionals, including a defense attorney, a prosecuting attorney, a former Supreme Court justice, and a police officer. The subject-juries were comprised of citizens who had previous experience as jurors. After viewing the trial each jury was randomly assigned to reach either a unanimous or a two-thirds majority verdict. There were, therefore, four experimental conditions—12-person unanimous, 6-person unanimous, 12-person quorum, and 6-person quorum juries. Several dependent measures were taken.

The results of Saks' experiment were complex, indicating that each kind of jury offered certain advantages. Compared to 6-person juries, some of the advantages of 12-person juries were longer deliberations, more communication per unit of time, better recall of testimony, and better representation of the community. On the other hand, in small juries there was more communication per member (although the overall amount of communication was greater in 12-person juries), more equally shared communications, and greater satisfaction with the group. Compared to quorum juries, unanimous juries deliberated longer, divided communications more equally, and were more certain when deciding to convict. Quorum juries, on the other hand, communicated more and were better able to remember arguments put forth during the deliberation. It is clear, therefore, that there are differences in the performance among the four types of juries. Which type is best is less clear. Saks suggests that to determine which is best one would need to begin by weighing the importance of each of the relevant measures. For example, in the *Williams* decision the Court stressed the importance of promoting deliberation, which would seem to favor unanimous 12-person juries. As an alternative to selecting one of the four types of juries, Saks suggests that a combination of the types might collectively produce more advantages than any one type. For example, he proposed the use of two simultaneous 6-person juries that would each be required to reach a two-thirds majority decision. To convict the defendant both juries would have to vote guilty. To the author's knowledge this proposal has never been put into effect in a real trial.

As a final note on jury size, in 1978 the Supreme Court (in *Ballew* v. *Georgia*) ruled that juries cannot have less than six members. Ironically, the Court cited social science data (including Saks, 1977) that indicated differences between 6- and 12-person juries. If 5-person juries are not allowed on the basis of these data, then why are 6-person juries allowed?

In summary, the Supreme Court has considered social science data when making decisions about jury size and decision rules. The Court has, however, misinterpreted the data, especially with regard to the differences between 6- and 12-person juries.

Death Qualification

In addition to the usual selection procedures, prospective jurors in capital cases must take part in a special voir dire to determine "death qualification." During this interview members of the jury panel are asked about their attitudes toward the death penalty. Anyone who is categorically opposed to capital punishment to the extent that he or she would not vote to impose the death penalty no matter what the circumstances is disqualified from serving as a juror in a capital case. The rationale for such excusals is that, since capital punishment is legal, a juror who would categorically refuse to impose it would not be able to carry out the law.

A possible negative side effect of death qualification is that it might produce juries that are biased toward convictions. In 1968 this complaint was brought before the Supreme Court in the case of *Witherspoon* v. *Illinois*. Eight years earlier Witherspoon had been convicted of first degree murder and sentenced to death by a death-qualified jury. In the qualification process 47 members of the jury panel were dismissed because of their attitudes about capital punishment. The argument that Witherspoon's attorneys presented to the Supreme Court was that people who are willing to impose the death penalty would be most likely to ignore instructions to presume innocence, to accept the prosecution's case, and to vote for conviction (Gross, 1983). At the time there was very little evidence to support these claims and the Supreme Court upheld the conviction. The Court was, however, sufficiently convinced to commute the death sentence. Of broader significance, the text of the Court's opinion suggested that subsequent modification, or elimination, of the death-qualifying voir dire might occur if it could be shown that the procedure is prejudicial to defendants (Gross, 1983).

Given that the *Witherspoon* opinion opened the door to further consideration of the possible biasing effect of the death-qualifying voir dire, several social scientists decided to study the effects of death qualification empirically. Indeed the National Jury Project supported relevant research studies that were directed by social psychologists Ellsworth and Haney (Gross, 1983). In general, the studies by Ellsworth and her associates clearly demonstrated that death-qualified subjects were significantly more pro-prosecution and conviction prone than were subjects who were excludable on the basis of death qualification but were otherwise eligible for jury service. These findings were obtained both in a survey of randomly selected citizens (Fitzgerald & Ellsworth, 1984) and in an experiment involving a videotape of a simulated murder trial (Cowan, Thompson, & Ellsworth, 1984) (see Table 8-2). The simulation also indicated that death-excludabe subjects remember the facts of the case better than the death-qualified subjects. In addition to the selection bias found by Ellsworth and her associates, Haney (1984) found that the process of death qualification may further bias jurors. A sample of subjects, who were all death-qualified, saw a videotape of a trial. For half of the subjects the videotape included a death-qualifying voir dire. It should be noted that it is common practice to have prospective jurors participate in a voir dire as a group, which means that each prospective juror will witness the questioning of other members of the jury panel. The other half of the subjects saw the same videotape without the death-qualifying voir dire. Afterward, subjects who saw the death qualification were more likely to think that the defendant was guilty than were those subjects who did not see that segment of the tape (see Table 8-3). Evidently, exposure to questioning about a punishment before the evidence is heard suggests that the defendant is guilty. In sum, the research indicates that death-qualified jurors are biased toward conviction and that this bias can be further exacerbated by the process of death qualification.

In 1980 the death-qualification studies (many in prepublication

Table 8-2. Percentages of Jurors Finding the Defendant Guilty Both Before and After Jury Deliberation

	Death-qualified (%)	Excludable (%)
Predeliberation	77.9	53.3
Postdeliberation	86.3	65.5

Adapted from Cowan, Thompson, & Ellsworth, 1984. Reprinted by permission of Plenum Publishing Corporation and the authors.

Table 8-3. Mean Estimate[a] of Likelihood of Defendant's Guilt and Likelihood of Death Penalty by Subject-Jurors Exposed/Not Exposed to Death Qualification Procedures

	Exposed to death qualification	Not exposed to death qualification
Guilt	46.7	36.2
Death penalty	39.6	24.5

[a]Estimates made on 100-point scales, with higher numbers meaning greater likelihood.

Adapted from Haney, 1984. Reprinted by permission of Plenum Publishing Corporation and the author.

form) were carefully reviewed by the California Supreme Court in the case of *Hovey* v. *Superior Court* (Gross, 1983). Similar to the *Witherspoon* case, Hovey's complaint was that his death-qualified jury was biased toward conviction. Although the court upheld Hovey's conviction, it did rule, mainly on the basis of Haney's data, that in California all future death-qualifying voir dires be sequestered. That is, to minimize the biasing effects of the process of death qualification, each prospective juror must be interviewed individually. Obviously, this ruling falls far short of what the social science data suggest, but it does seem to be a step in the right direction.

In summary, despite the Supreme Court's consideration of social science data indicating that death qualification leads to the selection of conviction-prone jurors and further biases those jurors toward conviction, the only change that has come about in the procedure is that in California the death-qualifying voir dire must now be sequestered.

Enhancing Utilization of Social Science Data

Given that relevant social science data have often been ignored or misused by the Supreme Court, Tanke and Tanke (1979) provide some suggestions to enhance utilization. First, they suggest that social scientists need to do a better job of anticipating which issues are likely to come before the Supreme Court. Once a case comes before the Court it is usually too late to collect data that will have a bearing on the case, and once a legal precedent has been set (e.g., legality of 6-person juries) it is difficult to change. To anticipate issues, Tanke and Tanke suggest that interested social scientists keep up-to-date with legal publications and with interest groups that are likely to raise legal questions. Second, once an issue has been identified, these social scientists should consult with legal experts in all phases of research, including formulating hypotheses, designing methodology, and analyzing results. Such consultation will help assure that the research addresses legally relevant questions in a manner that is compatible with legal decision making. Finally, Tanke and Tanke suggest that social scientists actively communicate their findings to the legal profession. This can be accomplished by publishing in legal journals, providing relevant findings to petitioners in appellate cases, presenting the Court with amicus curiae (friend of the court) briefs, and through expert testimony in a trial.

Summary and Conclusions

The potential applicability of social psychology to our legal system appears to be great. Legal proceedings are greatly influenced by interpersonal processes and legal decisions are often based on assumptions about human behavior that have been, and can be, studied by social psychologists. On the other hand, there are several barriers to the actual application of social psychology to law. There are problems with generalizing simulation experiments to actual legal phenomena. Legal practitioners are largely ignorant of relevant social psychological findings. The impact of legal applications of social psychology are hard to assess. Some steps have been taken to overcome these barriers. Greater care is being taken to design simulations that are as realistic as possible. Social psychologists are beginning to regularly publish in legal journals and work along with legal professionals. The issue of assessing impact remains, however, a particularly troublesome problem both for legal practitioners, who need to know what works, and for social scientists, who as scientists should carefully evaluate the effects of their applications. Further efforts to overcome the barriers, especially with regard to evaluation, may eventually help social psychology reach its potential as a contributor to the legal system.

Despite the barriers, there have been some actual uses of social psychology in legal matters. These applications have come in two (sometimes overlapping) general forms—direct intervention by social psychologists in legal proceedings, and utilization of social psychology findings by legal policy setters. The interventions include systematic jury selection and expert testimony about the accuracy of eyewitness testimony. The desirability of these interventions has been questioned on both ethical and scientific grounds. These criticisms underscore the problem raised above. Adequate evaluation of the impact of the techniques is important but lacking. With regard to utilization of social psychological findings, the Supreme Court has considered such data when making decisions about the size and decision rules of juries and about the process of death-qualifying jurors in capital cases. Although such utilizations could have potentially far-reaching effects, thus far there seems to have been as much misuse as use of the relevant findings.

One last point should be made. The classification of the applications described in this chapter as social psychological is admittedly more questionable than in other chapters of this volume. For one thing, applications to legal matters by social psychologists are typically more atheoretical than are applications to other social problems. That is, few of the legal applications are based on a social psychological theory. This may be because the questions (hypotheses) raised are determined more by what legal matters are of current importance than by the desire to test a scientific theory. In addition, almost all the applications described are multidisciplinary, involving the efforts of sociologists, cognitive psychologists, and lawyers, as well as social psychologists. This explains the frequent use of the term social science instead of social psychology in this chapter. Nevertheless, there are two good reasons to classify the applications reviewed here as social psychological: All the applications involve issues that fit into the general subject matter of social psychology, and there has been a substantial input by social psychologists in all the applications described.

Appendix

Glossary of Useful Social Psychological Theories, Principles, Concepts, and Techniques

Achievement motivation training involves a number of techniques designed to prompt striving for achievement. The main focus is on the characteristics of high achievers. These characteristics are described and the trainees are asked to think about them, discuss them, and incorporate them while participating in specially designed games. This kind of training has been used to help academic underachievers.

Attitude inoculation is a technique developed by McGuire (1964) that is used to strengthen resistance to attitudinal and behavioral change. Just as a medical inoculation involves exposing someone to a weak virus in order to activate defenses against a stronger contamination, attitude inoculation involves exposing someone to weak pressures to adopt an undesirable attitude or behavior in order to bolster defenses against stronger pressures. This technique has been used to help teenagers resist pressures to smoke, to drink, and to take drugs.

Attribution is the process by which all of us, as naïve psychologists, explain the behavior, motivations, and characteristics of people, including ourselves. Research on this process provides the basis for attribution therapy, which has been applied in the areas of clinical psychology and education.

Attribution therapy is a technique designed to help people overcome pathologically self-defeating explanations of their own behavior. Basically, it involves getting people to change attributions of their problem behaviors from causes that imply character flaws, which would be difficult to change, to more normal and more controllable causes. Once these new attributions are made, persons will realize that they can change their problem behaviors. This technique has been applied to a variety of problems in the areas of mental health and education.

Attributional-style therapy is a broadly focused form of attribution therapy. It is aimed at replacing a syndrome of habitually self-defeating attributions with a consistent pattern of self-enhancing attributions. This technique has been applied to the treatment of chronically low self-esteem and depression.

The *authoritarian personality,* identified by Adorno and his associates (1950), is characterized by a relatively unquestioning respect for authority. Authoritarians show great deference for superiors and expect great deference from subordinates. As part of a strategy of systematic jury selection, social scientists have advised defense attorneys to challenge the selection of authoritarian jurors when the defendants have had obvious antiestablishment views.

Body language refers to communication conveyed, often unintentionally, by body posture, hand movements, facial expressions, and eye contact. Interpretation of body language has been used in systematic jury selection.

The *bogus pipeline* is a technique developed by Jones and Sigall (1971) that is designed to increase the accuracy of self-report measures. Honest disclosures are induced by leading subjects to believe that their responses can be verified by a physiological measure. In applied research this technique has been used to increase the accuracy of self-reported cigarette smoking by teenagers.

A *cognitive coping strategy* is a technique designed to help people deal with stressful events. The basic strategy is to get people to attend to the positive aspects of an event rather than the negative aspects. This technique has been used to help surgical patients face upcoming operations.

Cognitive dissonance is a theory developed by Festinger (1957) that posits that people are motivated to maintain consistency among their attitudes and behaviors. Inconsistency, or dissonance, motivates attitudinal or behavioral change. For example, if I felt that violence is a good way to resolve problems but made a statement to the contrary, then I would feel pressure to change either my original attitude or my statement. This theory has been applied to mitigate the negative influence of televised violence on children and to increase the effectiveness of therapies in the areas of health and mental health.

The *commons tragedy* occurs when people use a widely available, but limited, resource for their own benefit without regard for the common need to conserve that resource. The tragedy is that the resource becomes depleted and all who rely on it suffer. This phenomenon has been used as a model for studying energy conservation.

The *communicator credibility effect* is a well-established principle of attitude and behavior change. Factors that increase a communicator's credibility, such as expertise and trustworthiness, have consistently been shown to enhance the persuasive impact of a communicator's message. The principle has been applied to inducing residential energy consumption.

A *community survey* is a technique used to gather information about people in a certain community. A sample of community members, usually selected at random, is asked questions about attitudes, beliefs, and behaviors. Demographic characteristics (e.g., race of respondent) are also noted. This technique has many uses in systematic jury selection.

Contingency model of leadership is a theory developed by Fiedler (1964) that holds that effective leadership depends on the relationship between one's leadership style and situational factors. According to the theory, good leaders are not born but rather emerge under the proper circumstances. An important implication of the theory is that an ineffective leader can become effective by changing the situation or by moving to a new situation. This theory has been applied to training leaders in various kinds of organizations, including business and the military.

Control, or at least the perception of control, over one's environment is important for maintaining both physical and mental health, whereas lack of actual or perceived control can have detrimental effects. This principle is the basis for reattribution therapy and for interventions designed to give the institutionally aged more control, or at least the perception of more control, over their everyday lives.

Cooperative classroom structures are teaching techniques that require students to work interdependently for common goals. The purpose of such structures is to mitigate some negative consequences of traditional classroom structures, which many social psychologists believe are overly competitive.

Coping models are used to enhance the therapeutic effects of vicarious extinction. A fearful person is shown a behavioral model who at first displays the same fears, but who also successfully overcomes those fears. This technique has been applied to help people overcome phobias, shyness, and anxiety about upcoming surgery.

Counterattitudinal advocacy is a technique of attitude change in which people are asked to argue against their own attitudes about a certain issue. According to the theory of cognitive dissonance, if people engage in counterattitudinal advocacy without feeling pressured to do so, they will tend to change their attitude toward the advocated position. This technique has been applied to mitigating the negative impact of televised violence on children.

Disinhibition is a principle that derives from social learning theory. Observing other people engage in socially disapproved behaviors reduces the observer's inhibitions about engaging in the same behaviors, thus increasing the likelihood of imitating the antisocial acts. This principle has been applied to the control of litter.

Effort justification is a principle that derives from cognitive dissonance theory. When people perceive that they have freely chosen to engage in an unpleasant or difficult task, they tend to justify their behavior, often by convincing themselves that the task was worthwhile. This principle has been used to increase the effectiveness of therapies in the areas of health and mental health.

Emotional role-playing is a technique developed by Janis and Mann (1965) designed to help people break self-destructive habits. Along with a psychologist, a person acts out several scenes in which he or she must deal with the negative consequences of a bad habit. The underlying rationale is that by "experiencing" the consequences, the person should become sufficiently motivated to break the habit. This technique has been used to help people quit smoking cigarettes.

Equity is a theory that provides a simple model of how people determine fairness in a wide variety of interpersonal relationships. According to the model, a feeling of fairness occurs when one perceives that his or her ratio of interpersonal inputs to outcomes is equal to that of other people. Inequity, which occurs when one's ratio of inputs to outcomes is not equal to that of others, produces unpleasant feelings, even for those who have the upper hand. Although the effects of inequity have been studied in such real-world settings as the workplace, there have been no real applications of the theory to solving the problems that inequity produces.

Even-a-penny is a technique developed by Cialdini and Schroeder (1976) that is designed to induce contributions to charity. The strategy is to finish a request for a donation by saying "even a penny will help." Presumably this phrase legitimizes small requests and takes away the convenient excuse of being short of money. Several studies have shown that this technique is highly successful in door-to-door campaigns.

Expectation effects generally refer to a tendency to observe what we expect to see. In one form, known as self-fulfilling prophecy, communication of one's expectations about others, even when subtle and unintentional, may actually cause those others to behave in a manner that is consistent with the expectations. Knowledge of this principle has led to interventions to help school teachers avoid communicating negative expectations to their students.

Field theory (Lewin, 1942, 1951) is a complex formulation of human social behavior that involves many constructs and mathematical representations. Borrowing from the gestalt view that "the whole is more than the sum of its parts," field theory emphasizes the interrelationships among elements. The most fundamental tenet of the theory is that behavior can be best understood by examining the context, or field, in which it occurs. Field theory was the basis for the technique of group (worker) participation in decision making.

Foot-in-the-door is a technique designed to induce compliance with a request by first asking for a small favor. Like the door-to-door salesperson who increases his or her chances of a sale by getting in the door, compliance with a small request increases the chances that a person will subsequently comply with a larger request (Freedman & Fraser, 1966). This technique has been successfully applied to encouraging conservation of resources, inducing donations to charity, and prompting involvement in a recycling program.

Group dynamics, which is a major area of inquiry in social psychology, generally refers to all the ways that individuals are influenced by other members of a group. The principles of group dynamics have been applied to many problems, including poor productivity in the workplace and prejudicial biases in jury trials.

Groups-investigation is a cooperative classroom structure in which small, multiethnic groups of students work together to investigate a topic with the goal of making group presentations. This technique has been applied to reducing ethnic prejudice in schools.

Group (worker) participation is a technique designed to reduce resistance to change. Based on Lewin's field theory, acceptance of change is facilitated by allowing people to actively participate in the decision-making process. This technique has been applied to such diverse goals as altering eating habits and instituting modifications in the workplace.

Hawthorne effects are inadvertent increases in morale and motivation that can occur when people realize that they are in a new experimental program. Such effects may make the specific aspects of an experimental program appear to be effective when, in fact, it is merely the attention and change that the participants experience that produce the positive results. In the Western Electric studies the discovery of these effects led researchers who were investigating scientific management to realize the importance of human relations in the workplace. Eventually, the human relations approach to organizations led to techniques designed to improve interpersonal relationships in the workplace, such as worker participation and sensitivity training.

Informational social influence is, according to Deutsch and Gerard (1955), one of two general reasons that people conform to the behavior of others. It is assumed that when people are uncertain about how to respond to a given situation they are particularly susceptible to social influence. Normative social influence is the pressure we feel to act in a manner that is acceptable to others and is motivated by fear of rejection from the group. In contrast, informational social influence is a more dispassionate process in which we use other people's behavior as a source of information about appropriate responses to a situation. Information designed to prompt informational social influence has been used to induce donations to charity.

Informal structure is a principle of group dynamics that serves as a basis for the human relations approach to organizations. Groups, especially organizations, typically have explicit rules that provide a formal structure for how things are to be done. In addition, implicit rules and ways of interacting usually develop spontaneously, thus providing an informal structure. The realization that informal structures exist and can have a great influence on morale and productivity helped pave the way for the human relations approach to organizations, which includes techniques such as worker participation and sensitivity training.

The *interracial contact hypothesis* suggests that bringing people of various races together for prolonged periods of time will help dispel negative stereotypes, thus providing conditions for reduced prejudice and discrimination. This notion was presented to the Supreme Court and apparently influenced its decision to order desegregation of public schools.

The *jigsaw classroom* is a cooperative classroom structure developed by Aronson and his associates (Aronson, Stephan, Sikes, Blaney, & Snapp, 1978) that is designed to reduce racial tension and to improve academic performance in desegregated schools. The basic strategy is to promote cooperation by requiring that each student learn a part of a lesson and teach his or her part to others.

Labeling is a technique that can induce behavior that is consistent with the label. The underlying principle is that people will tend to use feedback from others to form self-perceptions and to guide their behavior. Applications of this technique have prompted energy-conscious self-perceptions and charitable behavior.

Leader match is a technique of leadership training based on Fiedler's contingency model. By using a self-paced manual, leaders can identify their own leadership style and assess how well that style matches their leadership situations. A good match is predictive of success, while a poor match can be remedied by following suggestions in the manual. This technique has been applied to training leaders in various kinds of organizations, including business and the military.

Learned helplessness is a condition, prompted by experiences with uncontrollable outcomes, in which animals, including humans, fail to see the connection between what they do (behavior) and what happens to them (outcomes). This condition, first identified by Seligman (1975), leads to an impaired ability to learn, lack of motivation, and depression. The realization that for humans this condition is cognitively mediated has led to the development of attributional therapies designed to induce people to attribute their outcomes to controllable causes.

Minimal justification occurs when someone engages in an activity with little or no external incentive. Both cognitive dissonance and self-perception theories predict that subsequent motivation to engage in the minimally justified behavior should increase. This technique has been used to increase commitment to a variety of programs, including those designed to induce recycling and to maintain weight loss.

Misattribution occurs when a person attributes a physiological sensation to an incorrect cause. It has been hypothesized that such misattributions may account for many psychosomatic diseases. Knowledge of this principle has led to techniques for curing certain maladies that may not have a physical cause, such as insomnia.

Multiple regression is a statistical technique used to predict individual scores on a certain variable (generally called the criterion variable) from scores on a related set of variables (generally called predictor variables). First, sample data are used to calculate a mathematical equation that weights and combines the predictor variables in a manner that provides the best linear relationship between the set of predictors and the criterion. Once this equation is obtained it can be used to predict scores on the criterion variable when only data on the predictor variables are available. This technique has been applied to systematic jury selection in order to predict which prospective jurors are likely to be favorable or unfavorable to the defense.

Norm activation, a theory developed by Schwartz (1970), suggests that people are most likely to conform to a societal norm when they (a) are aware that noncompliance will have negative consequences for others, and (b) take personal responsibility for the negative consequences. Research indicates that when either of these two conditions is lacking people are not likely to comply with the norm.

Personal causation training involves training teachers to encourage their students to view themselves as independent initiators of their own behavior (Origins) rather than as dependent responders to other people's wishes (Pawns). The underlying rationale is that if students were treated like independent decision makers, then they would begin to view themselves as causal agents and develop intrinsic motivation to achieve.

Public commitment to an attitude, which basically means expressing an attitude to others, increases the probability that one's behavior will be consistent with the expressed attitude. This principle, first identified by Kiesler (1971), has been used by other social psychologists to induce energy conservation and to help teenagers resist the temptation to smoke cigarettes.

Reactance theory, developed by Brehm (1966), posits that we react to a threat to a freedom by trying to exercise that freedom. For example, some research indicates that "Don't Litter" signs, which may be interpreted as a command that leaves no freedom of choice, may actually elicit the behavior they are intended to inhibit.

Self-fulfilling prophecy is a kind of expectation effect in which one person's expectations about the behavior of a second person actually cause the second person to act in the expected manner. Knowledge of this principle, and its sometimes harmful effects on students' self-perceptions, has led to interventions to help school teachers avoid communicating negative expectations to their students.

Self-perception theory (Bem, 1972) suggests that we learn about ourselves by observing our own behaviors and the circumstances under which those behaviors occur. If a compelling circumstance precedes one of our behaviors, we tend to attribute the behavior to the situation, but if the situation is not so compelling, we tend to view our behavior as evidence about our enduring internal characteristics. It has been suggested that self-perception theory expains the foot-in-the-door effect, which has been successfully applied to encouraging conservation of resources, eliciting donations to charity, and prompting involvement in a recycling program.

Sensitivity training is a technique, based primarily on Lewin's principles of group dynamics, that is designed to improve interpersonal skills. Individuals, usually strangers, are put into small groups and are encouraged to interact with one another in an open, frank, and nearly unrestrained manner. The goal is to achieve greater sensitivity about how one influences, and is perceived by, others. This kind of training has been used to help foster better interpersonal relationships in the workplace.

Sensory deprivation is a treatment in which a person spends a period of time in the virtual absence of sensory stimuli. Light, sound, smell, taste, tactile stimuli, and movement are reduced to a minimum. It has been hypothesized that such deprivation produces hypersuggestibility, which may facilitate attitudinal and behavioral change. This treatment has been used to help cigarette smokers to quit smoking.

Simulation is a research technique in which some aspects of a real-world situation are mimicked in a laboratory study. The goal is to study the dynamics of a real-world situation in a controlled setting. Simulations have been used quite extensively to investigate the social psychology of the courtrooom.

Social comparison is a theory developed by Festinger (1954). Based on the premise that we all have a need to evaluate ourselves, the theory suggests that we will compare ourselves to similar others and modify our behavior so that we compare favorably. This theory has been applied to inducing people to conserve energy.

Social learning theory (Bandura 1977) suggests that people acquire behaviors primarily through observation and imitation of other people. Imitation of a behavioral model is especially likely under the following conditions: (a) the model is attractive, powerful, salient, or otherwise captures the observer's attention; (b) the behavior can be readily retained by the observer; (c) the observer has opportunities to reproduce or rehearse the behavior; and (d) the observer sees that the model is rewarded for the behavior. Applications of the theory have been successful in enhancing the effects of prosocial television, mitigating the effects of aggressive television shows, teaching leadership skills, and preventing behaviors that are dangerous for health.

The *specificity hypothesis* suggests that an attitude is predictive of a behavior when both are assessed at at a high level of specificity. For example, a favorable attitude about vegetables in general might not be predictive of eating asparagus, but a favorable attitude about asparagus should predict eating of that vegetable. An implication is that certain behaviors can be modified by changing specific attitudes.

Student teams is a technique developed by DeVries and Slavin (1978) that is designed to promote cooperation, cross-racial friendships, and greater academic achievement. Teams—each comprised of a mixture of students including both sexes, various ethnic groups, and various levels of ability— first tutor one another and then compete against other teams in an academic contest (Teams-Games-Tournament) or on more traditional academic tests (Student Teams and Achievement Divisions).

Superordinate goals are desired objectives that can be achieved only if individuals, or groups of individuals, pool their efforts and work together. Such goals have been used in educational settings to promote cooperation and mutual attraction among students.

Symbolic vicarious extinction is a social learning technique in which a fearful person is shown a filmed model who effectively deals with the source of anxiety. It has been used to help people overcome phobias, shyness, and the anxiety associated with upcoming surgery.

Systematic jury selection refers to social science techniques that have been used to help defense attorneys secure juries that are not unfavorably biased toward their clients. The techniques used include community surveys, observations of prospective jurors, applications of group dynamics, and statistical analyses, such as multiple regression.

The *Type A behavior pattern,* characterized by high levels of competitiveness, time urgency, and aggressiveness, is associated with an increased incidence of coronary heart disease. Although it has been hypothesized that this pattern of behavior may develop from, and be fostered by, social factors, as yet there are no social psychological interventions designed to reduce Type A behavior.

Veridical reattribution is a therapeutic technique that involves truthfully pointing out to a patient that behavior that may seem to be abnormal can be expained as normal reactions to certain events. This technique has been used to treat a number of psychological disorders.

Vicarious consequences are the rewards and punishments that we observe other people getting. According to social learning theory, vicarious rewards increase the probability that an observer will engage in the observed behavior, whereas vicarious punishments decrease the likelihood of imitative responses. This principle has served as the basis for some interventions designed to reduce the likelihood that children will develop the aggressive behaviors that they see on television.

Vicarious extinction is a technique designed to help people overcome anxiety about a certain event or object. Derived from social learning theory, the technique involves showing the anxious person a behavioral model who effectively deals with the source of anxiety. This technique has been used to reduce anxiety about a variety of objects and events, including phobias and upcoming surgery.

References

Adams, J. S. (1965). Inequity in social exchange. In L. Berkowitz (Ed.), *Advances in experimental social psychology* (Vol. 2). New York: Academic Press.

Adams, J. S., & Freedman, S. (1976). Equity theory revisited: Comments and annotated bibliography. In L. Berkowitz & E. Walster (Eds.), *Advances in experimental social psychology* (Vol. 9). New York: Academic Press.

Adams, J. S., & Rosenbaum, W. B. (1962). The relationship of worker productivity to cognitive dissonance about wage inequities. *Journal of Applied Psychology, 46,* 161–164.

Adorno, T. W., Frenkel-Brunswik, E., Levinson, D., & Sanford, N. (1950). *The authoritarian personality.* New York: Harper & Row.

Allen, C. T. (1982). Self-perception based strategies for stimulating energy conservation. *Journal of Consumer Research, 8,* 381–390.

Allport, G. (1954). *The nature of prejudice.* Reading, MA: Addison-Wesley.

Allport, G. W. (1968). The historical background of modern social psychology. In G. Lindzey & E. Aronson (Eds.), *The handbook of social psychology* (Vol. 1, 2nd ed., pp. 1–80). Reading, MA: Addison-Wesley.

Andrews, G. R., & Dubus, R. L. (1978). Persistence and the causal perception of failure: Modifying cognitive attributions. *Journal of Educational Psychology, 70,* 154–166.

Andrews, L. B. (1982, March). Mind control in the courtroom. *Psychology Today,* 66–73.

Arbuthnot, J., Tedeschi, R., Wayner, M., Turner, J., Kressel, S., & Rush, R. (1976–1977). The induction of sustained recycling behavior through the foot-in-the-door technique. *Journal of Environmental Systems, 6,* 355–368.

Arkin, R. M., Roemhild, H. F., Johnson, C. A., Luepker, R. V., & Murray, D. M. (1981, November). The Minnesota smoking prevention program: A seventh-grade health curriculum supplement. *Journal of School Health,* 611–616.

Aronson, E., & Mills, J. (1959). The effect of severity of initiation on liking for a group. *Journal of Abnormal and Social Psychology, 59,* 177–181.

Aronson, E., & Osherow, N. (1980). Cooperation, social behavior, and academic performance: Experiments in the desegregated classroom. In L. Bickman (Ed.), *Applied social psychology annual* (Vol. 1). Beverly Hills, CA: Sage Publications.

Aronson, E., Stephan, C., Sikes, J., Blaney, N., & Snapp, M. (1978). *The jigsaw classroom.* Beverly Hills, CA: Sage Publications.

Aronson, E., & Yates, S. (1983). Cooperation in the classroom: The impact of the jigsaw method on inter-ethnic relations, classroom performance and self-esteem. In H. H. Blumberg, A. P. Hare, V. Kent, & M. F. Davies (Eds.), *Small groups and social interaction.* New York: John Wiley.

Austin, W., & Walster, E. (1974). Reactions to confirmation and disconfirmations of expectancies of equity and inequity. *Journal of Personality and Social Psychology, 30,* 208–216.

Axsom, D., & Cooper, J. (1981). Reducing weight by reducing dissonance: The role of effort justification in inducing weight loss. In E. Aronson (Ed.), *Readings about the social animal* (3rd ed.). San Francisco: Freeman.

Ayllon, T. & Azrin, N. H. (1964). Reinforcement and instructions with mental patients. *Journal of the Experimental Analysis of Behavior, 7,* 327–331.

Babad, E. Y., Inbar, J., & Rosenthal, R. (1982). Teachers' judgement of students' potential as a function of teachers' susceptibility to biasing information. *Journal of Personality and Social Psychology, 42,* 541–547.

Backman, C. W., & Secord, P. F. (1968). *A social psychological view of education.* New York: Harcourt, Brace & World.

Bandura, A. (1963, October 22). What TV violence can do to your child. *Look,* pp. 46–52.

Bandura, A. (1965). Vicarious processes: A case of no-trial learning. In L. Berkowitz (Ed.), *Advances in experimental social psychology* (Vol. 2). New York: Academic Press.

Bandura, A. (1969a). *Principles of behavior modification.* New York: Holt, Rinehart and Winston.

Bandura, A. (1969b). Theoretical approaches to socialization. In D. A. Goslin (Ed.), *Handbook of socialization theory and research.* Chicago: Rand McNally.

Bandura, A. (1971). *Social learning theory.* New York: General Learning Press.

Bandura, A. (1977). *Social learning theory.* Englewood Cliffs, NJ: Prentice-Hall.

Bandura, A., Grusec, J. E., & Menlove, F. L. (1967). Vicarious extinction of avoidance behaviors. *Journal of Personality and Social Psychology, 5,* 16–23.

Bandura, A., & Menlove, F. L. (1968). Factors determining vicarious extinction of avoidance behavior through symbolic modeling. *Journal of Personality and Social Psychology, 8,* 99–108.

Bandura, A., Ross, D., & Ross, S. (1961). Transmission of aggression through imitation of aggressive models. *Journal of Abnormal and Social Psychology, 63,* 575–582.

Bandura, A., Ross, D., & Ross, S. (1963). Imitation of film-mediated aggressive models. *Journal of Abnormal and Social Psychology, 66,* 3–11.

Bandura, A., & Walters, R. H. (1963). *Social learning and personality development.* New York: Holt, Rinehart and Winston.

Becker, L. J., & Seligman, C. (1978). Reducing air conditioning waste by signalling it is cool outside. *Personality and Social Psychology Bulletin, 4,* 412–415.

Bem, D. J. (1965). An experimental analysis of self-persuasion. *Journal of experimental social psychology, 1,* 199–218.

Bem, D. J. (1968). Attitudes as self-descriptions: Another look at the attitude-behavior link. In A. G. Greenwald, T. C. Brock, & T. M. Ostrom (Eds.), *Psychological foundations of attitudes.* New York: Academic Press.

Bem, D. J. (1972). Self-perception theory. In L. Berkowitz (Ed.), *Advances in experimental social psychology* (Vol. 6). New York: Academic Press.

Berk, R. A. (1976). Social science and jury selection: A case study of a civil suit. In G. Bermant, C. Nemeth, & N. Vidmar (Eds.), *Psychology and the law: Research frontiers.* Lexington, MA: Lexington Books.

Berkowitz, L. (1974). Some determinants of impulsive aggression: Role mediated associations with reinforcement for aggression. *Psychological Review, 81,* 165–176.

Bernstein, D. A., & McAlister, A. (1976). The modification of smoking behavior: Progress and problems. *Addictive Behavior, 1,* 89–102.

Best, J. A., Flay, B. R., Towson, S. M. J., Ryan, K. B., Perry, C. L., Brown, K. S., Kersell, M. W., & D'Avernas, J. B. (1984). Smoking prevention and the concept of risk. *Journal of Applied Social Psychology, 14,* 257–273.

Best, J. A., & Suedfeld, P. (1982). Restricted environmental stimulation therapy and behavioral self-management in smoking cessation. *Journal of Applied Social Psychology, 12,* 408–419.

Bickman, L. (1972). Environmental attitudes and actions. *Journal of Social Psychology, 87,* 323–324.

Bickman, L. (1980). Introduction. In L. Bickman (Ed.), *Applied social psychology annual* (Vol. 1). Beverly Hills, CA: Sage Publications.

Blaney, N., Stephan, C., Rosenfield, D., Aronson, E., & Sikes, J. (1977). Interdependence in the classroom: A field study. *Journal of Educational Psychology, 69,* 121–128.

Bonora, B., Linder, R., Christie, R., & Schulman, J. (1983). Selecting a jury. In B. Bonora & E. Krauss (Eds.), *Jurywork: Systematic techniques* (2nd ed.). New York: Clark Boardman.

Bonora, B., & Krauss, E. (1979). *Jurywork: Systematic techniques.* Berkeley, CA: National Jury Project.

Bonora, B., & Krauss, E. (Eds.). (1983). *Jurywork: Systematic techniques* (2nd ed.). New York: Clark Boardman.

Bootzin, R. R., Herman, C. P., & Nicassio, P. (1976). The power of suggestion: Another examination of misattribution and insomnia. *Journal of Personality and Social Psychology, 34,* 673–674.

Bray, R., & Kerr, N. (1982). Methodological considerations in the study of the psychology of the courtroom. In N. Kerr & R. Bray (Eds.), *The psychology of the courtroom.* New York: Academic Press.

Brehm, J. W. (1966). *A theory of psychological reactance.* New York: Academic Press.

Bridgeman, D. L. (1981). Enhanced role taking through cooperative interdependence: A field study. *Child Development, 52,* 1231–1238.

Brigham, J. C., & Barkowitz, P. (1978). Do "they all look alike?" The effect of race, sex, experience, and attitudes on the ability to recognize faces. *Journal of Applied Social Psychology, 8,* 306–318.

Brigham, J. C., & Bothwell, R. K. (1983). The ability of prospective jurors to estimate the accuracy of eyewitness identifications. *Law and Human Behavior, 7,* 19–30.

Brigham, J. C., & Wolfskeil, M. P. (1983). Opinions of attorneys and law enforcement personnel on the accuracy of eyewitness identifications. *Law and Human Behavior, 7,* 337–349.

Brophy, J. E., & Good, T. L. (1974). *Teacher-student relationships: Causes and consequences.* New York: Holt, Rinehart and Winston.

Bryan, J. & Test, M. (1967). Models and helping: Naturalistic studies in aiding behavior. *Journal of Personality and Social Psychology, 6,* 400–407.

Buckhout, R. (1974). Eyewitness testimony. *Scientific American, 231* (6), 22–31.

Burn, S. M., & Oskamp, S. (1984, April). *Increasing recycling with persuasive communication and public commitment.* Paper presented at the meeting of the Western Psychological Association. Los Angeles.

Burnett, J. J., & Wilkes, R. E. (1980). Fear appeals to segments only. *Journal of Advertising Research, 20,* 21–24.

Campbell, J. P., & Dunnette, M. D. (1968). Effectiveness of T-group experiences in managerial training and development. *Psychological Bulletin, 70,* 73–104.

Carver, C. S., Coleman, A. E., & Glass, D. C. (1976). The coronary-prone behavior pattern and the suppression of fatigue on a treadmill. *Journal of Personality and Social Psychology, 33,* 460–466.

Center for Disease Control. (1975). *Ten leading causes of death in the United States.* Atlanta, GA: Author.

Chaikin, A., Sigler, E., & Derlega, V. (1974). Nonverbal mediators of teacher expectancy effects. *Journal of Personality and Social Psychology, 30,* 144–149.

Chapin, M., & Dyck, D. G. (1976). Persistence in children's reading behavior as a function of N length and attribution retraining. *Journal of Abnormal Psychology, 85,* 511–515.

Christie, R. (1976). Probability v. precedence: The social psychology of jury selection. In G. Bermant, C. Nemeth, & N. Vidmar (Eds.), *Psychology and the Law: Research frontiers.* Lexington, MA: Lexington Books.

Cialdini, R. B., & Schroeder, D. A. (1976). Increasing contributions by legitimizing paltry contributiions: When even a penny helps. *Journal of Personality and Social Psychology, 34,* 599–604.

Cialdini, R. B., Vincent, J. E., Lewis, S. K., Catalan, J., Wheeler, D., & Darby, B. L. (1975). A reciprocal concessions procedure for inducing compliance: The door-in-the-face technique. *Journal of Personality and Social Psychology, 21,* 206–215.

Clark, J. V. (1958). *A Preliminary Investigation of Some Unconscious Assumptions Affecting Labor Efficiency in Eight Supermarkets.* Unpublished Ph.D. dissertation, Harvard University, Cambridge, MA.

Clark, K. B. (1979). The role of social scientists 25 years after Brown. *Personality and Social Psychology Bulletin, 5,* 477–481.

Clark, K. B., & Clark, M. P. (1947). Racial identification and preference in Negro children. In T. M. Newcomb & E. L. Hartley (Eds.), *Readings in social psychology.* New York: Holt, Rinehart and Winston.

Clifford, M., & Walster, E. (1973). The effect of physical attractiveness on teacher expectation. *Sociology of Education, 46,* 248.

Coates, B., Pusser, H. E., & Goodman, I. (1976). The influence of "Sesame Street" and "Mister Rogers' Neighborhood" on children's social behavior in preschool. *Child Development, 47,* 138–144.

Coch, L., & French, J. R. P., Jr. (1948). Overcoming resistance to change. *Human Relations, 1,* 512–532.

Conger, J. C., & Keane, S. P. (1981). Social skills intervention in the treatment of isolated or withdrawn children. *Psychological Bulletin, 90,* 478–495.

Cook, T. D., & Flay, B. R. (1978). The persistence of experimentally induced attitude change. In L. Berkowitz (Ed.), *Advances in experimental social psychology* (Vol. 11). New York: Academic Press.

Cooper, H. M. (1979). Pygmalion grows up: A model for teacher expectation, communication and performance influence. *Review of Educational Research, 49,* 389–410.

Cooper, J. (1980). Reducing fears and increasing assertiveness: The role of dissonance reduction. *Journal of Experimental Social Psychology, 16,* 199–213.

Cooper, J., & Axsom, D. (1982). Effort justification in psychotherapy. In G. Weary & H. L. Mirels (Eds.), *Integrations of clinical and social psychology.* New York: Oxford University Press.

Cowan, C. L., Thompson, W. C., & Ellsworth, P. C. (1984). The effects of death qualification on jurors' predisposition to convict and on the quality of deliberations. *Law and Human Behavior, 8,* 53–79.

Craig, C. S., & McCann, J. M. (1978). Assessing communication effects on energy conservation. *Journal of Consumer Research, 5,* 82–88.

Crano, W. D. (1970). Effects of sex, response order, and expertise in conformity: A dispositional approach. *Sociometry, 33,* 239–252.

Crisci, R., & Kassinove, H. (1973). Effect of perceived expertise, strength of advice, and environmental setting on parental compliance. *Journal of Social Psychology, 89,* 245–250.

Crowne, D. P., & Marlowe, D. (1964). *The approval motive.* New York: John Wiley.

Davison, G. (1966). Differential relaxation and cognitive restructuring in therapy with a "paranoid schizophrenic" or "paranoid state." Proceedings of the American Psychological Association, 177–178.

deCharms, R. (1972). Personal causation training in the schools. *Journal of Applied Social Psychology, 2,* 95–113.

deCharms, R. (1976). *Enhancing motivation: Change in the classroom.* New York: Irvington.

Dembroski, T. M., Lasater, T. M., & Ramirez, A. (1978). Communicator similarity, fear growing communications, and compliance with health care recommendations. *Journal of Applied Social Psychology, 8,* 254–269.

Dembroski, T. M., MacDougall, J. M., & Shields, J. L. (1977). Physiological reactions to social challenge in persons evidencing the type A coronary-prone behavior pattern. *Journal of Human Stress, 3* (3), 2–9.

Deutsch, M. (1949). An experimental study of the effects of cooperation and competition upon group process. *Human Relations, 2,* 199–231.

Deutsch, M. (1980). Socially relevant research: Comments on "applied" versus "basic" research. In R. F. Kidd & M. J. Saks (Eds.), *Advances in applied social psychology* (Vol. 1). Hillsdale, NJ: Lawrence Erlbaum Associates.

Deutsch, M., & Gerard, H. (1955). A study of normative and informational social influences upon individual judgement. *Journal of Abnormal and Social Psychology, 51,* 629–636.

DeVries, D. L., & Slavin, R. E. (1978). Teams-Games-Tournament: Review of ten classroom experiments. *Journal of Research and Development in Education, 12,* 28–38.

De Young, R. (1984, May/June). Motivating people to recycle: The use of incentives. *Resource Recycling, 14–15,* 42.

Diener, E., & DeFour, D. (1978). Does television violence enhance program popularity? *Journal of Personality and Social Psychology, 36,* 333–341.

Dillehay, R. C., & Nietzel, M. T. (1980). Contructing a science of jury behavior. In L. Wheeler (Ed.), *Review of personality and social psychology* (Vol. 1). Beverly Hills, CA: Sage.

Drabman, R. S., & Thomas, M. H. (1975). Does TV violence breed indifference? *Journal of Communication, 25,* 86–89.

Dweck, C. S. (1975). The role of expectations and attributions in the alleviation of learned helplessness. *Journal of Personality and Social Psychology, 31,* 674–685.

Dweck, C. S., & Licht, B. G. (1980). Learned helplessness and intellectual achievement. In J. Garber & M. E. P. Seligman (Eds.), *Human helplessness: Theory and applications.* New York: Academic Press.

Dweck, C. S., & Repucci, N. D. (1973). Learned helplessness and reinforcement in children. *Journal of Personality and Social Psychology, 25,* 109–117.

Ebbesen, E. B., & Konečni, V. J. (1975). Decision making and information integration in the courts: The setting of bail. *Journal of Personality and Social Psychology, 32,* 805–821.

Edney, J. J. (1979). The nuts game: A concise commons dilemma analog. *Environmental Psychology and Nonverbal Behavior, 3* (4), 252–254.

Ekman, P., & Friesen, W. V. (1974). Detecting deception from body or face. *Journal of Personality and Social Psychology, 29,* 288–298.

Eron, L. D. (1982). Parent-child interaction, television violence, and aggression of children. *American Psychologist, 37,* 197–211.

Etgar, M., & Goodwin, S. A. (1982). One-sided versus two-sided comparative message appeals for new brand introductions. *Journal of Consumer Research, 8,* 460–465.

Etzioni, A. (1974). Creating an imbalance. *Trial, 10*(6), 28, 30.

Evans, R. I. (1976). Smoking in children: Developing a social psychological strategy of deterrence. *Preventive Medicine, 5,* 122–127.

Evans, R. I. (1980). A new applied challenge to social psychologists: Behavioral medicine. In L. Bickman (Ed.), *Applied Social Psychology Annual* (Vol. 1). Beverly Hills, CA: Sage Publications.

Evans, R. I., Hansen, W. B., & Mittelmark, M. B. (1978). Increasing the validity of self-reports of behavior in a smoking in children investigation. *Journal of Applied Psychology, 62,* 521–523.

Evans, R. I., Henderson, A. H., Hill, P. C., & Raines, B. E. (1979). Current psychological, social, and educational programs in the control and preventing of smoking: A critical methodological review. *Atherosclerosis Reviews, 6,* 203–245.

Evans, R. I., Rozelle, R. M., Lasater, T. M., Dembroski, T. M., & Allen, B. P. (1968). New measure of effects of persuasive communications: A chemical indicator of toothbrushing behavior. *Psychological Reports, 23,* 731–736.

Evans, R. I., Rozelle, R. M., Lasater, T. M., Dembroski, T. M., & Allen, B. P. (1970). Fear arousal persuasion, and actual versus implied behavior change: New perspective utilizing a real-life dental hygiene program. *Journal of Personality and Social Psychology, 16,* 220–227.

Evans, R. I., Rozelle, R. M., Maxwell, S. E., Raines, B .E., Dill, C. A., Guthrie, T. J., Henderson, A. H., & Hill, P. C. (1981). Social modeling films to deter smoking in adolescents: Results of a three year field investigation. *Journal of Applied Psychology, 66,* 399–414.

Evans, R. I., Rozelle, R. M., Mittelmark, M. B., Hansen, W. B., Bane, A. L., & Havis, J. (1978). Deterring the onset of smoking in children: Knowledge of immediate physiological effects and coping with peer pressure, media pressure, and parent modeling. *Journal of Applied Social Psychology, 8,* 126–135.

Evans, R. I., Rozelle, R. M., Noblitt, R., & Williams, D. L. (1975). Feedback and unintentional treatment effects as deterrents of behavior reversion in persuasive communication: New perspective utilizing a real life dental hygiene situation. *Journal of Applied Social Psychology, 5,* 150–156.

Festinger, L. (1954). A theory of social comparison processes. *Human Relations, 7,* 117–140.

Festinger, L. (1957). *A theory of cognitive dissonance.* Stanford, CA: Stanford University Press.

Festinger, L. (1961). The psychological effects of insufficient reward. *American Psychologist, 16,* 1–11.

Fiedler, F. E. (1964). A contingency model of leadership effectiveness. In

L. Berkowitz (Ed.), *Advances in experimental social psychology* (Vol. 1). New York: Academic Press.

Fiedler, F. E. (1978). The contingency model and dynamics of the leadership process. In L. Berkowitz (Ed.), *Advances in experimental social psychology* (Vol. 2). New York: Academic Press.

Fiedler, F. E., Chemers, M. M., & Mahar, L. (1976). *Improving leadership effectiveness: The Leader Match concept.* New York: John Wiley.

Fiedler, F. E., & Mahar, L. (1979a). The effectiveness of contingency model training: A review of the validation of Leader Match. *Personnel Psychology, 32,* 45–62.

Fiedler, F. E., & Mahar, L. (1979b). A field experiment validating contingency model leadership training. *Journal of Applied Psychology, 64,* 247–254.

Finnie, W. C. (1973). Field experiments in litter control. *Environment and Behavior, 5,* 123–144.

Fisher, R. J. (1982). *Social psychology: An applied approach.* New York: St. Martin's Press.

Fitzgerald, R., & Ellsworth, P. C. (1984). Due process vs. crime control: Death-qualification and jury attitudes. *Law and Human Behavior, 8,* 31–51.

Freedman, J. L., & Fraser, S. C. (1966). Compliance without pressure: The foot-in-the-door technique. *Journal of Personality and Social Psychology, 4,* 195–202.

French, J. R. P., Jr., Israel, J, & As, D. (1960). An experiment in participation in a Norwegian factory. *Human Relations, 13,* 3–19.

Friedrich, L. K., & Stein, A. H. (1973). Aggressive and prosocial television programs and the natural behavior of preschool children. *Monographs of the Society for Research in Child Development, 38* (4, Serial No. 151).

Friedrich, L. K., & Stein, A. H. (1975). Prosocial behavior and young children: The effects of verbal labeling and role playing on learning and behavior. *Child Development, 46,* 27–38.

Friedrich-Cofer, L. K., Huston-Stein, A., Kipnis, D. M., Susman, E. J., & Clewett, A. S. (1979). Environmental enhancement of prosocial television content: Effects of interpersonal behavior, imaginative play, and self-regulation in a natural setting. *Developmental Psychology, 15,* 637–646.

Geffner, R. (1978). *The effects of interdependent learning on self-esteem, inter-ethnic relations, and intra-ethnic attitudes of elementary school children: A field experiment.* Unpublished doctoral dissertation, University of California at Santa Cruz.

Geller, E. S., Chaffee, J. L., & Ingram, R. E. (1975). Prompting paper recycling on a university campus. *Journal of Environmental Systems, 5,* 39–57.

Geller, E. S., Witmer, J. F., & Orebaugh, A. L. (1976). Instructions as a determinant of paper-disposal behaviors. *Environment and Behavior, 8,* 417–438.

Getzels, J. W. (1969). A social psychology of education. In G. Lindzey & E. Aronson (Eds.), *The handbook of social psychology* (2nd ed.) (Vol. 5). Reading, MA: Addison-Wesley.

Glass, D. C. (1977). Stress behavior patterns, and coronary disease. *American Scientist, 65*(B), 177–185.

Goldstein, A. P., & Sorcher, M. (1974). *Changing supervisory behavior.* New York: Pergamon Press.

Goldstein, J. H. (1980). *Social psychology.* New York: Academic Press.

Gonzalez, A. (1979). *Classroom cooperation and ethnic balance.* Unpublished doctoral dissertation, University of California at Santa Cruz.

Good, T., & Brophy, J. (1972). Behavioral expression of teacher attitudes. *Journal of Educational Psychology, 63,* 617–624.

Gordon, R. M. (1976). Effects of volunteering and responsibility on the perceived value and effectiveness of a clinical treatment. *Journal of Counseling and Clinical Psychology, 44,* 799–801.

Greenberg, M. S., & Ruback, R. B. (1982). *Social psychology of the criminal justice system.* Monterey, CA: Brooks/Cole.

Gross, S. R. (1983). Constitutional challenges to the death-qualifying voir dire: *Witherspoon* to *Hovey.* In B. Bonora & E. Krauss (Eds.), *Jurywork: Systematic techniques* (2nd ed.). New York: Clark Boardman.

Grusec, J. E. (1973). Effects of co-observers evaluations on imitations: A developmental study. *Developmental Psychology, 8,* 141.

Guskin, A. E., & Guskin, S. L. A. (1970). *A social psychology of education.* Reading, MA: Addison-Wesley.

Haines, D. B., & McKeachie, W. J. (1967). Cooperative versus competitive discussion methods in teaching introductory psychology. *Journal of Educational Psychology, 58,* 386–390.

Haney, C. (1980). Psychology and legal change. *Law and Human Behavior, 4,* 147–199.

Haney, C. (1984). On the selection of capital juries: The biasing effects of the death-qualification process. *Law and Human Behavior, 4,* 217–302.

Hardin, G. (1968). The tragedy of the commons. *Science, 162,* 1243–1248.

Heberlein, T. A. (1972). The land ethic realized: Some social psychological explanations for changing environmental attitudes. *Journal of Social Issues, 28* (4), 79–87.

Heberlein, T. A., & Black, J. S. (1976). Attitudinal specificity and the prediction of behavior in a field setting. *Journal of Personality and Social Psychology, 33,* 474–479.

Heider, F. (1944). Social perception and phenomenal causality. *Psychological Review, 51,* 358–374.

Heider, F. (1958). *The psychology of interpersonal relations.* New York: John Wiley.

Hennigan, K. M., Flay, B. R., & Cook, T. D. (1980). "Give me the facts": Some suggestions for using social science knowledge in national policy-making. In R. F. Kidd & M. J. Saks (Eds.), *Advances in applied social psycholgy* (Vol. 1). Hillsdale, NJ: Lawrence Erlbaum Associates.

Hicks, D. J. (1968). Effects of co-observer's sanctions and adult presence on imitative aggression. *Child Development, 39,* 303–309.

Holmes, T. H., & Masuda, M. (1974). Life changes and illness susceptibility. In B. S. Dohrenwend & B. P. Dohrenwend (Eds.), *Stressful life events: Their nature and effects.* New York: John Wiley.

Horton, R. W., & Santogrossi, D. A. (1978). The effect of adult commentary on reducing the influence of televised violence. *Personality and Social Psychology Bulletin, 4,* 337–340.

Hosch, H. M. (1980). Commentary: A comparison of three studies of the influence of expert testimony on jurors. *Law and Human Behavior, 4,* 297–302.

Hosch, H. M., Beck, E. L., & McIntyre, P. (1980). Influence of expert testimony regarding eyewitness accuracy on jury decisions. *Law and Human Behavior, 4,* 287–296.

Hovland, C., Janis, I., & Kelley, H. H. (1953). *Communication and persuasion.* New Haven, CT: Yale University Press.

Hovland, C. I., & Weiss, W. (1951). The influence of source credibility on communication effectiveness. *The Public Opinion Quarterly, 15,* 635–650.

Huesmann, L. R., Eron, L. D., Klein, R., Brice, P., & Fischer, P. (1983). Mitigating the imitation of aggressive behaviors by changing children's attitudes about media violence. *Journal of Personality and Social Psychology, 44,* 899–910.

Ikard, F. F., Green, D. E., & Horn, D. (1968, April). *The development of a scale to differentiate between types of smoking as related to the management of affect.* Paper presented at the annual meeting of the Eastern Psychological Association, Washington, DC.

Jacobs, H. & Bailey, J. (1982–1983). Evaluating participation in a residential recycling program. *Journal of Environmental Systems, 12,* 141–152.

Jacoby, J. (1975). Consumer psychology as a social psychological sphere of action. *American Psychologist, 30,* 977–987.

Jakibchuk, Z., & Smeriglio, V. L. (1976). The influence of symbolic modeling on the social behavior of preschool children with low levels of social responsiveness. *Child Development, 47,* 838–841.

Janis, I. L. (1975). Effectiveness of social support for stressful decisions. In M. Deutsch & H. A. Hornstein (Eds.), *Applying social psychology: Implications for research, practice, and training.* Hillsdale, NJ: Lawrence Erlbaum Associates.

Janis, I. L., & Feshbach, S. (1953). Effects of fear-arousing communications. *Journal of Abnormal and Social Psychology, 48,* 78–92.

Janis, I. L., & Mann, L. (1965). Effectiveness of emotional role-playing in modifying smoking habits and attitudes. *Journal of Experimental Research in Personality, 1,* 84–90.

Janoff-Bulman, R., & Marshall, G. (1982). Mortality, well-being, and control: A study of a population of institutionalized aged. *Personality and Social Psychology Bulletin, 8,* 691–698.

Johnson, D. W. (1970). *Social psychology of education.* New York: Holt, Rinehart and Winston.

Johnson, D. W., & Johnson, R. T. (1975). *Learning together and alone.* Englewood Cliffs, NJ: Prentice Hall.

Johnson, W. G., Ross, J. M., & Mastria, M. A. (1977). Delusional behavior: An attributional analysis of development and modification. *Journal of Abnormal Psychology, 86,* 421–426.

Jones, E. E., Kanouse, D. E., Kelley, H. H., Nisbett, R. E., Valins, S., & Weiner, B. (Eds.). (1971). *Attribution: Perceiving the causes of behavior.* Morristown, NJ: General Learning Press.

Jones, E. E., & Nisbett, R. E. (1971). The actor and observer: Divergent perceptions of the causes of behaviors. In E. E. Jones, D. E. Kanouse, H. H. Kelley, R. E. Nisbett, S. Valins, & B. Weiner (Eds.), *Attribution: Perceiving the causes of behavior.* Morristown, NJ: General Learning Press.

Jones, E. E., & Sigall, H. (1971). The bogus pipeline: A new paradigm for measuring affect and attitude. *Psychological Bulletin, 76,* 349–364.

Jones, W. H., Hobbs, S. A., & Hockenbury, D. (1982). Loneliness and social skills deficits. *Journal of Personality and Social Psychology, 42,* 682–689.

Kahneman, D., & Tversky, A. (1973). On the psychology of prediction. *Psychological Review, 80,* 237–251.

Kairys, D., Schulman, J., & Harring, S. (Eds.). (1975). *The jury system: New methods for reducing prejudice.* Prepared by the National Jury Project and the National Lawyers Guild. Philadelphia: Philadelphia Resistance Print Shop.

Kaplan, R. M., & Singer, R. D. (1976). Television violence and viewer aggression: A reexamination of the evidence. *Journal of Social Issues, 32,* 35–70.

Kasl, S. V. (1975). Issues in patient adherence to health care regimens. *Journal of Human Stress, 1* (3), 5–17.

Katz, D., & Kahn, R. L. (1978). *The social psychology of organizations* (2nd ed.). New York: John Wiley.

Katzev, R. D., & Johnson, T. R. (1984). Comparing the effects of monetary incentives and foot-in-the-door strategies in promoting residential electricity conservation. *Journal of Applied Social Psychology, 14,* 12–27.

Keep America Beautiful. (1973). *Litter statistics compilation.* 99 Park Avenue, New York, NY: Author.

Keller, M. F., & Carlson, P. M. (1974). The use of symbolic modeling to promote social skills in preschool children with low levels of social responsiveness. *Child Development, 45,* 912–919.

Kelley, H. H. (1967). Attribution in social psychology. In D. Levine (Ed.), *Nebraska Symposium on Motivation* (Vol. 15). Lincoln: University of Nebraska Press.

Kellogg, R., & Baron, R. S. (1975). Attribution theory, insomnia and the reverse placebo effect. *Journal of Personality and Social Psychology, 32,* 231–236.

Kessler, J. (1973). An empirical study of six- and twelve-member jury decision making processes. *University of Michigan Journal of Law Reform, 6,* 712.

Kidd, R. F., & Saks, M. J. (1980). What is applied social psychology? An Introduction. In R. F. Kidd & M. J. Saks (Eds.), *Advances in applied social psychology* (Vol. 1). Hillsdale, NJ: Lawrence Erlbaum Associates.

Kiesler, C. A. (1971). *The psychology of commitment: Experiments linking behavior to belief.* New York: Academic Press.

Kolb, D. A. (1965). Achievement motivation training for underachieving high-school boys. *Journal of Personality and Social Psychology, 2,* 783–792.

Konečni, V. J., & Ebbesen, E. B. (1979). External validity of research in legal psychology. *Law and Human Behavior, 3,* 39–70.

Kornhaber, R. C., & Schroeder, H. E. (1975). Importance of model similarity on extinction of avoidance behavior in children. *Journal of Consulting and Clinical Psychology, 43,* 601–607.

Krantz, D., & Schulz, R. (1980). Personal control and health: Some applications to crisis of middle and old age. In A. Baum & J Singer (Eds.), *Advances in environmental psychology* (Vol. 2). New York: Academic Press.

Krauss, R. M., Freedman, J. L., & Whitcup, M. (1978). Field and laboratory studies of littering. *Journal of Experimental Social Psychology, 14,* 109–122.

Kraut, R. F. (1973). Effects of social labeling on giving to charity. *Journal of Experimental Social Psychology, 9,* 551–562.

Langer, E. J., Janis, I. L., & Wolfer, J. A.. (1975). Reduction of psychological stress in surgical patients. *Journal of Experimental Social Psychology, 11,* 155–165.

Langer, E. J., & Rodin, J. (1976). The effects of choice and enhanced personal responsibility for the aged: A field experiment in an institutional setting. *Journal of Personality and Social Psychology, 34,* 191–198.

Latham, G. P., & Saari, L. (1979). Application of social-learning theory to training supervisors through behavioral modeling. *Journal of Applied Psychology, 64,* 239–246.

Lawler, E. E., & Hackman, J. R. (1969). Impact of employee participation in the development of pay incentives: A field experiment. *Journal of Applied Psychology, 53,* 467–471.

Layden, M. A. (1982). Attributional style therapy. In C. Antaki & C. Brewin (Eds.), *Attributions and psychological change: Applications of attributional theories to clinical and educational practice.* New York: Academic Press.

Leventhal, H., Singer, R., & Jones, S. (1965). Effects of fear and specificity of recommendations upon attitudes and behavior. *Journal of Personality and Social Psychology, 2,* 20–29.

Lewin, K. (1947a). Frontiers in group dynamics. *Human Relations, 1,* 5–41.

Lewin, K. (1947b). Group decision and social change. In T. Newcombe & E. Hartley (Eds.), *Readings in social psychology.* New York: Holt, Rinehart and Winston.

Lewin, K. (1948). *Resolving social conflicts.* New York: Harper & Row.

Lewin, K. (1951). *Field theory in social science.* Chicago: University of Chicago Press.

Liebert, R. M., Sprafkin, J.N., & Davidson, E. S. (1982). *The early window: Effects of television on children and youth* (2nd ed.). New York: Pergamon Press.

Loftus, E. F., (1979). *Eyewitness testimony.* Cambridge, MA: Harvard University Press.

Loftus, E. F. (1980). Impact of expert psychological testimony on the unreliability of eyewitness identification. *Journal of Applied Psychology, 65,* 9–15.

Loftus, E. F. (1983a). Silence is not golden. *American Psychologist, 38,* 564–572.

Loftus, E. F. (1983b). Whose shadow is crooked? *American Psychologist,* 38, 576–577.

Loftus, E., & Monahan, J. (1980). Trial by data: Psychological research as legal evidence. *American Psychologist, 35,* 270–283.

Lowery, C. R., Denney, D. R., & Storms, M. D. (1979). Insomnia: A comparison of the effects of pill attribution and nonpejorative self-attribution. *Cognitive Therapy and Research, 3,* 161–164.

Lucker, G. W., Rosenfield, D., Sikes, J., & Aronson, E. (1976). Performance in the interdependent classroom: A field study. *American Educational Research Journal, 13,* 115–123.

Malpass, R. S., & Kravitz, J. (1969). Recognition for faces of own and other race. *Journal of Personality and Social Psychology, 13,* 330–334.

Mann, L. (1967). The effects of emotional role playing on smoking attitudes and behavior. *Journal of Experimental Social Psychology, 3,* 334–348.

Mann, L., & Janis, I. L. (1968). A follow-up study on the long range effects of emotional role playing. *Journal of Personality and Social Psychology, 8,* 339–342.

Marrow, A. J. (1969) *The practical theorist: The life and times of Kurt Lewin.* New York: Basic Books.

Matthews, K. A. (1979). Efforts of control by children and adults with the Type A coronary-prone behavior pattern. *Child Development, 50,* 842–847.

Matthews, K. A. (1981). "At a relatively early age . . . the habit of working the machine to its maximum capacity": Antecedents of the Type A coronary-prone behavior pattern. In S. S. Brehm, S. M. Kassin, & F. X. Gibbons (Eds.), *Developmental social psychology.* New York: Oxford University Press.

Mayo, C., & La France, M. (1980). Toward an applicable social psychology. In R. F. Kidd & M. J. Saks (Eds.), *Advances in applied social psychology* (Vol. 1). Hillsdale, NJ: Lawrence Erlbaum Associates.

McAlister, A., Perry, C., Killen, L. A., Slinkard, L. A., & Maccoby, N. (1980). Pilot study of smoking, alcohol, and drug abuse prevention. *American Journal of Public Health, 70,* 719–721.

McAlister, A. L., Perry, C., & Maccoby, N.(1979). Adolescent smoking: Onset and prevention. *Pediatrics, 63,* 650–658.

McAlister, A., Puska, P., Koskela, K., Pallonen, U., & Maccoby, N. (1980). Mass communication and community organization for public education. *American Psychologist, 35,* 375–379.

McClelland, D. C., Atkinson, J. W., Clark, R. A., & Lowell, E. L. (1953). *The achievement motive.* New York: Appleton-Century-Crofts.

McClelland, L., & Cook, S. W. (1980). Promoting energy conservation in master-metered apartments through group financial incentives. *Journal of Applied Social Psychology, 10,* 20–31.

McClintock, C. G., & Hunt, R. C. (1975). Nonverbal indicators of affect and deception in an interview setting. *Journal of Applied Social Psychology, 5,* 54–67.

McCloskey, M., & Egeth, H. E. (1983a). Eyewitness identification: What can a psychologist tell a jury? *American Psychologist, 38,* 550–563.

McCloskey, M., & Egeth, H. E. (1983b). A time to speak or a time to keep silence? *American Psychologist, 38,* 573–575.

McConahay, J., Mullin, C., & Frederick, J. (1977). The uses of social science in trials with political and racial overtones: The trial of Joan Little. *Law and Comtemporary Problems, 41,* 205–229.

McGuire, W. J. (1964). Inducing resistance to persuasion. In L. Berkowitz (Ed.), *Advances on experimental social psycholgy* (Vol. 1). New York: Academic Press.

McGuire, W. J. (1974). Communication-persuasion models for drug education: Experimental findings. In M. Goodstadt (Ed.), *Research on methods and programs of drug education.* Toronto, Canada: Addiction Research Foundation.

Mechanic, D. (1972). Social psychological factors affecting the presentation of bodily complaints. *New England Journal of Medicine, 286,* 1132–1139.

Meichenbaum, D. (1971). Examination of model characteristics in reducing avoidance behavior. *Journal of Personality and Social Psychology, 17,* 298–307.

Melamed, B. G., & Siegel, L. J. (1975). Reduction of anxiety in children facing hospitalization and surgery by use of filmed modeling. *Journal of Consulting and Clinical Psychology, 43,* 511–521.

Mendonca, P. J., & Brehm, S. S. (1983). Effects of choice on behavioral treatment of overweight children. *Journal of Social and Clinical Psychology, 1,* 343–358.

Miller, G., & Baseheart, J. (1969). Source of trustworthiness, opinionated statements and response to persuasive communication. *Speech Monographs, 36,* 1–7.

Miller, R., Brickman, P. & Bolen, D. (1975). Attribution versus persuasion as a means for modifying behavior. *Journal of Personality and Social Psychology, 31,* 430–441.

Morse, N., & Reimer, E. (1956). The experimental change of a major organizational variable. *Journal of Abnormal and Social Psychology, 52,* 120–129.

Murray, D. M., Johnson, C. A., Luepker, R. V., & Mittelmark, M. B. (1984). The prevention of cigarette smoking in children: A comparison of four strategies. *Journal of Applied Social Psychology, 14,* 274–288.

National Institute of Mental Health. (1982). *Television and behavior: Ten years of scientific progress and implications for the eighties* (DHHS Publication No. ADM 82–1195). Washington, DC: U.S. Government Printing Office: Author.

Nemetz, G. H., Craig, K. D., & Reith, G. (1978). Treatment of female sexual dysfunction through symbolic modeling. *Journal of Consulting and Clinical Psychology, 46,* 62–73.

O'Connor, R. D. (1969). Modification of social withdrawal through symbolic modeling. *Journal of Applied Behavior Analysis, 2,* 15–22.

O'Connor, R. D. (1972). Relative efficiency of modeling, shaping, and the combined procedure for modification of social withdrawal. *Journal of Abnormal Psychology, 79,* 327–334.

Orne, M. T. (1969). Demand characteristics and the concept of quasi-controls. In R. Rosenthal & R. L. Rosnow (Eds.), *Artifact and behavioral research.* New York: Academic Press.

Pallak, M. S., Cook, D. A., & Sullivan, J. J. (1980). Commitment and energy conservation. In L. Bickman (Ed.), *Applied Social Psychology Annual, 1,* 235–253.

Pallak, M. S., & Cummings, N. (1976). Commitment and voluntary energy conservation. *Personality and Social Psychology Bulletin, 2,* 27–31.

Pardini, A. U., & Katzev, R. D. (1983–1984). The effects of strength of commitment on newspaper recycling. *Journal of Environmental Systems, 13,* 245–254.

Perry, C., Killen, J., Slinkard, L.A., & McAlister, A. L. (1980). Peer teaching and smoking prevention among junior high school students. *Adolescence, 15,* 277–281.

Perry, C., Killen, J., Telch, M., J., Slinkard, L. A., & Danaher, B. G. (1980). Modifying smoking behavior of teenagers: A school-based intervention. *American Journal of Public Health, 70,* 722–725.

Peterson, C. (1982). Learned helplessness and attributional interventions in depression. In C. Antaki & C. Brewin (Eds.), *Attributions and psychological change: Applications of attributional theories to clinical and educational practice.* New York: Academic Press.

Pliner, P., Hart, H., Kohl, J., & Saari, D. (1974). Compliance without pressure: Some further data on the foot-in-the-door technique. *Journal of Experimental Social Psychology, 10,* 17–22.

Porras, J. I., Hargis, K., Patterson, K. J., Maxfield, D. G., Roberts, N., & Bies, R. J. (1982). Modeling-based organizational development: A longitudinal assessment. *Journal of Applied Behavioral Science, 18,* 433–446.

Pyszczynski, T. A., & Wrightsman, L. S. (1981). The effects of opening statements on mock jurors' verdicts in a simulated trial. *Journal of Applied Social Psychology, 11,* 301–313.

Reich, J. W., & Robertson, J. L. (1979). Reactance and norm appeal in anti-littering messages. *Journal of Applied Social Psychology, 9,* 91–101.

Reimer, T. C. (1965). *Serendipity and the three princes.* Norman, OK: University of Oklahoma Press.

Reingen, P. H. (1978). On inducing compliance with requests. *Journal of Consumer Research, 5,* 96–102.

Reingen, P. H. (1982). Test of a list procedure for inducing compliance with a request to donate money. *Journal of Applied Psychology, 67,* 110–118.

Reiter, S. M., & Samuel, W. (1980). Littering as a function of prior litter and the presence or absence of prohibitive signs. *Journal of Applied Social Psychology, 10,* 45–55.

Reyes, H., & Varela, J. A. (1980). Condition required for a technology of the social sciences. In R. F. Kidd & M. J. Saks (Eds.), *Advances in applied social psychology* (Vol. 1). Hillsdale, NJ: Lawrence Erlbaum Associates.

Richmond, J. B. (1979a). *Smoking and health: A report of the Surgeon General.* Washington, DC: U.S. Government Printing Office.

Richmond, J. B. (1979b). *Healthy people: The Surgeon General's report on health promotion and disease prevention.* Washington, DC: U.S. Government Printing Office.

Ring, K. (1967). Experimental social psychology: Some sober questions about frivolous values. *Journal of Experimental Social Psychology, 3,* 113–123.

Rodin, J. (1978). Somatophysics and attribution. *Personality and Social Psychology Bulletin, 4,* 531–540.

Rodin, J., & Langer, E. J. (1977). Long-term effects of a control-relevant intervention with the institutionalized aged. *Journal of Personality and Social Psychology, 35,* 897–902.

Rosenman, R. H., & Friedman, M. (1974). Neurogenic factors in pathogenesis of coronary heart disease. *Medical Clinics of North America, 58,* 269–279.

Rosenthal, R. (1974). *On the social psychology of self-fulfilling prophecy: Further evidence for Pygmalion effects and their mediating mechanisms.* New York: MSS Modular Publications.

Rosenthal, R. (1976). *Experimenter effects in behavioral research* (enlarged ed.). New York: Irvington.

Rosenthal, R., & Jacobson, L. (1968). *Pygmalion in the classroom.* New York: Holt, Rinehart and Winston.

Ross, R., Rodin, J., & Zimbardo, P. G. (1969). Toward an attribution therapy: The reduction of fear through induced cognitive-emotional misattribution. *Journal of Personality and Social Psychology, 12,* 279–288.

Saks, M. J. (1974). Ignorance of science is no excuse. *Trial, 10* (6), 18–20.

Saks, M J. (1976a). The limits of scientific jury selection: Ethical and empirical. *Jurimetrics Journal, 17,* 3–22.

Saks, M. J. (1976b, August). Social scientists can't rig juries. *Psychology Today, 9,* 48–50, 55–57.

Saks, M. (1977). *Jury verdicts: The role of group size and social decision rule.* Lexington, MA: Lexington Books.

Saks, M. (1980). Closing remarks. In M.J. Saks & C.H. Baron (Eds.), *The use/nonuse/misuse of applied social research in the courts.* Cambridge, MA: Abt Books.

Saks, M. J., & Hastie, R. (1978). *Social psychology in court.* New York: Van Nostrand Reinhold.

Schachter, S. (1964). The interaction of cognitive and physiological determinants of emotional state. In L. Berkowitz (Ed.), *Advances in experimental social psychology.* New York: Academic Press.

Schachter, S., Silverstein, B., Kozlowski, L. T., Herman, C. P., & Liebling, B. (1977). Effects of stress on cigarette smoking and urinary ph. *Journal of Experimental Psychology, 106,* 24–30.

Schachter, S., & Singer, J. E. (1962). Cognitive, social, and physiological determinants of emotional state. *Psychological Review, 69,* 379–399.

Schulman, J., Shaver, P., Colman, R., Emrick, B., & Christie, R. (1973, December). Recipe for a jury. *Psychology Today, 6,* 37–44, 77–84.

Schulz, R. (1976). Effects of control and predictability on the physical and psychological well-being of the institutionalized aged. *Journal of Personality and Social Psychology, 33,* 563–573.

Schulz, R., & Hanusa, B. H. (1978). Long-term effects of control and predictability enhancing interventions: Findings and ethical issues. *Journal of Personality and Social Psychology, 36,* 1194–1201.

Schwartz, S. H. (1970). Moral decision making and behavior. In J. Macaulay & L. Berkowitz (Eds.), *Altruism and helping behavior.* New York: Academic Press.

Schwarzwald, J., Bizman, A., & Raz, M. (1983). The foot-in-the-door paradigm: Effects of second request size on donation probability and social generosity. *Personality and Social Psychology Bulletin, 9,* 443–450.

Scott, C. A. (1977). Modifying socially-conscious behavior: The foot-in-the-door technique. *Journal of Consumer Research, 4,* 156–164.

Scott, T. H., Bexton, W. H., Heron, W., & Doane, B. K. (1959). Cognitive effects of perceptual isolation. *Canadian Journal of Psychology, 13,* 200–209.

Seashore, S. E., & Bowers, D. G. (1963). *Changing the structure and functioning of an organization.* Ann Arbor, MI: Institute for Social Research.

Seligman, C., & Darley, J. M. (1977). Feedback as a means of decreasing residential energy consumption. *Journal of Applied Psychology, 62,* 363–368.

Seligman, C., Kriss, M., Darley, J. M., Fazio, R. H., Becker, L. J., & Prior, J. B. (1979). Predicting summer energy consumption from homeowner's attitudes. *Journal of Applied Social Psychology, 9* (1), 70–90.

Seligman, M. E. P. (1975). *Helplessness: On depression, development, and death.* San Francisco: Freeman.

Settle, R. B., & Golden, L. L. (1974). Attribution theory and advertiser credibility. *Journal of Marketing Research, 11,* 181–185.

Sharan, S., Kussel, P., Hertz-Lazarow, R., Bejarano, Y., Raviv, S., & Sharan, Y. (1984). *Cooperative learning in the desegregated schools.* Hillsdale, NJ: Lawrence Earlbaum Associates.

Sherif, M., & Sherif, C. (1953). *Groups in harmony and tension.* New York: Harper & Row.

Sherman, S. J., Cialdini, R. B., Schwartzman, D. F., & Reynolds, K. D. (1985). Imagining can heighten or lower the perceived likelihood of contracting a disease: The mediating effect of ease of imagery. *Personality and Social Psychology Bulletin, 11,* 118–127.

Siegal, A. E. (1982). Introductory comments. In D. Pearl, L. Bouthilet, & J. Lazar (Eds.), *Television and behavior: Ten years of scientific progress and implications for the eighties* (Vol. 2, DHHS Publication No. ADM 82–1196). Washington, DC: U.S. Government Printing Office.

Skillbeck, W. (1974). Attributional changes and crisis intervention. *Psychotherapy Theory, Research, and Practice, 11,* 371–375.

Slavin, R. E. (1978). Student teams and achievement divisions. *Journal of Research and Development in Education, 12,* 39–49.

Smith, D. E., Gier, J. A., & Willis, F. N. (1982). Interpersonal touch and compliance with a marketing request. *Basic and Applied Social Psychology, 3,* 35–38.

Smith, R. E., & Hunt, S. D. (1978). Attributional processes and effects in promotional situations. *Journal of Consumer Research, 3,* 149–158.

Snyder, M. L., & Mentzer, S. (1978). Social psychological perspectives on the physician's feelings and behavior. *Personality and Social Psychology Bulletin, 4,* 541–547.

Soloman, D. S. (1982). Health campaigns on television. In D. Pearl, L. Bouthilet, & J. Lazar (Eds.), *Television and behavior: Ten years of scientific progress and implications for the eighties* (Vol. 2, DHHS Publication No. ADM 82–1196). Washington, DC: U.S. Government Printing Office.

Sparkman, R. M., & Locander, W. B. (1980). Attribution theory and advertising effectiveness. *Journal of Consumer Research, 7,* 219–224.

Steinberg, C. S. (1980). *TV Facts.* New York: Facts on File.

Stephan, W. G. (1978). School desegregation: An evaluation of predictions made in Brown v. Board of Education. *Psychological Bulletin, 85,* 217–238.

Stephan, W. G. (1980). The heart and mind of social psychology. In R. F. Kidd & M. J. Saks (Eds.), *Advances in applied social psychology* (Vol. 1). Hillsdale, NJ: Lawrence Erlbaum Associates.

Stern, P. C., & Gardner, G. T. (1980). A review and critique of energy research in psychology. *Social Science Energy Review, 3,* 1–71.

Stern, P. C., & Gardner, G. T. (1981). Psychological research and energy policy. *American Psychologist, 36,* 329–342.

Storms, M. D., Denney, D. R., McCaul, K. D., & Lowery, C. R. (1979). Treating insomnia. In I. H. Frieze, D. Bar-Tal, & J. S. Carroll (Eds.), *New approaches to social problems.* San Francisco: Jossey-Bass.

Storms, M. D., & McCaul, K. D. (1976). Attribution processes and emotional exacerbation of dysfunctional behavior. In J. H. Harvey, W. J. Ickes, & R. F. Kidd (Eds.), *New directions in attribution research* (Vol. 1). Hillsdale, NJ: Lawrence Erlbaum Associates.

Storms, M. D., & Nisbett, R. E. (1970). Insomnia and the attribution process. *Journal of Personality and Social Psychology, 16,* 319–328.

Suedfeld, P. (1973). Sensory deprivation used in the reduction of cigarette smoking: Attitude change experiments in an applied context. *Journal of Applied Social Psychology, 3,* 30–38.

Suedfeld, P. (1975). The benefits of boredom: Sensory deprivation reconsidered. *American Scientist, 63,* 60–69.

Suedfeld, P., & Ikard, F. F. (1974). The use of sensory deprivation in facilitating the reduction of cigarette smoking. *Journal of Consulting and Clinical Psychology, 42,* 888–895.

Suggs, D., & Sales, B. D. (1981). Juror self-disclosure in voir dire: A social science analysis. *The Indiana Law Journal, 56,* 245–271.

Surgeon General's Scientific Advisory Committee on Television and Social Behavior (1972). *Television and growing up: The impact of televised violence.* Report to the Surgeon General, United States Public Health Service. Washington, DC: U.S. Government Printing Office.

Tanke, E.D., & Tanke, T. J. (1979). Getting off a slippery slope: Social science in the judicial process. *American Psychologist, 34,* 1130–1138.

Tannenbaum, A. S. (1966). *Social psychology of work organization.* Belmont, CA: Brooks/Cole.

Taylor, S. E. (1978). A developing role for social psychology in medicine and medical practice. *Personality and Social Psychology Bulletin, 4,* 515–523.

Telch, M. J., Killen, J. D., McAlister, A. L., Perry, C. L., & Maccoby, N. (1982) Long-term follow-up of a pilot project on smoking prevention with adolescents. *Journal of Behavioral Medicine, 5,* 1–8.

Tornatzky, L. G., & Solomon, T. (1982). Contributions of social science to innovation and productivity. *American Psychologist, 37,* 737–746.

Triplett, N. (1897). The dynamogenic factors in pacemaking and competition. *American Journal of Psychology, 9,* 507–533.

U.S. Bureau of the Census. (1980a). *Social indicators III.* Washington, DC: U.S. Government Printing Office: Author.

U.S. Bureau of the Census. (1980b). *Statistical abstract of the United States* (101st ed.). Washington, DC: U.S. Government Printing Office: Author.

U.S. Department of Health, Education, and Welfare. (1964). *Smoking and Health* (Technical Report of the Advisory Committee to the Surgeon General of the Public Health Service, Public Health Service, Publication No. 1103). Washington, DC: U.S. Government Printing Office.

U.S. Department of Health, Education, and Welfare. (1980). *Nutrition and your health: Dietary guidelines of Americans.* Washington, DC: U.S. Government Printing Office: Author.

Valenti, A. C., & Downing, L. L. (1975). Differential effects of jury size on verdicts following deliberation as a function of the apparent guilt of a defendant. *Journal of Personality and Social Psychology, 32,* 655–663.

Valins, S., & Nisbett, R.E. (1971). Attribution processes in the development and treatment of emotional disorders. In E. E. Jones, D. E. Kanouse, H. H. Kelley, R. E. Nisbett, S. Valins, & B. Weiner (Eds.), *Attribution: Perceiving the causes of behavior.* Morristown, NJ: General Learning Press.

Van Liere, K. D., & Dunlap, R. E. (1978). Moral norms and environmental behavior: An application of Schwartz's norm-activation model to yard burning. *Journal of Applied Social Psychology, 8,* 174–188.

Walster, E., Walster, G. W., & Berscheid, E. (1978). *Equity: Theory and research.* Boston: Allyn and Bacon.

Watts, W., & McGuire, W. D. (1964). Persistence of induced opinion change and retention of the inducing message contents. *Journal of Abnormal and Social Psychology, 68,* 233–241.

Webster, F. E., Jr. (1975). Determining the characteristics of the socially conscious consumer. *Journal of Consumer Research, 2,* 188–196.

Weidner, G. (1980). Self-handicapping following learned helplessness treatment and the Type A coronary-prone behavior pattern. *Journal of Psychosomatic Research, 24,* 319–325.

Weigal, R. H., & Newman, L. S. (1976). Increasing attitude-behavior correspondence by broadening the scope of the behavioral measure. *Journal of Personality and Social Psychology, 33,* 793–802.

Weiner, B. (1974). An attributional interpretation of expectancy-value theory. In B. Weiner (Ed.), *Cognitive views of human motivation.* New York: Academic Press.

Wells, G. L., Lindsay, R., & Ferguson, T. (1979). Accuracy, confidence, and juror perceptions in eyewitness identification. *Journal of Applied Psychology, 64,* 440–448.

Wells, G. L., Lindsay, R. C. L., & Tousignant, J. P. (1980). Effects of expert psychological advice on human performance in judging the validity of eyewitness testimony. *Law and Human Behavior, 4,* 275–285.

Wells, G. L., & Murray, D. M. (1983). What can psychology say about the *Neil v. Biggers* criteria for judging eyewitness accuracy? *Journal of Applied Psychology, 68,* 347–362.

Westphal, R. C. (1977). *The effects of a primary grade inter-ethnic curriculum on racial prejudice.* San Francisco: R. & E. Research Associates.

Weyant, J. M. (1984). Applying social psychology to induce charitable donations. *Journal of Applied Social Psychology, 14,* 441–447.

Weyant, J. M., & Smith, S. L. (in press). Getting more by asking for less: The effects of request size on donations to charity. *Journal of Applied Social Psychology.*

Whyte, W. F. (1983). Worker participation: International and historical perspectives. *Journal of Applied Behavioral Science, 19,* 395–407.

Wicker, A. W. (1969). Attitudes versus actions: The relationship of verbal and overt behavioral responses to attitude objects. *Journal of Social Issues, 25,* 41–78.

Winett, R. A., Hatcher, J. W., Fort, T. R., Leckliter, I. N., Love, S. R., Riley, A. W., & Fishback, J. F. (1982). The effects of videotape modeling and daily feedback on residential electricity conservation, home temperature and humidity, perceived comfort, and clothing worn: Winter and summer. *Journal of Applied Behavior Analysis, 15,* 381–402.

Wolpe, J. (1958). *Psychotherapy by reciprocal inhibition.* Stanford, CA: Stanford University Press.

Woocher, F. D. (1977). Did your eyes deceive you? Expert psychological testimony on the unreliability of eyewitness identification. *Stanford Law Review, 29,* 969–1030.

Woodside, A. G., & Davenport, J. W. (1974). The effect of salesman similarity and expertise on consumer purchasing behavior. *Journal of Marketing Research, 11*, 198–202.

Woodside, A. G., & Davenport, J. W. (1976). Effects of price and salesman expertise on customer purchasing behavior. *Journal of Business, 49*, 51–59.

Wrightsman, L. S., & Deaux, K. (1981). *Social psychology in the 80's* (3rd ed.). Monterey, CA: Brooks/Cole.

Yarmey, A. D. (1979). *The psychology of eyewitness testimony*. New York: Free Press.

Yarmey, A. D., & Jones, H. P. T. (1983). Is eyewitness identification a matter of common sense? In S. Lloyd-Bostock & B. R. Clifford (Eds.), *Evaluating eyewitness evidence*. London: John Wiley.

Zeisel, H., & Diamond, S. S. (1976). The jury selection in the Mitchell-Stans conspiracy trial. *American Bar Foundation Research Journal, 1*, 151–174.

Zuckerman, M., De Paulo, B. M., & Rosenthal, R. (1981). Verbal and non-verbal communication of deception. *Advances in Experimental Social Psychology, 14*, 1–59.

Court Cases

Ballew v. Georgia, 435 U.S. 223 (1978).

Brown v. Board of Education of Topeka, 347 U.S. 483 (1954).

Colgrove v. Battin, 413 U.S. 149 (1973).

Hovey v. Superior Court, 28 Cal. 3d 1 616 P.2d 1301 (1980).

Neil v. Biggers, 409 U.S. 188 (1972).

Williams v. Florida, 399 U.S. 78C (1970).

Witherspoon v. Illinois, 391 U.S. 510 (1968).

Name Index

Subject Index